CONFLICT AND COMMUNICATION:
A Guide Through the Labyrinth of Conflict Management

☙❧

CONFLICT AND COMMUNICATION:
A Guide Through the Labyrinth of Conflict Management

☙❧

Conflict and Communication: A Guide Through the Labyrinth of Conflict Management was developed for the Open Society Institute's Regional Children and Youth Program for use in Central and Eastern European schools. The information and skills presented within this curriculum can also be implemented in other parts of the world.

Author: Daniel Shapiro
Editors: Lisa Pilsitz, Susan Shapiro
Content Editor: Fran Donelan
Assistant Editors: Sarah Aitken, Lara Davidovic, Jennifer Dellmuth

Published by

international debate education association

400 West 59th Street / New York, NY 10019

Copyright © 2004 by Open Society Institute

Conflict and Communication: A Guide Through the Labyrinth of Conflict Management was developed for the Open Society Institute's Regional Children and Youth Program for use in Central and Eastern European schools. The information and skills presented within this curriculum can also be implemented in other parts of the world.

Editors:	Lisa Pilsitz
	Susan Shapiro
Content Editor:	Fran Donelan
Assistant Editors:	Sarah Aitken
	Lara Davidovic
	Jennifer Dellmuth

All rights reserved. No part of this publication may be reproduced or transmitted in any form or by any means, electronic or mechanical, including photocopy, or any information storage and retrieval system, without written permission from the publisher.

THE PUBLISHER GRANTS PERMISSION FOR THE REPRODUCTION OF THE ACTIVITY SHEETS IN THIS WORK FOR NON-PROFIT EDUCATIONAL USE. THE ACTIVITY SHEETS MAY NOT BE USED IN A PROFIT-MAKING VENTURE WITHOUT THE WRITTEN PERMISSION OF THE PUBLISHER.

Activity sheets may be downloaded from
www.idebate.org/conflictandcommunication.htm

Library of Congress Cataloging-in-Publication Data

Shapiro, Daniel, 1971-
  Conflict and communication : a guide through the labyrinth of conflict
management / Daniel Shapiro.
      p. cm.
  Includes bibliographical references and index.
  ISBN 0-9720541-9-7 (alk. paper)
 1. Conflict management—Study and teaching. 2. Social conflict—Study
and teaching. 3. Conflict management—Study and teaching—Activity
programs. 4. Social conflict—Study and teaching—Activity programs.
I. Title.
  HM1126.S53 2004
  303.6'9'071—dc22
                                                            2004010121

Design by Hernan Bonomo
Printed in the USA

Acknowledgments

A major strength of this book lies in the joint efforts of a number of talented people who offered inspiration and ideas. Thank you to:

Dr. Jerome Frank, who has taught me that the mind, which "has proved capable of splitting the atom and putting satellites into space," is equally capable of creating a world free from violence and war.

The multitude of teachers and Soros Health Education Coordinators from Central and Eastern Europe who piloted and evaluated the lessons in this book. The lessons were modified and improved on the basis of the field-tests.

The participants of the workshops on communication and conflict management. You are the voice and body of this book.

The university professors, who dedicated many hours to reviewing the book and offering constructive suggestions—Ervin Staub, Social Psychologist, specializing in issues of violence (University of Massachusetts at Amherst), Carl Latkin, Industrial/Organizational Psychologist (Johns Hopkins University), Carol Beal, Developmental Psychologist (University of Massachusetts at Amherst), Joseph Folger, Expert Mediation (Temple University), Ghislaine Godenne, Professor of Psychiatry (Johns Hopkins University/Medical School).

My Mom, Dad, Grandma, and Nan, who have taught me how to teach, how to listen, and how to love.
Lisa Pilsitz, my "other Mom," whose sincere sense of humanity has touched every page of this book.

Elizabeth Lorant, for her friendship, as well as for her vision of an open society.

Fran Donelan, Consultant and Expert in Conflict Resolution, Peace Education Project Director (American Friends Service Committee and Faculty, Goucher College), for her diligent work, steadfast dedication, and devotion to the teaching of conflict resolution.

To Sarah Aitken, Sophie Ungvary, and Ben Chan for their insightful contributions to the curriculum.

Lara Davidovic, who day or night, unconditionally and sincerely offered insight and assistance.

The "co-facilitators," whose spirit, energy, and ideas have helped shaped the curriculum: Jennifer Dellmuth, Marius Mates, Craig Zelizer, Pedje Zivotic, Melissa Agocs, and Micah Murray.

Clare, Emily, and Lucas, for teaching me that life is much deeper than the mere beating of our hearts.
Those others who have added vitality, logic, and love to the curriculum:
Vera & Ivan Janik
Jamie Daneberg
Sarah Klaus
Lona Vinarski
Andrey Chadeav
Chris Fitz
Zina Baltreniene
Jeff Pilsitz
Mira Polazarevska
Dan Baciu
Darko Tot
Kathleen Curry
Rodica Cristea
Jana Hazirova
Jennifer Kreamer
and last, but not at all least, Madelyn Shapiro

Table of Contents

FOREWORD: A GLOBAL FRAMEWORK OF CONFLICT MANAGEMENT - Page IX

PART I - CONFLICT MANAGEMENT

INTRODUCTION - Page 2
This introduction highlights the overall intent of the curriculum, the importance of conflict management education, and the curriculum philosophy.

CHAPTER ONE: ME - Page 9
Students discover their personal values and beliefs, how they are formed, and how they relate to conflict. They also learn how their own self-esteem and self-concept relate to conflict.

CHAPTER TWO: YOU - Page 43
Sometimes misperceptions and misunderstanding arise and affect relationships. This chapter emphasizes the importance of appreciating others' differences and everyone's uniqueness.

CHAPTER THREE: ME AND YOU - Page 83
The focus of this chapter is communication: How can we effectively interact when we are in a conflict situation? How can we be better listeners? How can we clearly express ourselves? This chapter presents activities on listening strategies, effective conversation techniques, body language, and trust.

CHAPTER FOUR: ME VS. YOU - Page 111
This chapter allows students to examine the roots and consequences of conflict. It raises important issues, such as why people resort to violence during conflicts.

CHAPTER FIVE: ME WITH YOU - Page 137
This chapter presents a specific, five-step strategy for managing conflicts. Many of the activities emphasize the idea that in a conflict between people, both people can often win the conflict.

CHAPTER SIX: US - Page 177
This chapter consists of activities designed for students to discover basic human rights and their connection to conflict. It also offers exercises and ideas on how students can promote change within a system when they believe that the system infringes on their basic human rights.

PART II - STUDENT MEDIATION

INTRODUCTION - Page 202
This introduction defines mediation and explains its purpose.

THE TEN SESSIONS - Page 204
This part consists of sessions on setting up a student mediation program in your school. The necessary training materials are included.

APPENDIXES

APPENDIX I: STRESS-RELIEVING ACTIVITIES - Page 272
If discussions become sensitive or emotional, you can facilitate these activities to relieve some of the stress. They are useful for you as well as the students.

APPENDIX II: ICEBREAKERS - Page 276
This appendix lists quick activities that create a warm, accepting, comfortable environment for you and the participants.

APPENDIX III: THE THREE LOVELY LITTLE PIGS (A SHORT PLAY ABOUT MEDIATION) - Page 279
This short play, "The Three Lovely Little Pigs," captures the essence of mediation in a humorous manner.

APPENDIX IV: INTERDISCIPLINARY APPROACHES TO CONFLICT MANAGEMENT - Page 285
This appendix describes the roles of school, family, and peers in regard to conflict management. There are sample activities that highlight ways conflict management can be implemented into various subjects and settings.

APPENDIX V: DIVIDING STUDENTS INTO GROUPS - Page 288
This section offers suggestions on dividing students into random groups.

GLOSSARY - Page 289

INDEX OF LESSONS - Page 291

INDEX OF KEY CONCEPTS - Page 292

Foreword:
A Global Framework Of Conflict Management

Among the ubiquitous dangers facing humanity these days, only one threatens extinction of the human race: modern war. Until the advent of nuclear, chemical, and biological weapons, recurring conflicts have been compatible with survival and indeed have provided stimuli to scientific and technological breakthroughs, leading to major advances in health and welfare, albeit at great temporary cost in lives and human suffering.

As the last two world wars have shown, wars can escalate until combatants attack each other with the most destructive weapons at their disposal. Until today, even the worst of these weapons could cause only regional damage. With the abrupt emergence of weapons capable of worldwide destruction, any war waged by modern industrialized nations could endanger humanity, and indeed all life.

Those struggling to contain this unprecedented threat work toward achieving two interacting and mutually reinforcing goals: verifiable, enforceable universal disarmament and substitution of effective nonviolent for violent methods of resolving conflicts.

The search for disarmament, although making a little progress periodically, has always been frustrated by the underlying belief of all contending parties that superior destructive force still is the ultimate arbiter of international quarrels, as it always has been. Superior destructive power, however, has become a chimera, no longer achievable by industrially and scientifically advanced nations.

This realization forces those working for human survival to develop effective nonviolent means for resolving group conflicts. A major obstacle toward achieving this goal interacts with reliance on superior violence. It is that humans as group creatures regard survival of the group, not its individual members, as the paramount good. Witness the worldwide posthumous acclaim of heroes who have sacrificed their lives in battle for their comrades or their country.

Another aspect of psychological primacy of the group has been termed *ethnocentrism*. Members of each group typically regard its values, customs, and achievements as superior to all others. When two groups come into conflict over territory, food, or other limited resources, as well as for other reasons, each combatant sees its own goals and behaviors as the only legitimate, praiseworthy ones. Each demeans and ridicules its opponent who becomes the "enemy."

Each contender justifies its own atrocities by the atrocities of the enemy and seeks revenge. These mutual images and behaviors are powerfully supported by value systems, traditions, and codes of conduct. In consequence, armed conflict, often lasting generations, typically leads to escalation of violence until each combatant seeks exterminating the other, often including women and children, as a sacred duty. In a nuclear-armed world, this is a recipe for mutual extinction.

Two available and mutually reinforcing ways of breaking out of these traps are to work simultaneously for disarmament and nonviolent conflict resolution. The hope that this goal can be achieved rests on the workshops in conflict resolution and communication skills burgeoning throughout the world.

To be sure, one must be cautious in drawing conclusions as to the success of these workshops. In comparison to the enormous extent of the problem, the number of participants in them is still minuscule, which limits the generalizability of the results. Moreover, the conditions under which the workshops are being conducted and evaluated contain many inevitable sources of bias.

What makes this particular program especially appealing is that it is no armchair exercise. The participating teachers and students are living in some of the most conflict-ridden parts of the world, and the designer of this curriculum has spent months in these regions organizing and participating in the exercises. The curriculum is methodologically and conceptually sophisticated.

Since production of basic change in culturally ingrained attitudes is difficult and slow, humanity will have to live under the Damocles sword of civilization—destroying weaponry for a long time. Until the sword drops, however, there may be time for humans to achieve the massive psychological transformation eventually leading to exclusive reliance on nonviolent methods for resolving group disputes. A daunting task indeed, but there is no other alternative.

Hopefully, programs of conflict management like this one will in time become sufficiently widespread and sophisticated to mitigate and eventually replace violence in domestic and international conflicts. Only a distant hope, to be sure, but in the wise aphorism of Krishnamurti, an Indian philosopher: "A pebble can change the course of a river."

This curriculum is such a pebble. As more and more such pebbles accumulate, we may hope they will grow to form a dam mighty enough to divert the course of human events from its present destructive channels.

In the meanwhile, I heartily recommend serious perusal and implementation where possible of *Conflict and Communication: A Guide Through the Labyrinth of Conflict Management* to all who cherish hopes for the future of humanity.

Jerome Frank, Ph.D., M.D., Professor of Psychiatry (Emeritus of Johns Hopkins University)

A message to you, the teacher...

Welcome!

You have just entered the world of positive change: As a teacher you have the power to significantly influence the lives of your students. You have the power to guide them toward a clearer picture of themselves and society. You have the power to turn their conflicts into educational opportunities. You have the power to guide your students through the labyrinth of conflict management. But what are the practical steps for accomplishing these goals? Welcome to the curriculum.

PART I
Conflict Management

INTRODUCTION:
THE IMPORTANCE OF CONFLICT MANAGEMENT EDUCATION

Fighting. Indecision. Anger. Lack of acceptance. Conflict is such a natural, indispensable component of our everyday lives and relations with others that we do not usually analyze, think about, or study it.

However, on a daily basis, students encounter conflicts within themselves, as well as with classmates, family, and society. While most people view conflict as a negative and destructive force, it can be an opportunity for growth and learning. If taught specific conflict management skills, students can analyze social situations, decide on wise courses of action, and take responsibility for the consequences of their actions. Conflict management describes a range of skills and strategies useful in constructively handling conflicts.[1] The ability to deal with conflict in a constructive way not only adds to students' individual mental health, but also positively affects society as a whole.

The primary outcomes of this curriculum are that students will:
- Learn to critically analyze their attitudes and perspectives on a variety of issues;
- Develop useful skills for managing conflicts;
- Understand the importance of communication;
- Gain the ability to communicate in ways that defuse conflict.

Opening the Door to Conflict Management

What exactly is conflict, and how can we deal with it constructively? How can students learn to view conflict as a powerful stimulus for growth and change? This curriculum has five important features that help students learn and understand the nature of conflict:

1. *The activities are practical.* This curriculum is designed to help students understand the nature of conflict through practical activities. This book contains very few lessons explicitly explaining theories of conflict; rather, it allows students to critically analyze their own attitudes and perspectives on issues. The emphasis of this curriculum is not on having students memorize definitions, but instead on having them learn and understand useful, specific skills to enable them to deal with conflicts in their own lives.

2. *The activities allow students to experience and process.* Learning facts is often not sufficient for true understanding. We believe experience is the key to understanding. The activities in this curriculum are designed to allow students to experience concepts and then to think about (process) their experience, thereby learning. For example, many people know what discrimination is, and yet they still discriminate. Therefore, one of the goals of this curriculum is to have students experience and share the feelings involved in discrimination. The intended outcome is to reduce the likelihood of future discrimination or, at the very least, to increase the understanding of its implications.

3. *The activities stimulate discussion.* By stimulating discussion, students share different opinions, positions, and viewpoints; this process of exchanging is the foundation from which solutions for conflicts emerge. Discussions and shared experiences

---

1. The terms "conflict management" and "conflict resolution" are not synonymous. Conflict resolution is a narrow term describing skills and strategies useful solely in resolving conflicts. Conflict management is a broader term. Although certain conflicts cannot be resolved, they all have positive potential. For instance, two disputing students may not find a solution to their conflict, but their relationships may improve.

enable the students not only to become closer to one another, but also to learn something new about themselves. Students are encouraged to openly express their opinions. They also see that it is natural to disagree.

4. *The activities are fun and educational.* Many of the activities in this book are presented in the format of games. But do not be deceived: though the activities are fun, they each have specific objectives. It is not enough to teach theory and definitions of concepts such as discrimination or prejudice. Using games as an additional teaching tool allows students a safe environment in which to experience these concepts. Also, by presenting much of the information in the format of games, students develop a sense of excitement and joy for learning. You will find that they want to learn more about conflict. Games arouse their curiosity and create a classroom atmosphere where learning can be both productive and fun.

5. *The activities can be adapted.* Every classroom is different—students behave differently, learn at different rates, and have different beliefs, values, and needs. While the activities in this curriculum have been tested to ensure their effectiveness, no activity works perfectly in every situation. After you read activities, we encourage you to adapt them to meet the specific needs of your students.

Curriculum Philosophy: The Labyrinth of Conflict Management

This curriculum is built on a philosophy that can be easily communicated to students. The central concept is finding one's way through the labyrinth of conflict. Conflict management is like a complex labyrinth of choices. We must make decisions regarding our actions, thoughts, and emotions. What should we do when we arrive at a crossroads during a conflict situation and are not certain how to behave? With two or more paths staring at us, how do we choose the decision that will guide us through the labyrinth most efficiently? Just as the shortest path between two points is a straight line, the most accurate form of communication is clear dialogue between people. Skills and information empower us to communicate, cooperate, and manage our conflicts successfully.

How the Philosophy Applies to This Curriculum

This curriculum presents conflict management from the bottom up: the initial chapter deals with self-understanding, while the final ones deal with conflict on a global level. The chapters build on one another, teaching skills that guide students through the labyrinth of conflict. This curriculum is based on nine fundamental building blocks:

1. Conflicts are disagreements between two or more persons or ideas. Conflict means, above all, interaction or dialogue.[2]

2. Conflicts are necessary for development and growth. The way a person handles conflict is an important part of his/her personality.

3. Self-awareness and self-understanding contribute to constructive management of conflicts. For example, students with low self-esteem often handle conflict differently than students with high self-esteem. Every conflict has positive potential. Whether or not the conflict is resolved, there is a basis for recognizing and understanding each other's needs and wants; relationships can be preserved or enhanced.

4. Conflicts cannot be constructively resolved without positive interaction, which is a form of communication.

5. Specific skills are needed in order for conflict to be an experience of growth and development.

6. These specific skills can be taught.

7. Conflicts can be resolved in a manner that does not violate human rights.

8. For conflict management strategies and structures to be most effective, they must be institutionalized into as much of society as possible. Impor-

---

2. Specifically, conflict exists when two interdependent sides are apparently incompatible because of perceived differences in goals, values, resources, or needs. By interdependence, we mean that whatever one side does in the conflict affects the other side.

tant levels of systematic institution include the family, school, community, and nation.

THE CURRICULUM FORMAT

Please note that the book is divided into two parts. In Part I, students discover how a broad range of factors affects the process of conflict management, ranging from personal values to beliefs about human rights. Part II is a program on student mediation. This curriculum can be viewed as two separate books with similar underlying ideas.

Part I: Conflict Management

Part I of this curriculum contains six chapters, each with an explanatory introduction. The chapters consist of various lesson plans that relate to the chapters' main themes. Each lesson plan contains learning objectives, key concepts, background information, materials needed, activities, and discussion questions.

- The *objectives* are measurable outcomes of the activities.
- *Key concepts* are the main ideas of each activity. An index of key concepts is located in the back of the curriculum on page 292. Definitions for all of the key concepts can be found in the *glossary*, located on page 289.
- The *background information* prepares the teacher with the information necessary to present the activity to the students.
- Each *activity* presents step-by-step procedures for teaching the concepts of the lesson. Some lessons have *additional activities* that clarify or expand on the objectives.
- *Discussion questions* are included at the end of nearly every lesson. These questions guide students in thinking about the main ideas of each activity.
- Most lessons include activity sheets that can be photocopied and given to the students. If a photocopy machine is unavailable, many of the activity sheets can easily be adapted.

Part II: Student Mediation

Part II consists of an explanation of mediation, as well as ten sessions in student mediation. Each session contains learning objectives, materials needed, and step-by-step activities.

Appendixes

The appendixes assist the teacher in all aspects of the curriculum. The appendixes include stress-relieving activities, icebreakers, a short play, interdisciplinary approaches to conflict management, and a section on how to divide students into groups.

HOW TO USE THIS CURRICULUM

This curriculum is big! Where do I begin??? There are a number of different ways that you can use this curriculum to effectively teach students valuable life skills:

1. **Do it all!** The most effective way for students to learn all of the conflict management skills within this book is to facilitate the activities in the book from the beginning to end, activity by activity. Because the skills build on one another, it is helpful to facilitate the activities in the order they are presented.

2. **Do some of it!** Most teachers do not have enough time to facilitate all the activities in the book. (Most of the activities take between 45–50 minutes to complete.) So here are some other ways to use the curriculum:

   A. **Explore the curriculum!**
   Educational, fun activities are hidden within each of the chapters. Flip through the curriculum and read the different activities.

   B. **Assess the needs of your class.**
   - In the index you will see a list of key concepts of conflict management. Beneath each concept is a list of lessons within the curriculum that deal with that specific concept. Decide which concepts you think will most effectively meet the needs of your students.
   - If many of the students need to improve their self-concept and self-esteem, facilitate activities from Chapter One.
   - If many of the students need to develop an understanding of prejudice, discrimination, stereotyping, and propaganda, facilitate activities from Chapter Two.
   - If many of the students need to improve their communication skills (such as their verbal and non-verbal skills, their sensitivity and ability

to express feelings, and so on), facilitate activities from Chapter Three.
- If many of the students have difficulty managing conflicts effectively, we recommend that you facilitate activities from each of the chapters. However, if many of your students have developed effective communication skills, facilitate activities from all chapters except Chapter Three.
- Create your own compilation of activities, based on your assessment of your students' needs. Turn to the first page of each chapter to find a quick and thorough description of its contents.
- Ask the students from your class what key issues are that they would like to work on.

C. **Develop a short conflict management program.** The activities within this curriculum build on one another. For instance, students cannot manage conflicts successfully if they don't have communication skills, and they can't communicate very effectively if they have low self-esteem.

Therefore, to develop a short conflict management program, simply select activities from each of the chapters and present them in the order they are presented in this curriculum.

Think of the needs, personalities, and attention spans of the students in your class. What are most students' levels of self-esteem? How well do they communicate? How well do they understand concepts like prejudice, nationalism, or discrimination? Only choose activities from Part I of this curriculum. We have included the Create Your Own Conflict Management Program activity sheet below to help you organize your own conflict management program.

Following this sheet are two sample conflict management programs. You may decide to use one of them as a guide for which activities to facilitate. However, we suggest that you create a sheet that meets your students' specific needs. Remember that each activity takes approximately 45 minutes.

Once you have created your program and have started facilitating the activities, you may need to modify the list of activities, depending on how well students grasp the concepts. For example, suppose you only choose to facilitate one activity on discrimination. If the class does not fully understand what discrimination is from that one activity, it may be wise to facilitate another activity to clarify the concept.

Create Your Own Conflict Management Program

ACTIVITIES FROM CHAPTER ONE
_____
_____
_____
_____
_____

ACTIVITIES FROM CHAPTER TWO
_____
_____
_____
_____
_____

ACTIVITIES FROM CHAPTER THREE
_____
_____
_____
_____
_____

ACTIVITIES FROM CHAPTER FOUR
_____
_____
_____
_____
_____

ACTIVITIES FROM CHAPTER FIVE
_____
_____
_____
_____
_____

ACTIVITIES FROM CHAPTER SIX
_____
_____
_____
_____
_____

2004 © Open Society Institute

The Publisher grants permission for the reproduction of this worksheet for non-profit educational purposes only.
Activity sheets may be downloaded from www.idebate.org/conflictandcommunication.htm

CREATE YOUR OWN CONFLICT MANAGEMENT PROGRAM

• SAMPLE I

ACTIVITIES FROM CHAPTER ONE

Mountains and Valleys
Me and the Mirror
The Two Sides of Me

ACTIVITIES FROM CHAPTER TWO

The Evening News
What's the Stereotype?
The Bargots and the Rooters!
Prejudice's Many Sizes and Shapes
Friend or Foe

ACTIVITIES FROM CHAPTER THREE

Watch Your Step
Tangled
Body Talk
The Guessing Game
The Feeling List

ACTIVITIES FROM CHAPTER FOUR

My Picture of Conflict
The Roots of Conflict
Where is Violence?

ACTIVITIES FROM CHAPTER FIVE

My Pounding Heart
Mind and Heart
The Milk Bottle
Bottle Caps
The Right Choice
Climbing the Ladder

ACTIVITIES FROM CHAPTER SIX

My Protective Shield
Stepping Across the Line

• SAMPLE II

ACTIVITIES FROM CHAPTER ONE

Mountains and Valleys
The Feel-Good Chair
Me and the Mirror
The Two Sides of Me

ACTIVITIES FROM CHAPTER TWO

The Evening News
The Bargots and the Rooters!
What's the Stereotype?
Prejudice's Many Sizes and Shapes
The Same Side of the Road
Friend or Foe

ACTIVITIES FROM CHAPTER THREE

Watch Your Step
The Mirror
Body Talk
The Feeling List
The Guessing Game
Susan Says
Why Ask Why?

ACTIVITIES FROM CHAPTER FOUR

My Picture of Conflict
The Roots of Conflict
The Conflict Dictionary
Where is Violence?

ACTIVITIES FROM CHAPTER FIVE

My Pounding Heart
Mind and Heart
The Milk Bottle
Bottle Caps
The Right Choice
Climbing the Ladder
The Factory

ACTIVITIES FROM CHAPTER SIX

My Protective Shield
Stepping Across the Line
Same Script, Different Play
Creating a Conflict Management Activity

2004 © Open Society Institute

The Publisher grants permission for the reproduction of this worksheet for non-profit educational purposes only.
Activity sheets may be downloaded from www.idebate.org/conflictandcommunication.htm

Chapter One:

ME

Our beliefs, perceptions, values, needs, and feelings are inescapable parts of every conflict in which we are involved. The way we resolve conflicts is influenced by how we feel about ourselves, how we relate to others, and how we value and view the world.

The activities in this chapter help students explore the relationship between conflict and their beliefs, feelings, thoughts, and life experiences. Students will become aware of what kinds of people they are, what their strengths are, how they feel about themselves, what their potentials are, and what their hopes, goals, and dreams are. The activities in later chapters will then help students develop strategies for dealing with conflicts, strategies that build on their own personalities, strengths, and potentials.

Many of the activities in the present chapter are designed to improve students' sense of self-esteem and self-worth. With an increased sense of self-worth, students will be better equipped for dealing with the complexities of conflict management.

An increased sense of self-worth may help prevent conflicts from escalating, since people with a healthy sense of self-worth are less likely to be prejudiced against others. Also, those with a healthy sense of self-worth are less likely to react defensively to others, and they are more able to see the other person's perspective in a conflict.

Thoughts On Conflict Management

OBJECTIVES
Upon completion of this exercise, the student will be able to:

1. Describe their views of conflict prior to learning the material within this conflict management program.

2. Describe their views of conflict after learning the material within this conflict management program.

3. Compare their initial views of conflict with their newer views.

KEY CONCEPTS
Analytical Thinking
Conflict Analysis

BACKGROUND
This activity is similar to a pre/post test. Both before and after teaching the skills and information presented in this curriculum, students complete the activity sheet located on page 12. You and the students can informally assess what the students learned from the conflict management program by comparing their initial views of conflict with their new views.

This lesson's activity allows students to see how their views change as they learn more about conflict. Before implementing the program, you may discover that many students view conflict as negative, destructive, and bad. However, on completion of the conflict management program, students will become aware of the positive, constructive potential of nearly every conflict.

MATERIALS
Thoughts on Conflict Management activity sheet, pencils, paper

TEACHER TIPS
Emphasize that the students should write candid, honest answers to the questions. To help your students feel more comfortable writing honest answers, you could have them not write their names on their papers. Instead, they could each draw a unique sign on their papers. Suggest to them that they draw their unique signs in their notebooks so they can refer to it later. When they have completed the activity sheet for the second time (after the conflict management program has been implemented), return the original completed sheets to each student by having each person draw or describe to you his/her unique sign.

ACTIVITY

1. Tell the students to complete the "Thoughts on Conflict Management" activity sheet. Students should not talk to anyone or compare answers with others while completing the sheet.

2. Once students have completed their answers, have them fold their sheet and draw their unique symbol on the outside.

3. Collect the sheets and tell students that you will return the sheets later in the year (after the conflict management program has been taught).

4. Put the sheets away, to be returned at the end of the program. After the conflict management program has been completed (days, weeks, or months later), have students complete new activity sheets. Pass back the original sheets so that the students can compare their initial views on conflict with their present ideas about conflict.

5. Have a discussion about how students' views of conflict have changed.

ACTIVITY SHEET
THOUGHTS ON CONFLICT MANAGEMENT

1. What is conflict?

2. When I think of the word *conflict*, I think of...

3. What types of conflicts have you experienced in your life?

4. Pretend that you are having a conflict with a friend of yours. What are some different ways the conflict can be resolved?

5. When you are in a conflict situation with a friend, how can you show your friend that you are listening?

6. Do the words "conflict" and "violence" mean the same thing to you? Explain.

DRAWING ME

OBJECTIVES

Upon completing this lesson, students will be able to:

1. Express aspects of themselves through artwork and discussion.
2. Describe their own interests and activities through their artwork and discussion.
3. Recognize positive and unique qualities about themselves.

KEY CONCEPTS

attitudes
behavior
feelings
pride
self-esteem

BACKGROUND

All students possess unique qualities that make them individually special. This activity is designed to give students pride in their interests, while at the same time increasing their levels of self-esteem. Increasing self-esteem primarily means promoting students' positive views of themselves. You, the teacher, should also take part in the activity.*

MATERIALS

crayons, pencils, paper

TEACHER TIPS

This activity can allow you the opportunity to break out of your role as teacher. By showing some of your interests, students can view you as a whole person, not just a teacher.

To set a supportive environment, tell students to respect each other. No one should make fun of anyone's drawings.

Before students share their pictures, you can evaluate the group process by asking the following

---

* Researeh shows that modeling is an effective method of transmitting knowledge. In other words, if you do something, the students will follow your example. For instance, it is more likely that your students will choose to read silently if you sit at your desk and quietly read.

questions: 1) Did everyone get a chance to share? 2) Was everyone treated with respect? The questions could be written on the chalkboard.

Additional Activity II can be very revealing. If a supportive environment is established, the activity can allow students to deeply explore their emotions and gain new self-awareness.

ACTIVITY

1. Divide the students into groups of three to five. (Include yourself in one of the groups.)
2. Distribute crayons, pencils, and paper to each group.
3. Write the following list on the board. Have everyone think of their:
   a. favorite type of music
   b. interests
   c. favorite subject in school (besides lunch)
   d. favorite color
   e. hobbies

Tell everyone to draw these different aspects of themselves on the paper. Stress that they should keep the drawings simple (this may reassure those who are self-conscious about drawing).

> *NOTE: If students say that they cannot express certain activities in drawing, tell them that they should be creative. You could offer students the following example: If a student's hobby is swimming, that person could draw a swimming pool or a lake or even a fish! If a student still insists that he/she cannot think of a way to express a particular activity, tell the student that he/she may use words also.*

4. Have students (and you!) show the drawings to the other members of their small groups. Tell everyone to explain:
   a. What each drawing represents, and
   b. Why each activity or interest is so special.

5. OPTIONAL: After the activity is finished, tell students to put their names on their drawings. Collect the students' drawings and hang them on the classroom wall.

ADDITIONAL ACTIVITY I

On another day, you could proceed with the same activity. But instead of having the students draw their activities and interests, tell them to draw themselves participating in an activity that they feel they do well.

ADDITIONAL ACTIVITY II

Have students think of something or someone they have lost. Have them either draw a picture or write a story or poem about that loss. Stress that no one has to show their project to anyone else unless they so desire. After the projects are completed, discuss aspects of them. This activity can help the healing process. Note that students should be given the choice of whether or not to participate.

An alternative way of presenting this activity is to tell the students to draw a picture or write a story or poem about what they imagine children can lose in a war.

DISCUSSION QUESTIONS

1. Was it difficult to figure out what to draw?
2. How did you feel before you did the project?
3. What thoughts went through your head while you were working on the project?
4. How do you feel now that the project is completed?

PRECAUTION: If it is apparent to you that a student has a serious problem due to a loss (e.g. of a family member, etc.), seek out psychiatric help for the child. If that is not possible, be sensitive to the child's needs. It may be useful for you to use some of the communications skills presented in Chapter Three.

WHO AM I ?

OBJECTIVE

Upon completing this lesson, students will be able to state their thoughts and feelings about personal topics.

KEY CONCEPTS

pride
self-esteem

BACKGROUND

This activity is designed for students to consciously acquaint themselves with feelings and thoughts about personal topics. Students will realize positive elements of themselves, and they will think about admirable qualities of others.

MATERIALS

"Who Am I?" activity sheet, pencils

TEACHER TIPS

Depending on your sense of what would be best for your students, the information could be shared. Everyone benefits when people share such things as what we are proud of and who we admire. However, make sure to create a safe, affirming environment. Emphasize that students should respect and listen to each other.

If there are less than ten students in your class, this activity could be facilitated as a discussion. Or, if you have a large class, you could divide it into groups of four to six. In small groups, the students could discuss the statements.

ACTIVITY

1. Have students individually fill out the "Who Am I?" activity sheet, finishing the statements honestly. Explain that they will be asked to share only one of the qualities of the people they most admire. Tell them that no one, not even you, will look at what is written on their worksheet.

2. After all students have completed the sheet, ask them to share one of the qualities they said they admire. Write these on the chalkboard. If there are duplications, add check marks next to those qualities to indicate how many students offered them.

3. After the discussion questions are completed, tell the students that they are free to do whatever they wish with the worksheet.

DISCUSSION QUESTIONS

1. Were the questions on the worksheet difficult to answer? Explain.

2. Did you feel embarrassed or find it difficult to write positive things about yourself, even though no one is going to read them? Explain.

3. How does it make you feel to spend time thinking about your positive qualities?

4. Have students read the qualities on the chalkboard. Ask:

   a. Does the list tell you anything about the types of people we admire? (This list usually includes only positive qualities.)

   b. Do we admire negative traits in people? Explain.

STUDENT ACTIVITY SHEET
WHO AM I ?

The people I care most about in my life are...

I feel proud of myself when I...

I am a likable person because...

The people I admire most in my life are...

The qualities I admire most about them are...

Two of my outstanding qualities are that I...

One of the kindest things I ever did was...

2004 © Open Society Institute

The Publisher grants permission for the reproduction of this worksheet for non-profit educational purposes only.
Activity sheets may be downloaded from www.idebate.org/conflictandcommunication.htm

MOUNTAINS AND VALLEYS

OBJECTIVES

Upon completing this lesson, students will be able to:

1. Describe influential positive and negative life experiences.
2. Recognize emotions connected with life experiences.
3. State common life events.

KEY CONCEPTS

attitudes
behavior
feelings
group bonding
self-esteem
trust
values

BACKGROUND

We all have unique life experiences, for we all lead our own lives. However, we all share certain common experiences, such as childhood. In the following activity, students gain an understanding of their unique and shared experiences, thus fostering a group spirit.

MATERIALS

paper, pencils

TEACHER TIPS

This is a powerful activity that awakens students' feelings and creates an atmosphere of openness and sharing. To help the activity work effectively, it may be useful to facilitate a quick icebreaker (see Appendix II) before beginning.

After students have completed their drawings, you could ask them to circle all events that they had control over or chose in their lives. For example, students do not have control over the natural death of grandparents. You could initiate a discussion about the relationship between the events in students' lives and the amount of control they had over those events.

ACTIVITY

1. Divide the class into groups of four or five. Direct each group to a separate area of the room and have them sit in a small circle.

2. On the left side of their papers, students make a dot and write their dates of birth.

3. On the right side of the paper, students make a dot and write today's date.

4. Tell students to think about the biggest events in their lives—both positive and negative—that have shaped their lives.

5. Students draw a line from the dot on the left side of the page to the other dot. For every positive event, the students bend the line upward so it makes a mountain. The more positive and great the event, the larger the mountain should be drawn. For every negative event, the students bend the line downward so it makes a valley like a hole. The more negative the event, the deeper the valley.

6. Students should label and date each event.

7. Once everyone in the group has completed the lifeline, each student individually explains his/her lifeline to the rest of the group. Stress that everyone should listen attentively while someone else is talking.

8. Read the following discussion questions to the class. Each student in each group should share his/her answers to the questions:

    a. What events in your life would you like to repeat?
    b. What would your perfect life be like?
    c. What events do you share in common with other students?

MOVIE AUDITIONS

OBJECTIVES

Upon completing this lesson, students will be able to:

1. List their accomplishments.
2. Speak in front of their classmates.
3. Express positive statements about themselves in front of others.

KEY CONCEPTS

attitudes
behavior
feelings
pride
self-esteem
values

BACKGROUND

A healthy outward acceptance of one's positive attributes relates to a high level of self-esteem. That is, a person who has confidence and self-worth often has a high level of self-esteem.

This activity allows students to proclaim publicly some of their positive attributes for the entire class to hear. In the process, the students develop a sense of self-worth because the class listens to them respectfully.

This activity also builds students' confidence levels because the students must muster the strength to tell the class something positive about themselves. It takes a great deal of confidence and courage to stand up in front of classmates and say something good about oneself!

MATERIALS

podium (placed at the front of the class), pencils, paper

TEACHER TIPS

This activity works very well, especially if you create an atmosphere of warmth and acceptance. Before facilitating this activity: 1) it may helpful to do an icebreaker with the class (see Appendix II) and 2) tell the students to be supportive of everyone.

Make it clear to the class that no one will be forced to participate. If students feel uncomfortable or shy, you can ask them if they would like to say their accomplishments without standing at the podium.

If you feel that the students are uncomfortable bragging in the presence of classmates, refer to the Teacher Tips of Self-Esteem Boosters (page 40) for advice.

ACTIVITY

1. Tell students that they have the chance to be in a major motion picture that will be seen all over the world. If they get the part, they will act beside famous movie stars. In order to try out for the part students must do the following:
    a. Make a list of five things accomplished in their lives of which they are proud. For example, students may be proud that they can get along so well with their friends or family, that they always finish their homework, etc.
    b. Have students look at their list and choose the one accomplishment of which they are most proud.
    c. You, the teacher, select one volunteer to stand at the podium at the front of the class. The student says, "I don't want to brag, but..." He/she completes the sentence with the accomplishment. The rest of the class is told that they are directors, and so they must listen to what the actor has to say.
    d. After the first student is finished, the class applauds, and he/she sits down. The student whose last name is next alphabetically stands at the podium and explains his/her accomplishment.
    e. This same procedure is followed until each student in the class has had a chance to speak.
    f. After the auditions end, have the class give itself a congratulatory round of applause. It will help the students relax before the discussion questions begin.

DISCUSSION QUESTIONS

1. How did it feel to stand at the podium and share accomplishments with the class?
2. Were you nervous or frightened to speak in front of the whole class? Explain.
3. What was it like to listen to others?
4. Do you think everyone felt the same way you did when they stood up on the chair and spoke? Explain.
5. Do you think you got the part in the movie? Explain.

Special People of the Week

OBJECTIVES

Upon completing this lesson, students will be able to:

1. Explain how it feels to be special.
2. Describe how it feels to be complimented.
3. State how it feels to compliment someone else.

KEY CONCEPTS

pride
self-esteem
values

BACKGROUND

Students often say negative comments to each other, such as when they tease each other. This can make individuals feel picked on or, at least, not appreciated. The following activity tries to make students aware of how important positive comments are to their self-images.

MATERIALS

pencils, paper

TEACHER TIPS

This activity works better in some classrooms than others, depending on the social maturity of the class.

When this activity works, it works very well. You may find that students initially may be reserved about openly writing compliments, but once students see positive evaluations, they feel proud and happy.

There is the possibility that students may tease the special people of the week. If you notice that students do tease each other, you could facilitate a discussion about teasing. You can ask the class questions such as: Why do people tease? What makes us all unique people? How does it feel when you are teased? What kind of person might someone be if he/she teases others?

ACTIVITY

1. Tell the class that every week there are going to be three special people of the week chosen at random. (You can choose your own method for selecting students.) These people's names will be written on a sign hanging on the wall. Students should be given the choice of whether they would like to be a special person of the week.

2. Students can also be given the opportunity to decide how the special people should be honored. For example, students could compliment the special people of the week whenever they see them. They could tell the special people of the week that they think the people have a pretty smile or are very clever. Alternately, you could list the names of the special people of the week on a poster and have students write complimentary notes on it throughout the week. Be clear to the students that the compliments must be sincere and honest. We all have good qualities and strengths. Others may see our strengths differently than we see them. This activity allows us to learn about others' perceptions of us in a non-threatening way.

DISCUSSION QUESTIONS

These questions can be asked at the end of every week, or whenever you think they are appropriate to ask:

1. How does it feel to be one of the special people of the week?
2. What are some reasons people feel more special when they are a special person of the week?
3. Is it possible to always feel special? How?
4. What makes a person feel special?
5. How did it feel to compliment someone?
6. How did it feel to receive compliments?
7. Why is it sometimes difficult to accept compliments?

How Many people am I?

OBJECTIVES
Upon completing this lesson, students will be able to:
1. Define the term *self-concept*.
2. Relate the term *self-concept* to themselves.
3. Describe the complexity of factors that influence their self-concepts.

KEY CONCEPTS
analytical thinking
attitudes
self-concept
self-esteem

BACKGROUND
Self-concept is the way people view themselves. It consists of people's attitudes, perceptions, and ideas about themselves. Each student (and each person in the world) has a unique self-concept, and therefore each student is unique. No two people see things exactly the same way. For instance, all of the students in the classroom might be able to see the teacher, but each one sees the teacher from a different point of view. The boy sitting in the corner might only see the right side of the teacher's face, while the girl in the front row might see the teacher's entire face. Similarly, each student has a unique self-concept partially based on common experiences with others. We all might participate in an activity, but we will not all have the same feelings within us while this activity takes place.

Also, the self-concept helps a person maintain stability and consistency. For example, if I feel I am a good person, I will have a positive outlook on much that I do because I will have a positive self-concept. On the other hand, if my self-concept is bad and inferior, many of my responses will probably be consistently hostile and contemptuous. So, the next activities focus on how to understand and increase one's positive self-concept.

This activity allows us to critically analyze how we view ourselves. A quotation is presented that provides insight into the variety of ways we can think about ourselves.

MATERIALS
chalkboard, chalk

TEACHER TIPS

This activity may be more appropriate for older, more intellectually mature students. The emphasis of this activity is on having students practice analysis of an issue.

If your students are younger, you can adapt this activity. First, you could explain what a self-concept is. Next, the students could draw a picture of how they view their self-concept. In small groups of four to six, the students could share their pictures with each other.

Also, for younger students, you could illustrate the activity by explaining that people act differently depending on the situation. For example, children act differently with parents, friends, and others.

ACTIVITY

1. Write the following quotation on the board, explaining that a famous psychologist named William James wrote it:

   "Whenever two people meet there are really six people present—there is each man [or woman] as he sees himself, each man [or woman] as the other sees him, and each man [or woman] as he really is."
   (William James, Principles of Psychology; 1890)

2. Write the word *self-concept* on the board.
3. Discuss its meaning with the students.
4. Divide the students into pairs.
5. Tell them that they will have approximately 10 minutes to decide what William James meant by the quote and how the quote relates to our self-concept.
6. Each pair briefly explains what it thinks the quotation means and how it relates to our self-concept.
7. Divide the students into groups of three. Ask them to discuss:
   a. What does it mean to be a happy person?
   b. How do people's self-concepts relate to contact with friends, teachers, siblings, and parents?
   c. What are some different ways that people accept praise?
   8. Have everyone gather a large circle. Have each small group share its answers to the questions.

DISCUSSION QUESTIONS

1. What things influence your self-concept?

   NOTE: Make sure that students answer this question specifically. (That is, if a student responds by saying, "attitudes," ask him/her what kinds of attitudes.)

2. How does self-concept relate to the quote on the board?
3. How positive do you think your self-concept is?
4. What are some ways that people can work to improve their self-concept?
5. What are signs of someone who has a positive self-concept?

POSITIVE SELF-TALK

OBJECTIVE

Upon completing this lesson, students will be able to apply positive self-talk, a powerful technique that helps to create a positive self-concept.

KEY CONCEPTS

self-concept
self-esteem

BACKGROUND

Students learn early from certain parents, friends, and teachers how to criticize and blame themselves. If students learn to turn negative thoughts into positive ones, they will in turn improve their self-concept. With a more positive self-concept, the students will be better able to deal constructively with problems at home, at school, or elsewhere.

The following activity is designed to promote positive *self-talk*. In other words, the activity is intended to teach students that praising themselves is beneficial to their self-concept.

In order for this activity to be effective, you as a teacher must play an active role in teaching the skill. Students look up to their teachers as role models, and because students often imitate their role models, you have one specific task: As a teacher, you should not only encourage your students to praise themselves, but you should openly and out loud praise your own positive qualities. Why? You must model the skill that you want the students to learn. As Donald Felker, an expert on self-concept, says, "Imagine for a moment a teacher who stands up and says, 'This is the way to work a problem.' She then stands for a few seconds and says, 'Now do you all see?' But no one sees anything because the teacher worked the problem in her head."*

Here is an example on how you can individualize the concept:

>Teacher: "Joseph, you really did well on the test. What do you feel like telling yourself?"
>
>Student: "I'm not sure."
>
>Teacher: "Well, what do you think I would say? Tell yourself what I would say."

MATERIALS

none

---

* Donald Felker. *Building Positive Self-Concepts* (Minneapolis: Burgess Publishing, 1974), 66.

TEACHER TIPS

Explain that self-talk is not the same as bragging, which can be negative because it may include putting down another person or their accomplishment. Bragging may even be exaggerated or untrue. Explain also that in a later activity, "Self-Esteem Boosters," the class will be looking at bragging in a positive way.

This activity is an important part of helping students develop a positive self-concept. As a role model for your students, you as the teacher should also model the skills of positive self-praise on a daily basis. See "How Many People Am I?" (page 25) for a more thorough description of self-concept.

ACTIVITY

1. Discuss with the students that it is important to learn how to praise oneself. Verbal praise is like giving yourself a reward when you feel you have done well and deserve credit. Tell them that for a while they should praise themselves out loud until the idea is completely understood. Then, students will begin to practice self-talk in their heads.

2. You, the teacher, should begin by praising yourself in areas that are not highly personal to you. For example, you could say, "I really like how well I put your drawings on the wall."

3. Make a list of praise phrases with your students to hang on the wall. A sample phrase might be, "I was proud of myself today when I…"

4. Set goals. For example, have the students praise themselves once a day. Possibly, introduce the concept to the class by saying something like, "Whose class believes it is a great class?" Have the class respond with, "Our class believes it is a great class!"

ADDITIONAL ACTIVITY

First, divide the class into groups of approximately seven to ten students. Each small group sits in a circle. Instruct the students to individually think of a quality that they like about themselves.

Second, the students in each small group compare the sizes of their hands; the person with the smallest hand is the first to share his/her quality.

Third, going clockwise, ask each student to share his/her quality and then repeat the others' qualities in the order in which they were stated.

ME AND THE MIRROR

OBJECTIVES

Upon completing this lesson, students will be able to:

1. Explain the difference between a positive and a negative outlook on life.
2. State positive aspects to situations and experiences that appear negative.
3. Brainstorm.

KEY CONCEPTS

brainstorming
self-concept
self-esteem

BACKGROUND

The self-concept is something that we learn from birth. It is affected by the way we look, the way we act, and the way others respond to us. It is essential to understand that the self-concept is learned; because of this, it can be changed and more positively shaped. The following activity teaches students how to focus on the positive aspects of life experiences and situations.

The activity also introduces students to brainstorming, a simple, effective method for generating ideas. In many conflict situations, people may feel that there is no workable resolution to their problem. But by brainstorming a list of solutions, a creative, workable resolution may be found.

MATERIALS

chalkboard, chalk

TEACHER TIPS

During this activity, students may think about sensitive life issues. Therefore, it is important to set a supportive environment. Tell students that they should listen to, respect, and not tease each other.

For a more thorough description of self-concept, see "How Many People Am I?" (page 25) and "Positive Self-Talk" (page 27).

After facilitating this activity, you may want to discuss with students why it is often easier to say unkind statements about other people or ourselves rather than kind, positive statements.

To reinforce the importance of this activity, it may be helpful to facilitate this same activity more than once.

ACTIVITY

1. Write the word *brainstorming* on the chalkboard. Tell the students that it is sometimes difficult to think of ideas, so one helpful tool is to brainstorm. Explain to the students the four rules of brainstorming:

    - **Write down every idea you can think of.** Some ideas may sound impossible or silly, but that's okay. Sometimes the most outrageous ideas cause us to think of other, useful ideas.
    - **Think of as many ideas as possible.** The more ideas you think of, the greater the chance that useful ideas will be found.
    - **Don't judge any idea as good or bad.**
    - **Don't talk or think about the ideas.** Just write them down.

2. Have students divide a sheet of paper into two columns. In the left column, tell students to brainstorm negative experiences and situations in their lives.

3. In the right column, ask them to brainstorm, writing down positive aspects of the same experiences or situations. For instance, in the left-hand column a student may write, "My parents yell at me a lot when I get bad grades." In the right-hand column, the student may write, "My parents care about me and want me to succeed in school."

4. Discuss with students the importance of interpreting situations positively.

5. Give the students the following example of how to focus on the positive aspects of a situation:

    The situation: Andras, your best friend, asked Barbara to play soccer with him. He didn't ask you.
    Negative thought: Andras didn't ask me. I guess I'm not as fast a runner. And I'm not as funny or as nice as Barbara.
    Positive thought: Even though Andras didn't ask me to play soccer with him, I know that I am a good soccer player and a nice, fun person.

6. Have students divide into pairs. Make sure pairs are spread out from one another. Tell the students to stand face to face.

7. Give students different situations. Have one person explain the situation negatively and the other person mirror the first person's statement, but reinterpret the situation positively.

    Possible Situations:
    a. You forget to do a chore for your mother.
    b. You do badly on a test.
    c. You ask a friend to play with you, and he/she says no.
    You and the class can think up more ideas.

DISCUSSION QUESTIONS

1. How does it feel to view the world positively?

2. What were some negative thoughts that were difficult to convert into positive thoughts? (Have the class brainstorm possible ways of turning those negative thoughts into positive ones.)

3. How can you use brainstorming in a conflict situation? Ask the students to describe a specific conflict and have them brainstorm possible resolutions to it.

IN TRUST WE TRUST

OBJECTIVES

Upon completing this lesson, students will be able to:

1. Explain essential qualities needed to trust people.
2. Brainstorm.

KEY CONCEPTS

brainstorming
self-esteem
trust

BACKGROUND

An important part of a student's growth is done through sharing. In this activity, students think about trust and with whom they trust enough to share their personal thoughts. Trust is defined as a confident reliance on another individual.

MATERIALS

"In Trust We Trust" activity sheet, pencils, paper

TEACHER TIPS

You may want to discuss with students what qualities make someone untrustworthy. For instance, you could ask them what happens when someone they trust does or says something unkind to them. How do they feel in such situations?

Another powerful trust lesson is "Watch Your Step" (page 84).

ACTIVITY

1. Ask students to write down five qualities that a person must have in order to be trusted. Example qualities could include: sensitivity, intelligence, caring, honesty, loyalty, and so on.
2. Divide the students into groups of four to six.
3. Have students share and discuss the qualities they wrote on their lists.

4. Ask each group to agree on two qualities it feels are most important for trusting someone.

5. Have each group report its findings.

6. Have students fill out the "In Trust We Trust" activity sheet.

7. Explain brainstorming. Write the four rules of brainstorming on the chalkboard. (Brainstorming is explained in the previous lesson.)

8. Ask students to brainstorm and tell you as many different words as they can that describe the people they trust. Write all the words on the chalkboard. Once the students can think of no more words, add words that they might not have thought about.

ACTIVITY SHEET
In Trust We Trust

DEFINE TRUST:

The people I trust are:

The reason I trust them is because:

The people who trust me are:

The reason they trust me is because:

The Feel-Good Chair

OBJECTIVES

Upon completing this lesson, students will be able to:

1. Define the concept of self-esteem
2. Relate the concept of self-esteem to themselves.
3. Explain how self-esteem relates to conflict.

KEY CONCEPTS

attitudes
behavior
conflict analysis
feelings
self-esteem

BACKGROUND

Self-esteem (how one feels about oneself) affects how one acts and reacts in conflict situations. Suppose two students have just failed a test and think they are not good at anything. If they become involved in a conflict situation, they are liable to act much differently than if they earned a good grade on the test and feel good about themselves.

MATERIALS

"The Feel-Good Chair" activity sheet; chair placed at the front of the classroom

TEACHER TIPS

Before facilitating this activity, it may be helpful to have the class do an icebreaker (see Appendix II).

While facilitating this activity and the discussion, emphasize the importance of self-respect. It is healthy to believe that we are unique, good people. Make sure that students don't conclude that having a great deal of self-respect is negative and having just a little self-respect is positive.

ACTIVITY

1. Before beginning this activity:

    a. Cut out the six different descriptions on "The Feel-Good Chair" activity sheet.
    b. Place a chair in the front of the room.
    c. Write the discussion questions on the chalkboard.

2. Ask the class to describe what they think self-esteem is. Explain that self-esteem is how you feel about yourself. For example, when you feel good about yourself and are proud to be you, you have high self-esteem. When you feel that you are a worthless failure, you have low self-esteem. Most of us have times of both low and high self-esteem. Some people have a higher self-esteem than other people. And, if someone feels that they have a low self-esteem, there is good news: Your level of self-esteem can change!

3. Randomly hand out the six descriptions to students in the class.

4. Have student 1 and student 2 walk up to the front of the room and read his/her description out loud.

5. Ask the class whether each description described a student with high or low self-esteem. Discuss with them their reasons for thinking that the person has high or low self-esteem.

7. Tell students 1 and 2 that they just walked into the classroom. Each one of them is very tired and wants to sit down, but there is only one chair in the room. While acting out their characters (that is acting the way they think that person would react in that situation), students 1 and 2 must now role play, arguing over who should sit in the seat. (Caution them that pushing and shoving aren't allowed.)

8. Repeat this entire process (steps 5–8) with students 3 and 4 and then with students 5 and 6.

9. Have the class divide into groups of four to six and discuss the questions listed on the chalkboard.

10. Have one representative from each group share the group's answers with the class.

DISCUSSION QUESTIONS

1. How are students described in the activity similar to students at school?

2. What is self-esteem? How is self-esteem different from being conceited?

3. How do people act when they have low self-esteem?

4. How do they act when they have high self-esteem?

5. When people with high self-esteem get into conflicts, how are they likely to act?

6. When people with low self-esteem get into conflicts, how are they likely to act?

7. Do you think a bully has high or low self-esteem? Why?

8. What happens when two people with high self-esteem get into a conflict? How might they typically try to resolve the conflict?

9. What happens when two people with low self-esteem get into a conflict? How might they typically try to resolve the conflict?

10. How can someone with low self-esteem make himself/herself feel important and special?

11. What kinds of things do you do to make yourself feel good about yourself?.

Activity Sheet
The Feel-Good Chair

Student 1: I have a sister. She is angry with me and said that I am stupid. I think that I am stupid, too, but I don't tell anyone that. My parents say that I don't study hard. I do try, but not hard enough, I guess. I just found out that I failed my mathematics test. I am not very happy now.

Student 2: I have a sister. She thinks I am very smart. I think I am smart, also. I study hard and am proud of myself, even though I don't get very good grades. I know that I have always tried my hardest. My parents are happy that I study so much. I did well on a history test today.

Student 3: I am the best football player on the team. My brother got married yesterday, and my family is very happy. The teacher told me that I am a very good student. Last week, I won an award for drawing beautiful artwork.

Student 4: I love to read and had a lot of time last week to read my favorite book. My best friend and I are getting along with each other very well. I failed a mathematics test, but I realize that I am simply not good at math. Although I failed the test, I still like myself.

Student 5: Everyone makes fun of me. My friends say that they care about me, but I don't think they really like me—not at all. My parents always ask me why I don't get grades as good as my older sister. I try as hard as I can, but even if I get good grades, they're never as good as my sister's grades. I don't think that I am very good at anything.

Student 6: Last week I was told that I was the best-looking student in the entire class. But I don't think I am attractive. I think I am ugly. My parents always tell me how smart I am. But even though I do well in school, I never get the best grades in the class. Friends sometimes tell me that they wish they were me, but I don't know why they would want to be me.

2004 © Open Society Institute

The Publisher grants permission for the reproduction of this worksheet for non-profit educational purposes only.
Activity sheets may be downloaded from www.idebate.org/conflictandcommunication.htm

BIGGER AND BIGGER

OBJECTIVES

Upon completing this lesson, students will be able to:

1. Set a goal and reach it.
2. Create a project on their own.

KEY CONCEPTS

self-efficacy
self-esteem

BACKGROUND

Self-efficacy is the feeling of confidence that one can successfully complete a task. If students set a goal and then reach it, they feel a sense of mastery over that task. The next time that they have a task, they may feel more confident that they can complete it. Their feeling of self-efficacy has increased. By giving students projects or tasks that they can successfully complete, their self-efficacy increases; they feel more confident and may try harder when given a more difficult, challenging task.

MATERIALS

A variety of student-created projects (see activity)

TEACHER TIPS

During this activity, emphasize that everyone should be respectful while students present their projects. Tell students to be supportive of one another.

A variation of this activity is to have students complete weekly projects; each week, the projects to complete become more challenging, but as long as students successfully complete their projects from week to week, their self-efficacy should increase.

ACTIVITY

1. Have students individually create projects (for example, artwork, stories, puzzles, games, songs, poems, etc.). Help students discover what kind of project they would like to create, but do not give them guidance in the actual project. Let them create the projects on their own.
2. Allow students to present their projects to the class.
3. Display the projects in the classroom. For instance, hang pictures and stories on the walls for everyone to see.

The Two Sides of Me

OBJECTIVES

Upon completing this lesson, students will be able to:

1. Explain what internal conflicts are.
2. Describe some of the dynamics behind their internal conflicts.

KEY CONCEPTS

conflict analysis
internal conflicts
self-understanding

BACKGROUND

Most people think of conflicts as arguments or battles between two or more people. However, we all experience internal conflicts in which we have apparently incompatible sides within ourselves. For example, a student may be unable to decide whether or not to smoke cigarettes with his/her friends.

When faced with internal conflicts, it is necessary to define specifically what the conflict is about. What are the issues involved? What feelings are connected to the different sides of the conflict?

MATERIALS

none

TEACHER TIPS

This lesson helps students become more aware of the dynamics of internal conflicts. The lessons in Chapter Five can easily be adapted to offer strategies for dealing with internal conflicts.

ACTIVITY

1. Explain to students what an internal conflict is. Ask them how an internal conflict is different from an interpersonal conflict (interpersonal conflicts involve more than one person).

2. Ask the class to offer internal conflicts that people their age encounter.

3. Have each student think of an internal conflict in his/her own life. Tell the students that they will be sharing the conflicts with each other, so make sure they think of a conflict they do not mind sharing.

4. Divide the class into groups of three.

5. Ask each group to find out which person in the group likes bread the most. That person becomes director of that group. The other two people are actors.

6. For 30 seconds, the director tells one actor in the group one side of his/her internal conflict. For 30 additional seconds, the director tells the other actor in the group the other side of his/her internal conflict.

7. The director watches the two actors act out the internal conflict. For instance, suppose the director's internal conflict deals with whether or not to skip school. One actor would argue that it is very important to stay in school and learn, while the other actor would argue about the boredom and uselessness of staying in school.

8. After approximately 2 minutes, the actors stop. The director then comments on what happened and how it felt to watch the internal conflict.

9. The students in each group switch roles and repeat steps 6–9. Each student should have an opportunity to be director.

DISCUSSION QUESTIONS

1. What is an internal conflict?
2. How did it feel to have your internal conflict acted out?
3. How do you normally resolve internal conflicts?

Self-Esteem Boosters

OBJECTIVE

Upon completing this lesson, students will be able to identify positive aspects of themselves and others.

KEY CONCEPTS

self-esteem
group bonding
trust

BACKGROUND

The following activities are effective in raising students' self-esteem. They can be used any time that you feel they would be appropriate. When the weather is persistently dark and dreary (especially during the winter months in many countries), people often become depressed and gloomy. During those times, self-esteem-boosting activities might be particularly beneficial.

MATERIALS

paper, pencils

TEACHER TIPS

These activities deal with bragging. In most cultures, bragging and complimenting oneself are not traditionally approved. So students may find it difficult to brag, or they may become shy. Three ways to make the activities work well are:

1. Before facilitating the activities, do an icebreaker (see Appendix II).

2. Explain to students that you realize that bragging is not traditionally accepted in most societies, but that today we are going to brag. Today, during this activity, it is okay to brag.

3. Create a supportive environment by telling students not to tease or make rude comments about others. Also, be supportive to both boys and girls. In some cultures, girls may find it more difficult to complete the activity.

ACTIVITY 1: THE PARTY SPEECH

All students gather into a circle and pretend that they are at a party. They pretend to have a glass of juice in their hands. One by one, students raise their glasses and make a complimentary speech about themselves. After each speech, everyone pretends to take a sip of his or her drink in agreement with the speech.

ACTIVITY 2: BRAGGING

All students gather into a circle. One by one, students say the following phrase, completing it with something positive about themselves: "I don't want to brag, but..." Students might be shy in admitting achievements, so it might be helpful if you (the teacher) go first.

Stress to the students that bragging during this activity should be positive and should not make anyone feel bad about themselves or their accomplishments.

ACTIVITY 3: BRAGGING THROUGH ART

This activity may be more effective than the previous two if many students in the class are reserved or shy. Have students draw something positive about themselves. It may take students a few minutes to decide what to draw. Have students share their drawings with the class.

Chapter Two:

YOU

As humans, we all have unique experiences and we all perceive the world from a different point of view. Our uniqueness is one of our strengths: No two people are exactly alike, so everyone can add to the color and excitement of life. However, our uniqueness can also be a source of trouble and conflict. Because we all do not perceive the world precisely the same, misperceptions, misunderstandings, and differences in values and needs may arise. These differences affect the way we act, think, feel, and react.

Through the activities of the previous chapter, students learned about themselves. They explored who they are and what their values and perceptions of the world are. This chapter's activities allow students to broaden their views and perceptions of the world. They will develop conflict management skills necessary to perceive situations in many different ways. And they will begin to understand that what looks like a rock to one student may look like a diamond to another.

Students will learn about and experience the processes, thoughts, and feelings involved in very powerful topics such as prejudice, discrimination, and stereotyping. Through their learning process, they will gain an appreciation of and sensitivity to the similarities and differences of all people. Also, they will learn to appreciate the value of diversity.

The following are definitions of some of the important words used in this book:

Prejudice—An opinion, often unfavorable, about a subject or group, that is formed before exploring all of its facets. Often, prejudice is formed due to a lack of effort to understand perceived differences.

Discrimination—The act of treating someone differently on the basis of age, religion, ethnicity, nationality, handicap, gender, class, race, and so on. It is prejudice acted out. Discrimination is similar to scapegoating, which is when a person or group is blamed for mistakes or events caused by others.

Stereotype—The belief that a group of people possesses certain similar qualities and does not have individual differences.

SNOWFLAKES

OBJECTIVES
Upon completing this lesson, students will be able to:
1. Describe how different people view the world from different perspectives and interpret concepts in different ways.
2. Describe why there is a diversity of perspectives on issues.

KEY CONCEPTS
appreciating diversity

BACKGROUND
This activity stresses the concept that, though differences in perspectives on an issue might exist, this does not mean there is only one correct perspective. In many scenarios, there is no right answer: Each person's perspective on the issue can be correct. For example, suppose two students argue about whether it is more important to learn algebra or science. One student firmly believes that algebra is the most useful subject in school, for it helps people to develop useful analytical skills. The other student holds the opinion that science is more important, for it promotes rational, scientific thinking. Who is correct? Both of them. Why? Because each student has a different value system. From each student's perspective, his/her values are correct.

Of course, certain values may be considered more important for ethical or humanitarian reasons. For instance, in most societies humans have the right to own property. If a person decides to steal from another person, his/her perspective on ownership may be considered less correct than most people's perspectives (which value all humans' rights to own property).

MATERIALS
one piece of notebook paper for the teacher and each student

TEACHER TIPS
Some students may hold views that may not be acceptable on ethical or humanitarian grounds. If these students voice their opinions, what should you do? Here are some possibilities:
1. You could ask open questions that allow students to fully express their thoughts.
2. You could ask other students for their views, making sure that everyone is respectful of one another.

3. You could have students switch roles and argue from the other side. So, for example, if a boy thinks girls are stupid, have boys and girls switch roles and argue from the other gender's point of view.

ACTIVITY

1. Give each student a piece of paper.

2. Explain that the following activity is not graded. Stress that it is important that each student not watch anyone else while doing the activity. Everyone must follow the teacher's instructions while remaining quiet. Tell the students that no one is allowed to ask any questions on how to do the activity. If students do ask a question, tell them to do the activity the way they think they should.

3. Instruct the students to:
    a. Pick up the piece of paper.
    b. Fold it in half.
    c. Tear off the top right corner of the paper.
    d. Fold the paper in half again.
    e. Tear off the top right corner of the paper.
    f. Fold the paper in half again.
    g. Tear off the top right corner of the paper.
    h. Fold the paper in half again.
    i. Tear off the top right corner of the paper if they can. If students insist that it is too hard to tear the corner off, tell them that they do not need to.
    j. Unfold the piece of paper.

4. Tell students to look around the room, noticing how different each classmate's piece of paper is.

DISCUSSION QUESTIONS

1. Is anybody's paper torn incorrectly? Why not?

2. Why are so many students' papers torn differently?

3. If students' papers are torn differently from yours, does that make them bad people? Why not?

4. Do we judge people as good or bad depending on whether they do things exactly like us? What's an example of when this happens?

5. In what ways do you think people from other countries (from different religious, ethnic backgrounds, etc.) view the world differently? How is their view different from your own? Whose view is correct?

6. What would the world be like if everyone saw everything the same way? How is the world more interesting because of the many different ways of seeing?

ADDITIONAL ACTIVITY I

Tell the students to draw what you tell them without asking questions or directions. Tell to them how to draw a teacup (or some other object), but only use geometric terminology. Do not tell them the object you are describing. For example, you could tell them to draw two ovals and connect the edges of the ovals with two straight lines. Of course, in this manner it is difficult to understand what is being described. Repeat the activity. However, this time, the students can ask questions to clarify how to draw the unknown object. Have students share their first and second pictures.

The objective of this activity is to show how interpretation affects our view of the world. This can also be done in small groups in which one student describes what to draw to the others.

ADDITIONAL ACTIVITY II

1. Have three volunteers stand at the front of the room. Ask them to form a human statue about a conflict.* They can design the statue any way they would like, but tell them that they must make the statue within one minute. After the minute has ended, they must not move.

2. Once the statue has been constructed, ask each student in the class to write down what he/she thinks the name of the statue should be. Stress that no one should discuss his/her title with anyone else.

3. Ask the students in the class to share what they wrote down as the title of the statue.

4. Ask the three students who made the statue to offer a suggestion of what they thought the name should be.

ADDITIONAL DISCUSSION QUESTIONS

1. Everyone in the class looked at the same statue. But did everyone give it the same title? Why not? What influenced people's titles? (Values, experiences, feelings, perceptions, personal needs, and so on.)

2. Can people look at the same situation and see different things?

---

* A human statue is created when the students in each group depict an incident or idea by using their bodies. For example, the statue could illustrate a scenario in which discrimination is taking place, or a scene in which prejudice affects someone. Each group needs to select a "sculptor" who will help the other students in the group to position their bodies. The students then practice creating the statue and standing still in those positions, as if they are in a photograph.

THE SAME DIFFERENCES

OBJECTIVE

Upon completing this lesson, students will be able to identify similarities and differences among people.

KEY CONCEPTS

appreciating diversity
discrimination
self-understanding

BACKGROUND

All humans have certain similarities and certain differences with other humans. A major aspect in stereotyping and the formation of prejudice is that differences are overemphasized while similarities are de-emphasized. This activity allows students to gain perspective on differences and similarities.

MATERIALS

"The Same Differences" activity sheet, pencils

TEACHER TIPS

Students may need your guidance in understanding that differences do not define a person or group as better or worse than others. Differences are simply qualities that make a person or group unique.

If students have difficulty completing the activity sheet, encourage them to be creative! It may also be helpful to refresh the ideas of brainstorming (explained in the lesson "Me and The Mirror" on page 29).

ACTIVITY

1. Have students complete the activity sheet.
2. Randomly divide students into pairs, and have them compare their answers with each other. Instruct students to look for similarities and differences with each other.
3. Have students compare their answers three more times with three different students.

DISCUSSION QUESTIONS

1. In what categories do you have the same responses as others?
2. How are you similar to the others with whom you talked?
3. How are you different from the others with whom you shared similarities and differences?
4. Have you ever been treated badly because of your differences from other people? You could offer them the example that adults sometimes treat children negatively, excluding them from certain activities, just because they are children.

ACTIVITY SHEET
THE SAME DIFFERENCES

In the following columns, list at least three similarities and three differences that you have for each of the categories.

CATEGORY	SIMILARITIES	DIFFERENCES
FAMILY MEMBERS	Three similarities between the members of my family and me are: 1. 2. 3.	Three differences between the members of my family and me are: 1. 2. 3.
FRIENDS	Three similarities between my friends and me are: 1. 2. 3.	Three differences between my friends and me are: 1. 2. 3.
ANIMALS	Three similarities between animals and me are: 1. 2. 3.	Three differences between animals and me are: 1. 2. 3.
PEOPLE BORN INTO OTHER RELIGIONS	Three similarities between people born into other religions and me are: 1. 2. 3.	Three differences between people born into other religions and me are: 1. 2. 3.
PEOPLE FROM OTHER COUNTRIES	Three similarities between people from other countries and me are: 1. 2. 3.	Three differences between people from other countries and me are: 1. 2. 3.

2004 © Open Society Institute

The Publisher grants permission for the reproduction of this worksheet for non-profit educational purposes only.
Activity sheets may be downloaded from www.idebate.org/conflictandcommunication.htm

What's the Stereotype?

OBJECTIVES

Upon completing this lesson, students will be able to:

1. Name common stereotypes.

2. Identify the benefits and dangers of using stereotypes.

KEY CONCEPTS

stereotypes

BACKGROUND

A stereotype is a belief that all the members of a certain group possess certain similar qualities. Basically, stereotyping is claiming that all the members of a certain group are the same and do not have individual differences. Suppose I met a person from Antarctica who treated me unkindly. A stereotypical remark would be to say, "All Antarctican people are rude." But how about the other people who live in Antarctica? Are they all rude? Probably not. Some Antarctican people may be rude, but some may not be.

MATERIALS

"What's The Stereotype?" activity sheet

TEACHER TIPS

Make sure students understand how stereotypes affect them. You may want to discuss stereotypes they have of others or stereotypes others have of them. You could ask, "How does it feel when others stereotype you?"

The discussion may become sensitive, so after this activity you may want to facilitate a stress-relieving activity (see Appendix I).

ACTIVITY

1. Have students fill out the activity sheet "What's the Stereotype?" You may want to tell the students not to put their names on the sheet. (The activity sheet will not be collected, though each stu-

dent will share his/her answers with others.) In this way, the students may feel more comfortable responding to the questions. Stress that students should be honest when completing the sheet.

2. Randomly divide students into groups of four to six.

3. Have students, in their groups, share their responses from the activity sheet.

4. Have each group present these answers to the class.

DISCUSSION QUESTIONS

1. Where did you learn the different stereotypes?

2. In what ways do stereotypes affect us daily?

3. In what ways are stereotypes helpful to us?

4. In what ways are stereotypes harmful to those who are stereotyped?

ACTIVITY SHEET

WHAT'S THE STEREOTYPE?

Stereotyping is supposing that all of the members of a group have the same qualities. When people stereotype, they assume no one in that group is at all different from anyone else.
We encounter people being stereotyped every day.

What is the stereotype of:

A smart student?

An unintelligent student?

A teacher?

A parent?

A rock star?

A religious fanatic?

A poor person?

A rich person?

An old person?

A boy your age?

A girl your age?

DISCUSSION QUESTIONS

1. Were everybody's stereotypes the same? If not, why not? If yes, why?

2. What is the effect of stereotyping on that individual? On the community? On the person believing that stereotype?

2004 © Open Society Institute

The Publisher grants permission for the reproduction of this worksheet for non-profit educational purposes only.
Activity sheets may be downloaded from www.idebate.org/conflictandcommunication.htm

The Same Side of the Road

OBJECTIVE

Upon completing this lesson, students will be able to identify similarities and differences among all people, thereby challenging their use of stereotypes.

KEY CONCEPTS

appreciating diversity
discrimination
nationalism/ethnocentrism
prejudice
self-worth
stereotypes

BACKGROUND

A major aspect of negative discrimination and prejudice arises when people view others as being dissimilar, and in certain cases, as not even sharing similar human functions. This activity stresses that all humans have certain similarities and differences, and that, because we are not all exactly the same, we are all unique and special.

MATERIALS

none

TEACHER TIPS

This is a fun activity, so try to keep the spirit light. You can make up new qualities or have the students take turns offering ideas. For example, students may say, "Go to the right side of the room if you like running races (or if you like writing letters, dressing fancy, and so on)."

Encourage students to be honest and respectful. This activity can be used:

1) as an icebreaker or
2) to re-energize your students when you teach activities in other chapters.

ACTIVITY

1. Have all the students stand in the middle of the room. Explain that a road runs through the middle of the room. Tell them that you are going to name different qualities, and that those who have that quality should go to the right side of the road; those who do not have the named quality should go to the left side of the road. You might want to write these rules on the chalkboard to reduce confusion.

2. Tell students to go to the right side of the road if they:

>   * Have had two or more cavities.
>   * Have a younger brother or sister.
>   * Have a pet.
>   * Have their hands in their pockets.
>   * Like their parents a lot.
>   * Ride a bicycle.
>   * Like to sing.
>   * Go to the same school.
>   * Play soccer well.
>   * Exercise at least twice a week.
>   * Live within two blocks of the school.
>   * Get angry easily.
>   * Wear glasses.
>   * Like ice cream.
>   * Like to wake up early in the morning.
>   * Like to stay awake until very late at night.
>   * Wear a watch.
>   * Wear a watch on their right wrist.
>   * Brush their teeth at least twice a day.
>   * Love to eat lunch.

DISCUSSION QUESTIONS

1. Were the same people always on the same side of the road? Why not?

2. How is everybody in our class similar?

3. How are all people in our country the same?

4. How are all people in the world the same?

5. How is everyone in our class different?

6. How are all people in our country different?

7. How are all people in the world different?

8. What is wrong with saying that certain people are not as good as other people?

9. What makes people different from one another?

ADDITIONAL ACTIVITY

1. Tell students to draw a house (or something else) without using any straight lines. This activity shows how everyone is given one point of similarity—to draw a house—but that each person approaches that challenge with a different, unique response. Of course, no one's response is incorrect.

2. Have a discussion with students. Ask them under what circumstances some people's views may be more correct than others' views. For instance, ask them, "What if someone believes that stealing is a good idea. Is that a correct or incorrect belief? Why or why not?"

NOTE: Be prepared. Students may reveal personal, controversial beliefs. Allow students to tell their opinions, uninterrupted by others. Remind students that all that is said is confidential.

THE EVENING NEWS

OBJECTIVES

Upon completing this lesson, students will be able to:

1. Explain the importance of objectively evaluating beliefs.
2. See two sides to an issue.
3. Explain the dangers of stereotyping.

KEY CONCEPTS

analytical thinking
discrimination
prejudice
stereotypes

BACKGROUND

Stereotyping occurs when we believe that a group of people possesses certain similar qualities and does not have individual differences. Note that stereotypes are beliefs. Because beliefs can be both positive and negative, it is important for students to learn how to critically analyze both their own and others' beliefs. A critical analysis includes having the students investigate possible flaws in their own beliefs, as well as exploring all angles of that belief. Students can use this new awareness to gain a deeper understanding of the nature of prejudice and stereotyping. They can realize the importance of being tolerant of others' beliefs. It is essential for students to show respect for others while discussing beliefs, because they will inevitably differ on some issues, although they may be in agreement on others.

MATERIALS

"The Evening News" activity sheet, two desks with chairs in the front of the classroom, paper, pencils, tape, small pieces of paper with stereotypes written on them.

TEACHER TIPS

Explain that this exercise will give the students a chance to analyze their own beliefs and hear others' beliefs. Respect must be maintained even when disagreeing.

If disagreements arise, or if you notice students expressing frustration or disagreement through body language, stop the activity for a few minutes and allow students to express their thoughts and feelings. Make sure that students respect each others' opinions by stressing that when one person is talking, all others should listen quietly; also emphasize that no one should blame anyone else or call him/her rude names.

ACTIVITY

1. Have each student write down a belief he/she holds about another group of people. Suggest that some possible groups to think about are:

    a. People of a different religion (or who speak a different language).
    b. People from another country (or who are of a different ethnic group).
    c. Students from another class, grade, or school.

Make it clear to the students that they will be sharing this belief with other classmates.

2. Hand out the activity sheet. Read the sample on the sheet with the entire group. (This may help students to think of a belief they hold about another group of people.)

3. Have students divide into groups of three.

4. Have students in each group designate two members of the group as television news reporters. The third member, being interviewed, reads his/her belief about a group.

5. One of the TV news reporters listens to the student's belief and writes a very short news report agreeing with the belief. The other news reporter writes a very short report disagreeing with the belief.

6. After the reports are written, tell the students to exchange roles and repeat the exercise until every person has shared his/her belief with the others in the group.

7. Bring two chairs and desks to the front of the class. Have volunteer TV news reporters sit at the desks, pretending they are on television. Tell them to read their opposing views on the same subject.

DISCUSSION QUESTIONS

1. Why is it so important to see two sides to every issue?
2. What are possible instances when seeing only one side to an issue could be a problem?
3. How does it feel when someone does not understand your side of an issue?

ADDITIONAL ACTIVITY I

1. Have students bring in two newspaper articles, one depicting a group in a negative sense and the other depicting a group in a positive way. You may want to have several articles on a variety of topics available.

2. Discuss how newspapers and television often show different groups in either positive or negative ways. Ask students to express their opinions about the impact newspapers and television have regarding how a group is perceived.

ADDITIONAL ACTIVITY II

This activity exemplifies many of the key concepts behind the dangers of stereotyping.

Ask students to list stereotypes that they use about themselves or their group. For instance, a student may claim that he/she is not good at something because of the gender to which he/she belongs. Next, ask students to list stereotypes others say about them. Also discuss how a group may become stereotyped by the way it is depicted in the media.

ADDITIONAL ACTIVITY III

On separate slips of paper, write words that stereotype people. Tape a slip of paper either on each student's forehead or back. Make sure each student does not see the label he/she is wearing. Then have the students walk around interacting with each other as if they were the stereotype that each is labeled. Allow this to proceed for about 10 minutes. Tell students to sit down when they figure out what is written on their slip of paper. Hold an open discussion about how it felt to be treated according to the stereotype and how they figured out what word was on their forehead or back.

ACTIVITY SHEET
THE EVENING NEWS

SAMPLE NEWS BROADCAST

State belief: Girls are not good athletes.

Reporter A: Good evening. This is the *Eight O'Clock News.* In today's news, we discovered that there are girls who cannot play soccer. They are not as strong as guys. (Sorry Girls!) That is all that is in the news today. Good night.

Reporter B: Good evening and hello! This is the *Six O'Clock News.* Today in the news, Satellite Television News made an exciting discovery. We discovered that many girls are very good at sports. As a matter of fact, some girls can run faster than some guys and some girls can lift more weight than some guys. Some girls can play soccer as well as some boys. Go Girls! And that's the news. Good night.

STATE BELIEF:

REPORTER A:

REPORTER B:

STATE BELIEF:

REPORTER A:

REPORTER B:

The Bargots and the Rooters!

OBJECTIVES

Upon completing this lesson, students will be able to:

1. Define prejudice.
2. Explain how prejudice and discrimination originate and develop.
3. Describe how it feels to hold a prejudice.

KEY CONCEPTS

attitudes
discrimination
nationalism/ethnocentrism
prejudice

BACKGROUND

Prejudice is an opinion, often unfavorable, about a subject or group that is formed before exploring all of its facets. Discrimination is the act of treating a person unfairly based on prejudiced attitudes. Prejudice is the belief, and discrimination is the act. Prejudice can be formed easily; the following activity allows students to understand the dangers of beliefs made rashly without fully understanding issues.

MATERIALS

"The Bargots and the Rooters!" activity sheets (A & B), pencils, crayons. You may substitute a blank piece of paper for activity sheet B.

TEACHER TIPS

This is a very powerful and effective activity. Because it deals with sensitive issues, it may be helpful to begin the activity with an icebreaker (see Appendix II). Also, students may voice their opinions on sensitive issues. For advice on how to respond to their comments, see the Teacher Tips of the activity "Fact And Fiction," (page 68).

ACTIVITY

1. Give each student crayons, a pencil, and the activity sheets.
2. Explain to the class that they are going to read about two groups of people, the Bargots and the Rooters.
3. Write the names of the two countries and their citizens' names on the board (that is, Bargonia, Bargots, Rutris, Rooters).
4. Read activity sheet A with the students. Explain to the students that a citizen of Bargonia wrote the essay.
5. Instruct the students to draw and crayon a picture of a typical Bargot from Bargonia on the left side of activity sheet B and a typical Rooter on the right side of activity sheet B. Tell the students that they will have approximately 20 minutes to draw the two humans.
6. After time has passed, have the students sit in a large circle. Have the students hold their drawings on their laps so that everyone can see them.

NOTE: This can be a fun activity, so it's okay if your students laugh when they show their pictures.

DISCUSSION QUESTIONS

1. What kind of people do you think the Rooters are? Do you think all Rooters are that way?
2. What kind of people do you think the Bargots are? Do you think all Bargots are that way?
3. Why did you draw the Bargots like that?
4. Why did you draw the Rooters like that?
5. What made you think that the Rooters are all mean?
6. What made you think that the Bargots are all wonderful?
7. How do you think the descriptions might have been different if each group had written its own description?
8. Explain the definition of prejudice. Then discuss: How do your views and drawings show a prejudiced attitude toward a certain group of people?

ACTIVITY SHEET (A)
THE BARGOTS AND THE ROOTERS!

The Bargots and the Rooters!
(written by a Bargot)

The Bargots live in a country called Bargonia. This country is on the other side of the world and is located between the islands of Zether and Treebonia. The people of Bargonia are very wonderful people. The children rarely fight with one another, and the adults all work in peace. The main food of Bargonia is rice, but the plates of the Bargots are never empty. The weather in Bargonia stays the same throughout the year: slightly breezy and always warm and sunny.

The Rooters are from a country called Rutris. This country is on the other side of the world, too, and is located between the islands of Bilbo and Treblin. The people of Rutris are very mean people. The children always yell at one another, and the adults often hit one another. Nothing ever gets accomplished when the adults are at work because everyone is always sleeping or screaming instead of working. The days in Rutris are always very cold, windy, and rainy.

Activity Sheet (B)
The Bargots and the Rooters!

What do they look like ???

A TYPICAL BARGOT	A TYPICAL ROOTER

Prejudice's Many Shapes and Sizes

OBJECTIVES

Upon completing this lesson, students will be able to:

1. Define prejudice.

2. Name types of prejudice.

3. Describe different types of prejudice.

KEY CONCEPTS

appreciating diversity
discrimination
prejudice

BACKGROUND

Prejudice is an opinion, often unfavorable, about a subject or group, that is formed before exploring all of its facets. There are many different areas in which we can form opinions, and likewise, there are many different areas in which we may have prejudices. For instance, our opinions about an ethnic minority may be influenced by media portrayals, the attitudes of those with whom we socialize, and our own experiences with them. This activity helps students recognize some of the many forms of prejudice.

MATERIALS

"Prejudice's Many Shapes and Sizes" activity sheet

TEACHER TIPS

Emphasize that the different types of prejudice are not just ways of thinking: they are also realities. People suffer from the effects of prejudice daily.

Make sure that students understand the distinction between prejudice and dislike. Usually, people have prejudices toward groups and dislikes toward individuals. However, prejudice can be shown against individuals because they are members of a particular group.

ACTIVITY

1. Divide students into pairs.

2. In pairs, have students complete the activity sheet. If the students are having trouble thinking of situations, tell them that you will give them a sample situation for one of the kinds of prejudice

listed. For example, you could offer an example of age prejudice, saying, "Two students are thinking about who they would like to play football with after school. They decide to invite everyone in the class except for one person, Martin. They don't invite him because he is the youngest person in the class. They don't like him because he is younger than they are."

NOTE: You might need to define what an ethnic (cultural) group is to the students. It might be simplest to give examples of different ethnic groups within your country or region.

3. Tell students to form new pairs. Try to have students experience discussion with both male and female partners.
4. In their new pairs, the students now compare their activity sheet answers.

DISCUSSION:

1. What types of prejudice do you think are most common? Why?
2. With what types of prejudice have you been faced?
3. What can you do when you encounter someone who prejudges you?
4. Some people never change their opinions no matter what! Suppose there is a new boy in the classroom. One of the girls in the class quickly forms an opinion about how much she likes the new student. The only information she knows about the new student is his religion and what he looks like. Why is it important for her to be willing to change her opinion if she finds out new information about him?
5. What are some times when prejudice might not be harmful?

ADDITIONAL ACTIVITY I

In groups of four to six, have students write one thing they could do to lessen the prejudice against each group listed on the activity sheet. Students could also write one thing your school could do. These ideas could be written on large paper and kept posted all year. The ideas for school involvement in the reduction of prejudice could be put in the form of a letter to the principal, parent-teacher organization, or school board.

ADDITIONAL ACTIVITY II

Invite someone from groups listed under the types of prejudice (on the activity sheet) to talk with students. Another day might be set aside for a cultural or diversity celebration. Family members could be included to:

    1) cook the food their ethnic group enjoys,

    2) speak to classes,

    3) have their own discussion groups to talk about how to lessen prejudice and teach tolerance,

    or

    4) talk about religious or ethnic beliefs or values.

ACTIVITY SHEET
Prejudice's Many Shapes and Sizes

1. What is prejudice?

2. There are many different kinds of prejudice. Some of the different kinds are explained below. Underneath each kind of prejudice, write a situation in which someone may express that type of prejudice.

   Age Prejudice: When someone prejudges others because of how old they are.

   Religious Prejudice: When someone prejudges others because of what their religious beliefs are.

   Ethnic Prejudice: When someone prejudges others because of what ethnic group they belong to. Others are prejudged because of their culture, language, customs, dress, food, or social structure.

   National Prejudice: When someone prejudges others because of their family's country of origin.

   Physical Prejudice: When someone prejudges others because of the way they look.

   Disability Prejudice: When someone prejudges others because of a physical limitation such as blindness, deafness, learning disability, or use of a wheelchair.

   Gender Prejudice: When someone prejudges others depending on whether they are male or female.

   Economic or Class Prejudice: When someone prejudges others depending on how rich or poor they are.

   Racial Prejudice: When someone prejudges others because of the color of their skin or other identifying features of their group.

The Yellows and the Blues

OBJECTIVES

Upon completing this lesson, students will be able to:

1. Define discrimination.
2. Explain how discrimination feels.

KEY CONCEPTS

discrimination
prejudice

BACKGROUND

Discrimination occurs when one acts out a prejudiced belief and, therefore, treats people unfairly. Suppose John holds the prejudiced belief that all girls are not good athletes. If John does not let the girls play football with him, and he lets all the boys in the class play, he is discriminating against the girls. He is treating them unfairly.

This activity divides students into two groups. The students are explained the rules of the game. To follow the rules, the students in each group consequently discriminate against the other group. Therefore, students experience discrimination.

MATERIALS

Two pieces of paper for each student, and an empty space in the middle of the classroom

TEACHER TIPS

This is a quick, simple activity that is useful with younger students.

For this activity to work effectively, stress that the students must follow the rules precisely. Specifically, if a student looks at another student, he/she must do what the rules explain (students should disregard their true feelings for each other).

After this activity and the discussion questions have been completed, students could divide into small groups (four to six students) and discuss incidents of discrimination that they have experienced, witnessed, or heard about.

This can be an emotional activity, so you may want to end the class with an icebreaker that brings the group together. Stress relievers may be more appropriate with some classes.

ACTIVITY

1. Divide the class into two groups. The two groups move to opposite corners of the room. Make sure that all of the students have two pieces of paper in their hands.
2. Tell one group that their group name is The Yellows, and tell the other group that their group name is The Blues.
3. The students should shake hands with each member of their group.
4. All the students now walk toward the center of the room.
5. Give the students the following instructions:

    The paper in your hands is not paper. It is actually gold. And you want to get as much of the gold as possible. You are going to walk around the room. You will have to ask every person you look at if you can have a piece of gold (a piece of paper). If someone from your group asks for a piece of gold, you must smile and hand over a piece of gold (if you have any left). If someone from the other group asks for a piece of gold, you frown and answer, "No, you little, little child. You can't have a piece of gold."

    Stress to the students that if they give their gold away, they still should continue walking around the room and participating. (If they look at someone from their group, they can acquire gold again.)

6. Let this activity run for approximately 5 minutes, then have everyone sit in one big circle.

DISCUSSION QUESTIONS

1. How did it feel when you asked someone in your group for a piece of gold?
2. How did it feel when you asked someone from the other group for a piece of gold?
3. Did you find yourself avoiding members of the other group? Why?
4. Explain to the class what discrimination is.
5. How does this activity relate to discrimination?
6. Why is discrimination unfair to people?
7. Have you or someone you know ever been discriminated against? How?

Fact and Fiction

OBJECTIVES

Upon completing this lesson, students will be able to:

1. Define discrimination.
2. Recognize acts of discrimination that affect people in their own surroundings.
3. Specify emotions linked with discriminatory events.
4. Critically analyze beliefs that result in discrimination.

KEY CONCEPTS

analytical thinking
discrimination
prejudice

BACKGROUND

Discrimination is the act of treating someone differently on the basis of age, religion, ethnicity, nationality, handicap, gender, class, race, and so on. It is prejudice acted out. Because discrimination excludes certain people from activities or groups, these people may feel resentful, angry, or hurt.

MATERIALS

paper, pencils

TEACHER TIPS

Note that this may be a very sensitive activity for students because descriptions of discrimination may involve members of ethnic, racial, or other groups of students within your class.

If students make prejudicial remarks, do not ignore the remarks. Turn them into topics for discussion and learning. For example, ask the class how people learn such thoughts and what effects those remarks have on others. Ask them: "When someone says a prejudicial remark, what kind of person does it make him/her? Why?"

Try not to make students feel defensive. Don't impose certain views on them. Let them express their views equally with others. In most cases, ask the entire class to comment on remarks. Usually it is not wise to single out disruptive students.

ACTIVITY

1. Discuss the meaning of discrimination.

2. Divide students into groups of four. Each student in the groups shares a time when a friend, someone in his/her family, or he/she was discriminated against. For instance, the discrimination might have been: feeling excluded because of being considered overweight, nonathletic, not pretty, the wrong gender, and so on.

3. After each student describes an incident of discrimination, the group discusses ways of combating the discrimination.

To help students understand the directions, offer an example: Suppose a student describes an incident of discrimination in which the president of a youth club did not permit him to belong to the club because of his ethnic background. To combat the discrimination, he could report it to the school administration, he could get students to protest the club, he could talk to the club president and discuss the issues, he could talk to other club members, and so on.

ADDITIONAL ACTIVITY

1. Have each student interview an older person (grandparent, older friend, family member).

2. Tell students to ask the elder questions about times when they witnessed or experienced discrimination or prejudice. Students should write answers to the questions on paper. Set a due date for the assignment.

   NOTE: Make sure that the students explain to the elders that the content of the interview will be shared with classmates.

3. Have the students bring the sheet back to class.

4. In class, have the students write a short paragraph about what the older person said.

5. Have students read their reports to the class. If the class is very large, you may want to divide the class into groups of six to ten students.

6. After each student reads his/her report, ask students to think of other possible sides to each belief about discrimination. (See the activity "The Evening News," on page 55, to understand how different sides can be clarified and expressed.)

The Tower of Babel

OBJECTIVE
Upon completing this lesson, students will be able to explain the problems connected with labeling

KEY CONCEPTS
attitudes
behavior
discrimination
feelings
prejudice
stereotypes

BACKGROUND
We often label other people. Labeling can be helpful, for it helps us to organize our world. For instance, when people have stomachaches, we may label them as sick. We use the label as a quick description of how they behave and feel. However, labeling is not a totally harmless way of organizing the world. When we label people, we often treat them in ways that reinforce the behavior and feelings. By treating people with stomachaches as sick, we develop a new way of relating to them, and they develop a new way of relating to us. Our relationship changes, and it becomes difficult for the sick people to break out of that label.

Stereotyping is a way of labeling groups of people. When we stereotype, we affect others' behavior as well as our own. We may, for example, treat all tall people as athletic; our treatment of them affects how they relate to us, and in turn, this affects how we relate to them.

MATERIALS
plenty of space, tape, index cards, or small pieces of paper for each student
On each index card, write one of the following messages:
- Smile at me
- Frown at me
- Make a face at me and tell me I don't know anything
- Listen to everything I say
- Do everything I do
- Keep changing the subject
- Don't listen to anything I say
- Talk to me as if I am six years old

You may need to write the same message on more than one card so there are enough cards for each student.

TEACHER TIPS

For more information on stereotyping, prejudice, and discrimination, see the background sections of "The Yellows and The Blues" (page 66) and "What's The Stereotype?" (page 50).

To personalize this activity, you may want to ask students to describe their own experiences of prejudice, discrimination, and stereotyping. Because these are emotional issues, encourage students to respect each other. That is, no one should tease, interrupt, or blame anyone. Ask the students to help you enforce the rules of respect inside and outside the classroom.

If there is tension at the end of the activity, you may want to use one of the activities from Appendix II that builds group unity, such as "10 Seconds" or "The Guesser."

ACTIVITY

1. Hand an index card with a message on it to each student, telling him or her not to show it to anyone else.
2. Hand each student a small piece of tape.
3. Have each student tape an index card onto the back of the person beside them, making sure that person does not see what is written on the card.
4. Divide the class up into groups of four to six, and tell the class that they are going to make a human statue about an incident in which someone helps someone else.* For example, they could make a human statue of a few children helping an old lady across the street, of children helping parents clean the house, and so on.
5. Each group must decide among themselves what they are going to sculpt.
6. Each group must work together to create the statue, but each student must treat the other students in accordance with the message on the person's back. For instance, suppose John has the message "Tell me what to do" on his back. Every time I see John, I would tell him what to do.
7. After about 20 minutes, have the groups sit down in their regular seats and have each group display their human statue. Tell the groups that they still cannot take the tags off their backs, nor can they look at them. Everyone must still treat everyone else in accordance with the message on each student's back.
8. After all the groups have displayed their statues, tell the students that they can take the messages off their backs.

DISCUSSION QUESTIONS

1. How did it feel to be treated in a certain way?
2. Ask students to name what message was on their back. How did that message influence the productivity of the group?

---

*A human statue is created when the students in each group depict an incident by using their bodies. After creating the statue, they stand still in these positions, as if they are on a photograph. Normally, when creating a human statue, one student in each group is a sculptor, telling everyone how to stand or sit. However, there should be no sculptor for this activity.

3. Would your group have been more productive without the labels on your backs? Why or why not?

4. Do people label each other in real life? Do children and adults label others as good, bad, bossy, nice, or mean without even knowing them very well?

5. What is wrong with labeling people?

6. Has anyone ever labeled you in a way you did not like? How?

7. Suppose someone thinks you are a bad person because you have brown hair. How could you change this person's view of you?

8. Where do we learn many of our thoughts and beliefs about others? (From friends, parents, siblings, teachers, and so on.)

9. Is it easy or hard to get rid of a label once it becomes known? How can you get rid of it?

FRIEND OR FOE

OBJECTIVES

Upon completing this lesson, students will be able to:

1. Explain the difference between nationalism and ethnocentrism.
2. Describe the concept of the enemy image.
3. Name feelings that are associated with discrimination and prejudice.

KEY CONCEPTS

discrimination
enemy image
nationalism/ethnocentrism
prejudice

BACKGROUND

Nationalism is pride in one's own country. This pride is often beneficial to the optimistic working attitudes of the citizens of a country. But sometimes nationalistic thoughts are transformed into notions that one's own country, and the citizens within it, are superior to those in other countries.

This is *ethnocentrism*: when citizens create images of foreigners as inferior. Usually the notions of the foreigners are based on generalized and/or inadequate information.

When two countries are involved in hostile conflict, a negative enemy image often emerges, becoming part of the citizens' patterns of thinking. With the enemy image, all members of the opposing warring nation are viewed as evil, unworthy, cold-hearted people who are unable to be trusted. For example, if Country X is at war with Country Y, some citizens of both countries may view all of the other country's citizens as evil, dirty, and blood-hungry. When people adopt the enemy image notion, they stereotype an entire group without investigating all the factors necessary to judge fairly.

The following activity allows students to experience the feelings of nationalism, ethnocentrism, and the enemy image on a small scale.

MATERIALS

plenty of room to move around

TEACHER TIPS

Stress the difference between nationalism and ethnocentrism. You could create a comparison to exemplify the difference: students, just like countries, sometimes form close, intimate cliques of friends. The cliques are healthy, for students feel included and desirable. But sometimes cliques are so tight and close that others are insensitively excluded and looked down on. Others may feel rejected, isolated, depressed, or even angry and vengeful. Similarly, nationalism is healthy, but ethnocentrism can create resentment by foreigners.

ACTIVITY

1. Divide the class into groups (each group should not be larger than six to eight). Have each group move to a different area of the classroom.

2. Tell the class that it will be creating human statues. Explain that a human statue is created when the students in each group depict an incident or idea by using their bodies. For example, the statue could illustrate a scenario in which discrimination is taking place, a scene in which prejudice affects someone (e.g., boy gets hurt because his classmates do not like red-haired students), or anything else they can think of. Each group needs to select a sculptor who will help the other students in the group position their bodies. The students then practice creating the statue and standing still in those positions, as if they are on a photograph.

3. Before the groups begin designing their statues, explain to each group that the sculpting activity is competitive. Tell the group that you will be judging the statues and that the students in the group that wins will gain a substantial award. Explain also that the students in the losing groups will suffer considerable losses. As the teacher, design these awards and losses at your own discretion, heeding the purpose of this exercise.

4. Tell the groups that they will each have 15 minutes to design a human statue about prejudice or discrimination. Each group should think of a name for its statue.

5. After the groups have designed their statues, have them display the statues to the others. The sculptor from each group tells the class the name of the statue and explains the statue's idea or incident. Make sure that while the students observe the other groups' statues, they remain in their groups and do not go back to their classroom seats.

6. Tell the class that you are having a difficult time deciding which group is the winner. Ask volunteers in each group why they think their statue is better than the other group's. Encourage students to be honest and to say whatever comes to mind. Make it clear that while an individual in one group is speaking, everyone must listen carefully to what that person is saying. The students in each group will most likely promote their group's positive aspects and de-emphasize the positive factors of the other group. Each group will think that it is better than the others.

7. Ask the groups the following questions:
    a. How will you feel about the other groups if your group loses? If your group wins?
    b. How did you feel about the students in the other group before the activity? How has your view of them changed? What do you think has caused your change of view about the students in the other group?

8. Tell the students that you will give them all an equal reward to emphasize the fact that all people are equal; people sometimes seem different because they are seen through prejudiced eyes.

DISCUSSION QUESTIONS

1. How do you view the students in the other groups now that you know there is no winner and no loser?

2. Many countries compete with one another; some countries even fight with each other in wars. How do you think your feelings for the other groups might be similar to those between countries at war? How were your feelings different? (Explain the concepts of the enemy image, nationalism, and ethnocentrism.)

TELEPHONE GAME

OBJECTIVE

Upon completing this lesson, students will be able to identify instances in which propaganda is used to attempt to persuade them.

KEY CONCEPTS

analytical thinking
media
propaganda

BACKGROUND

Propaganda is the spread of information to further a group's goals. Many companies and businesses use propaganda to make their products or ideas seem more attractive. Sometimes, governments and individuals also use propaganda techniques to persuade people that their ideas are the best ideas. This lesson introduces students to the power of propaganda.

MATERIALS

none

TEACHER TIPS

If the message in the activity seems too complicated for your students, you may want to create your own or have a student create one.

To reinforce this lesson, you could bring in an article or advertisement from a newspaper or magazine that clearly uses propaganda techniques. Have students discuss what technique(s) are used and how people are affected by them.

ACTIVITY

1. Have all the students stand in a straight line.
2. Whisper the following message into the first student's ear, "The short boy with brown hair yelled at the tall boy with blonde hair because the sister of the short boy with brown hair was very rude to the brother of the tall boy with blonde hair, but now they are all friends again."

3. Each student should whisper the message to the next person after he/she receives it.

4. When finished, compare the final message with the one that you whispered to the first student.

DISCUSSION QUESTIONS

1. Did the message change? Why?

2. What are some ways that you know that something is true? For instance, pretend you have two friends named Julian and Klara. After class, Klara walks up to you and whispers in your ear that she heard that Julian stole a bag of tea from the cafe. How do you know whether Julian did steal the tea? How can messages become confused?

3. How might the news in a newspaper be incorrect? Think about the game just played to help you answer that question.

4. How do you know if the news in newspapers, radio, and TV is true?

5. How can you discover what news is true and what news is not true?

THE PROPAGANDA PARTY

OBJECTIVES
Upon completing this lesson, students will be able to:
1. Describe common propaganda techniques.
2. Describe examples of how propaganda techniques are used.
3. Explain how propaganda techniques can be used to influence people's opinions.
4. Describe how large groups use propaganda.

KEY CONCEPTS
media
propaganda

BACKGROUND
Propaganda is the spread of information to further a group's goals. It is a kind of advertising that can often make products or ideas appear more attractive than they might be otherwise.
Propaganda can be used to persuade people, and depending on how it is used, its effects can be either helpful or harmful to its audience. For example, propaganda could be used to persuade people to use toothpaste; a television commercial might say, "Everybody uses X toothpaste to prevent cavities." On the other hand, propaganda could be misused to show how great sugar is. A television commercial might say, "Many experts agree that sugar is good for you."

MATERIALS
"The Propaganda Party" resource sheet, large sheets of paper, pencils

TEACHER TIPS
To reinforce this lesson, you could bring in an article or advertisement from a newspaper or magazine that clearly uses propaganda techniques. Have students discuss what technique(s) are used and how they affect people.

ACTIVITY

1. Hand out the resource sheet.
2. Discuss the different forms of propaganda and how they are used to influence people.
3. Have the class think of an example of how each propaganda technique is used.
4. Divide the class into groups of approximately four members.
5. Tell the class that there is going to be a party at school. This party is going to be advertised on television.
6. Each small group needs to create two television commercials. The first one will tell only the facts of the party. All of the facts need to be stated. The second commercial will use propaganda techniques to make the party seem like it will be unbelievably great and fun, using made-up facts or exaggeration. Students may want to draw pictures to go along with their television commercials.

DISCUSSION QUESTIONS

1. What propaganda techniques did each use? How were they effectively persuasive?
2. How is propaganda used to persuade people?
3. How can learning about propaganda techniques help you?
4. In what ways has propaganda been used to influence people?
5. How do schools, companies, and governments use propaganda to influence people?
6. How do people use propaganda when they are in a conflict? (The following lesson, "Propaganda Fight," addresses this question.)

RESOURCE SHEET
THE PROPAGANDA PARTY

The following are common propaganda techniques:

1. **Bandwagon**: Everybody's doing it, so you should, too!

2. **Picking Facts:** Let's advertise the facts that make our idea or product seem good! But let's not tell about the bad aspects of our product or idea.

3. **Expert Opinion:** A famous person or an expert claims that the product is good, so it must be good!

4. **Playing with Emotions:** If you are in love or sad or happy, then this is the product or idea for you!

5. **Repeating the Product Name or Idea:** This is the best product or idea! This is the best product or idea! This is the best product or idea! This is the best product or idea! This is the best product or idea! This is the best product or idea! This is the best product or ideal!

6. **Saying Negative Things About the Competition:** They lie and try to persuade you that their bread is fresh, but ours is the freshest by far.

2004 © Open Society Institute

The Publisher grants permission for the reproduction of this worksheet for non-profit educational purposes only.
Activity sheets may be downloaded from www.idebate.org/conflictandcommunication.htm

Propaganda Fight

OBJECTIVE

Upon completing this lesson, students will be able to identify ways in which people utilize propaganda techniques in arguments.

KEY CONCEPTS

conflict analysis
peer conflicts
propaganda
school conflicts

BACKGROUND

When people argue, they often attempt to persuade others that their argument is correct. Without even realizing it, many people use propaganda techniques to support their arguments. Understanding how these propaganda techniques are utilized can aid people in differentiating argument from fact and truth from fiction.

MATERIALS

"Propaganda Fight" activity sheet, "The Propaganda Party" resource sheet (page 79)

TEACHER TIPS

To help students understand propaganda techniques, it may be useful to facilitate "The Propaganda Party" (page 77) before facilitating this activity.

ACTIVITY

1. Hand out the activity sheets.
2. Have two volunteers, one boy and one girl, come to the front of the room.
3. Have the two volunteers act out the role play on Propaganda Fight. While watching the role play, the class writes down every propaganda technique each person uses. Answers to the propaganda techniques used in the role plays:

a. Bandwagon
   b. Playing with emotions
   c. Expert opinion
   d. Picking facts
   e. Repeating the idea
   f. Using negative comments
4. Review the propaganda techniques used in "The Propaganda Party."
5. Divide students into groups of four to six.
6. Have half the groups create role plays showing the positive aspects of school through propaganda techniques. For example, students could create a commercial that shows that everyone loves school. The other half of the groups create role plays showing the negative aspects of school through propaganda techniques. For example, students could create a commercial showing that experts agree that school is boring.

DISCUSSION QUESTIONS

1. What are some times when you have seen propaganda techniques used?
2. What is an example of a time when you or someone you know used a propaganda technique in an argument?
3. How could you use propaganda techniques to emphasize the positive aspects of school?
4. How could you use propaganda techniques to emphasize the negative aspects of school?

ACTIVITY SHEET
PROPAGANDA FIGHT

	TYPE OF PROPAGANDA USED
Liz: Hey, Peter, did you do your math homework? It's due today, isn't it? Peter: Yeah, I did it. Liz: Let me copy it. I don't want to get a bad grade in that class. Peter: No way! I worked all night on my homework.	
Liz: Come on. Everybody copies everybody's homework all the time. Peter: I don't care.	a.
Liz: If you are really my friend, if you really care about me and like me as a friend, you'd let me copy your homework. Please... Peter: Look, you're really starting to annoy me. I said no.	b.
Liz: But it's not bad to let me copy your homework. I read in a magazine that copying someone's homework is just as good as doing it yourself. Peter: Yeah, right. If you don't stop talking to me now, I'm going to tell the teacher about this.	c.
Liz: What's so bad about me copying your homework? Think about it. You will still get a good grade in math. And I would get a good grade, too. Peter: But what if the teacher catches us? What if our parents find out that you and I cheated?	d.
Liz: Peter, don't be silly. We won't get caught. So let me copy your homework, ok? Let me copy your homework. Just let me copy your homework! Peter: No.	e.
Liz: You're acting just like Michael, and we both know what a loser he is. Peter: You're not going to convince me by insulting Michael.	f.
Liz: I thought we were friends. Peter: I thought you were honest.	

2004 © Open Society Institute

The Publisher grants permission for the reproduction of this worksheet for non-profit educational purposes only.
Activity sheets may be downloaded from www.idebate.org/conflictandcommunication.htm

Chapter Three:
ME AND YOU

What would the world be like if no one ever communicated with anyone else? Indeed, it would be a lonely, sad place. Fortunately, as humans, we have many ways of communicating with one another. We express our feelings and thoughts through body language, writing, talking, shouting, blushing, and so on.

Effective communication is essential to managing conflicts. However, when we find ourselves in conflict situations, communication often becomes complicated and troubling. We may find it difficult to express our true emotions, or we may become frustrated that others don't understand exactly how we feel.

An important element of effective communication is keeping an open mind and listening to what others say. Conflicts frequently arise when we think we know other people's positions; without communicating effectively, we may not realize that our assumptions are incorrect. For example, silence could be assumed to mean many different things: anger, fatigue, resentment, confusion, or even a sore throat.

As discussed in Chapter One, everyone is unique. We may know different things, hold different beliefs, and have different points of view. When we focus on our differences, communication often becomes difficult. This communication difficulty in turn contributes to conflict. Conflict further interferes with communication, and a vicious cycle of worsening communication and increasing conflict may begin.

When we begin with a prejudiced view of others, our understanding and communications with them become less effective. For instance, if we have very prejudiced opinions about a group of people, we are likely to discriminate against them. We also reinforce our prejudices by reading and listening to only that information that agrees with our prejudice. Instead of exchanging feelings and thoughts, we develop more prejudiced views. Consequently, there is a communication breakdown. The vicious cycle of conflict becomes more and more destructive.

Fortunately, there are skills that we can all learn to prevent the vicious cycle of conflict from ever occurring. The skills are easy to learn and easy to use. This chapter's activities allow students to develop powerful communication skills to help them effectively manage conflicts.

WATCH YOUR STEP

OBJECTIVES

Upon completing this lesson, students will be able to:

1. Describe how it feels to rely on another person.
2. Explain the importance of trust in conflict management.

KEY CONCEPTS

conflict analysis
friendship
group bonding
trust

BACKGROUND

Trust is an integral part of conflict management. If disputants do not trust one another, nothing can ever be permanently resolved.

Suppose two students were in a fight this afternoon. Early this evening, they tried to make peace with one another. They talked, but they felt that the first few minutes were not productive. However, it was during those first few minutes that the students built trust.

Before students can resolve conflicts, they must trust one another. The decision to work together is the first step toward conflict resolution.

MATERIALS

"Walk of Trust" activity sheet

TEACHER TIPS

It is important to carefully supervise this activity to ensure everyone's safety. It may be helpful to facilitate the activity in a place as free of obstacles as possible. Avoid stairs, holes, rough ground, or any place where students might stumble and hurt themselves.

At first, students may be reserved about participating. However, in the end, most students will claim that this is one of their favorite activities.

This activity can be a lot of fun if students are permitted to guide their partners down school halls or outside. It is organizationally easier if the pairs stand in a line and follow a leading pair.

ACTIVITY

1. Students divide into pairs.
2. One of the students in each pair closes his/her eyes and holds on to the arm of the partner. The partner guides him/her on a walk around the room (or outside if possible and desired). Stress that the partner must be very careful while guiding.
3. After approximately 5 minutes (or more, depending on where you allow the students to guide one another) tell the guides not to hold on to their partner. Now, the guides us only their voices to direct their partners.
4. Reverse roles, and repeat steps 2 and 3.
5. Have a short discussion. Then have students complete the activity sheet.
6. Have students share their responses on the activity sheet.

DISCUSSION QUESTIONS

1. How did it feel to walk with your eyes closed?
2. Did you open your eyes at all during the walk? Why or why not?
3. How did it feel to rely on another person to help you walk?
4. What does trust have to do with this activity?
5. Why is trust important when you are involved in a conflict situation?

ACTIVITY SHEET
WALK OF TRUST

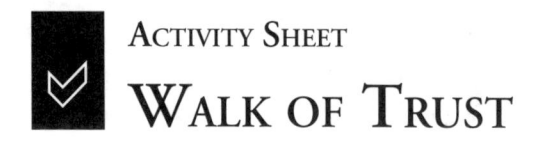

Write about an experience or situation in which you had to rely on someone else for help.

Imagine you have been fighting with your best friend for two weeks, and you don't even trust your friend anymore. But you are tired of arguing, you miss talking with your friend, and you want to make peace. How can you and your friend learn to trust each other again?

Why is trust so important when trying to resolve a conflict?

CAN YOU KEEP A SECRET ?

OBJECTIVES
Upon completing this lesson, students will be able to:
1. Describe the importance of confidentiality.
2. Explain when confidentiality should be broken.

KEY CONCEPTS
Confidentiality
Group Bonding
Trust

BACKGROUND
Confidentiality is the maintenance of a secret or something private. It is an important part of trust, and trust is an important part of conflict management. People in conflict sometimes do not reveal their true feelings because they may be afraid or nervous that others will find out the details of the conflict. Also, revealing emotions leaves one in a very vulnerable position, for others discover how one truly feels.

By respecting confidentiality, communication is enhanced: people feel more comfortable and are more likely to speak honestly. Therefore, it is essential that people who desire constructive conflict respect confidentiality.

MATERIALS
paper, pencils, chalkboard and chalk (or a large piece of paper and a pen)

TEACHER TIPS
Make sure that when students try to guess each other's secrets, they whisper; otherwise, students could eavesdrop.

ACTIVITY
1. Hand out one piece of paper to each student. Students should not put their names on the paper.
2. Tell the students that we are all special people. Each of us has secrets that we tell to nobody else.
3. Have students write down something special about themselves, something that nobody else in the class knows about them. For example, students might write down a nickname that only their father calls them, a hobby, something they would like to learn to do, a place they would like to visit, etc. Explain that later in the day, they will be sharing these secrets with the rest of the class;

so stress that they should only write down a secret that they do not mind sharing with the whole class.

4. Collect the papers, making sure that the students do not talk about their secrets.

5. Write down the secrets on the chalkboard or on a large piece of paper, consecutively numbering each secret.

6. Meanwhile, have students make a list from one to however many students are in the class. So, if there are thirty students in the class, the students should make a list from one to thirty.

7. Once you have written all the secrets, have students stand up and find as many matches as they can. That is, students must walk around the room and guess whose secret is whose. Once a student guesses correctly, he/she writes down the other person's name beside the secret's number corresponding to that person's secret. Warn the students that if they correctly guess, the other person should whisper that he/she was correct (otherwise, students may overhear correct answers).

8. After 10–15 minutes, ask how many students found over five matches? Over ten? Over fifteen?

9. Go through the secrets on the board and whose they were.

DISCUSSION QUESTIONS

1. What are secrets?

2. If you told your best friend a secret and your best friend told other people that secret, how would you feel?

3. When someone tells you about a problem or conflict that they are having, why is it important not to tell others about it? When might it be important that you do tell someone?

4. A friend tells you a secret. He/she says that he/she is thinking about either hurting himself/herself or someone else. Should you tell another person? (Yes.) Who should you tell? (An older person, like a teacher or parent.) Why? (When someone is in danger of being hurt, his/her safety is more important than keeping the promise. Also, the fact that the person told you may be an indication that he/she is asking for help.)

TANGLED

OBJECTIVES
Upon completing this lesson, students will be able to:
1. Identify ways in which people communicate by voice and body language.
2. Explain the importance of paying attention to both verbal and nonverbal communication.
3. Describe the experience of cooperating and problem solving in a group.

KEY CONCEPTS
conflict analysis
cooperation
group bonding
perceptions
problem-solving
nonverbal communication
verbal communication

BACKGROUND
A large portion of how we communicate is through our body language. To be an effective listener, it is important to pay attention to both a person's words and his/her behavior. Sometimes people do not immediately admit in words that they are angry, sad, and so on. That is why careful listeners also notice nonverbal cues, such as how people stand or sit, what their facial expressions imply, and so on. By becoming aware of other people's body language, we can become better listeners. And by becoming aware of our own body language, we can become better communicators.

Of course, the most effective form of communication between people occurs when they take cues from both verbal and nonverbal expressions.

MATERIALS
none

TEACHER TIPS
If a group does not have an even number of members, you could join the group. The activity is a lot of fun!

ACTIVITY

1. Divide the class into groups of six or eight. Each group must have an even number of members.

    NOTE: Just for fun, after your students have mastered groups of six and eight, you can challenge them with groups of ten or twelve. Smaller groups make this activity too easy.

2. Each group stands in a circle with its members shoulder to shoulder.

3. Everyone reaches into the middle of the circle, grasping hands with two different people. Students should not hold the hand of someone beside them.

4. The students try to untangle the knot without letting go of anyone's hands. When completed, they should all be standing in a circle holding hands.

    NOTE: Some knots are impossible to untangle. Perform the following to test to see if the knot can be untangled: Before attempting to untangle, have one student in each group send a squeeze (hand pressure) from his right hand. As each student receives the squeeze in one hand, he/she should send the squeeze in the other. By the time the squeeze returns to the original student, every student in the group should have felt it. If not, the students should let go and try the activity again. Remember to check that 1) no one is holding both hands with the same person, and 2) no one is holding hands with someone beside him/her. When all of these tests work, the students should try to untangle the knot.

5. After the groups have untangled knots a few times, tell the students to form a new knot.

6. The students must try to untangle their knot, but now, their vocabulary is limited to one word: knot. They must express themselves only by using body language and their tone of voice when saying the word *knot*.

7. After the groups have untangled the knot, tell them to form a new knot.

8. The students must again try to untangle their knot, but this time they cannot speak at all. The only way they can express themselves is through body language.

9. The activity can proceed one step further with students closing their eyes and not talking.

DISCUSSION QUESTIONS

1. How do the different versions of this game show the importance of communication?

2. Did anyone get frustrated in the silent version? Did you get frustrated when you wanted to communicate one thing and someone interpreted you incorrectly? How so? How did you feel?

3. Sometimes people misinterpret what others are thinking or feeling. What are some examples of when this happens in real life?

4. When has someone misinterpreted what you were thinking or feeling?

5. Sometimes people get into arguments and conflicts because feelings and thoughts are misinterpreted. What is an example of when this happens?

6. Do people sometimes misinterpret what you say? What is an example of when this happens?

7. Can teachers misinterpret what students are thinking? How?

8. Can students misinterpret what teachers are thinking? How?

9. How can the same problem of misinterpretation happen between nations?

BODY TALK

OBJECTIVE
Upon completing this lesson, students will be able to describe and illustrate the role of body language in effective communication.

KEY CONCEPTS
nonverbal communication
verbal communication

BACKGROUND
The power of basic nonverbal listening skills is often underestimated. For example, simple actions such as nodding the head or leaning forward express interest and empathetic understanding. In conflict situations, when tempers are high and tolerance is low, positive body language shows one's desire to understand and be understood. It lets people know that you are listening and you care enough to listen.

You may want to mention to your students that different cultures have different ways of expressing themselves with their bodies. For example, in Hungary, when one nods his/her head up and down, that means yes, while in Bulgaria it means no.

MATERIALS
"Body Talk" activity sheet

TEACHER TIPS
Before facilitating this activity, take a few minutes to analyze your own body language. Work on ways to make your nonverbal listening skills more powerful and effective. Students learn a great deal not only from what you say, but also from how you nonverbally express yourself.

In many cultures, nonverbal listening skills include:

1. Leaning slightly forward.

2. Nodding the head occasionally.

3. Looking (but not staring constantly) into the other person's eyes.

4. Expressing interest through facial expressions.

ACTIVITY

1. Discuss with students why positive body language is very important.

2. Have students complete the activity sheet by writing examples of positive and negative body language.

3. Divide students into pairs.

4. In each pair, one student, the talker, talks about an argument or conflict he/she recently had. The other student, the listener, listens using negative body language.

5. After a few minutes, tell the listener to use positive body language while listening to the talker. The listeners can use the activity sheet to help them remember what some of the ways are.

6. After a few more minutes, stop everyone. Ask the talker in each group:
   - How did it feel when the listener had negative body language?
   - How did it feel when the listener had positive body language?

7. Reverse roles (the talker is now the listener and the listener is now the talker). Repeat steps 4–6.

8. In the pairs, have students discuss the following:
   - Without talking, how can you show someone that you are listening? Be specific.
   - How did your partner show positive body language?
   - When you have a dispute with someone, why is it important to have positive body language?

ADDITIONAL ACTIVITY

Here's a fun activity that demonstrates the importance of being a good listener: Divide students into pairs. At the same time, have both students talk about anything for one minute. While talking, each student should also try to listen to what the other student is saying. After one minute has ended, students tell each other what they heard and remembered. Have the class form a circle. Discuss the experience with the entire class.

ACTIVITY SHEET
BODY TALK

Positive Body Language	Negative Body Language
List some ways that you can show others you are listening to them.	List some ways that you can show others that you are NOT listening to them.

THE GUESSING GAME

OBJECTIVES

Upon completing this lesson, students will be able to:

1. Describe the uses of open and closed questions.

2. Use open and closed questions to promote or hinder conversation.

KEY CONCEPTS

conflict analysis
group bonding
verbal communication

BACKGROUND

Open questions are questions that invite people to talk. Instead of making people feel defensive, these questions encourage them to talk. Open questions usually begin with the words *how* or *what*. Closed questions are conversation stoppers. They discourage conversation because usually the questions can be answered in a word or two, such as with the word *yes* or *no*.

During conflict situations, each disputant wants to be certain that the other person understands his/her point of view. By asking open questions, disputants allow the other person to talk freely about what they deem important. This facilitates discussion. Suppose two students, Monika and Simona, are arguing. If Simona asks Monika many closed questions, the intensity of the conflict might escalate.

Simona: Do you think I hate you?

Monika: No.

Simona: Do you trust me?

Monika: Not now.

Simona: Do you think I really told everyone that you like David?

Monika: No! And stop asking me so many questions!

Now suppose that Simona asks Monika open questions. The conflict quickly becomes more focused because the disputants themselves can say what they are thinking.

Simona: What do you think is the problem?

Monika: I was so embarrassed yesterday. Everybody kept walking up to me and asking me if I liked David. The only person I remember telling was you.

As you can see, in the second example, Monika was able to discuss what she wanted to discuss. The open question was very helpful in this situation.

Closed questions can sometimes be helpful, also. When a person does not stop talking, you can ask a closed question. This type of question is useful to end conversations.

MATERIALS
none

TEACHER TIPS
When the rules of the game change (at step 5 of the activity), it may be necessary to encourage students to ask questions that begin with the words *what* or *how*. Often, it takes a few minutes for students to discover how to ask open questions.

It is useful for students to learn the skills of how to ask open questions, for they encourage others to express their thoughts and feelings. The skill of knowing how to ask open questions is also useful for teaching purposes. By asking students open questions, you allow students to express themselves freely.

ACTIVITY
1. Have a student come to the front of the room.
2. Ask that student to think of a person, place, or object. For instance, the student could think of an animal, fruit, vegetable, famous person, etc. Tell the student not to tell anyone what he/she is thinking of.
3. Have the rest of the class try to guess what the student is thinking of. The students can only ask questions that can be answered with yes or no. Count how many questions it takes the class to guesses correctly. Inform the class of the final number.
4. Repeat steps 1–4 with a few different students.
5. Now tell the students that the game has new rules. Instead of asking questions that can be answered with yes or no, the class can now ask any question. The only question students cannot ask is, "What is it?" The student thinking of something must now answer every question fully (he/she is no longer required to say only yes or no).
6. Again have students come to the front of the room, think of something, and have the class guess. Count how many questions it takes the class until it guesses correctly.

DISCUSSION QUESTIONS
1. What was the difference between the two different ways in which this game was played?
2. Which way was the object guessed sooner?
3. Describe open and closed questions to the class.
4. How did the guessing game we played show the difference between open and closed questions?
5. When are open questions useful?
6. When are closed questions useful?
7. What are some examples of open questions? (These questions can be about anything.)
8. What are some examples of some closed questions? (These questions can be about anything.)

Why Ask Why?

OBJECTIVE
Upon completing this lesson, students will be able to word questions in a non-accusatory way that promotes conversation.

KEY CONCEPTS
conflict analysis
group bonding
verbal communication

BACKGROUND
Certain words facilitate conversation, while other words tend to make people feel defensive. When a question begins with the word *why*, people often feel as if they are being threatened or ordered to do something. For example, "Why don't you take out the garbage?" sounds more like advice than a question. The speaker doesn't seem to care about the response, and the listener will probably respond defensively.

It is often more facilitative to ask questions using words other than "Why." For instance, you could ask, "What are the reasons you didn't take out the garbage?" The question is friendlier, and there are more ways in which it could be answered.

During conflict situations, it is especially important for the disputants to ask questions that facilitate discussion. Defensive questions can escalate the conflict.

MATERIALS
none

TEACHER TIPS
Have students become more aware of how people phrase sentences in conversations. For example, you could tell students to listen carefully to what they say when they talk with others, and note when they ask a question that begins with *why*. How did the other person react to the question? What if it were phrased differently? Have the students discuss their experiences.

ACTIVITY

1. Divide the class into pairs. One of the students in each pair is the storyteller and the other is the questioner.
2. Have the storyteller in each pair explain how to do something. For example, the storyteller could explain how to bake a cake, how to get to his/her house, how to play football, and so on.
3. After every sentence, the questioner must ask the storyteller, "Why?" The storyteller must try to finish the story while also responding to each "Why?" asked.
4. Reverse the pair's roles after approximately 5 minutes.

DISCUSSION QUESTIONS

1. How did this activity make you feel?
2. In what ways was this conversation difficult?
3. When you are in an argument with a friend, why is it important not to ask many questions that begin with "Why?"

ADDITIONAL ACTIVITY

Students can do two role plays: In the first role play, two students are in a fight and they ask each other "Why" questions. For example, they could ask each other "Why did you hit me?" In the second role play, the two students act out the same argument, but they do not ask each other "Why" questions.

Discuss the difference between the two role plays. How did the role plays show the importance of not asking questions that begin with the word *why*.

THE MIRROR

OBJECTIVES

Upon completing this lesson, students will be able to:

1. Describe reflective listening.
2. Describe how to reflect body language.
3. Reflect feelings, thoughts, and body language.

KEY CONCEPTS

nonverbal communication
peer conflicts
verbal communication

BACKGROUND

Reflective listening is a technique used to facilitate conversation.* With reflective listening, one paraphrases either the factual information or the feelings the other person has said. This usually clarifies what that person is feeling or thinking.

When using reflective listening, it is important to reflect the exact feeling words that were used. Every person interprets the world slightly differently, and so may not define the different feeling words in the same way. For example, suppose Ron is in an argument with Zina:

Ron: I am so mad that you told my mother that I cheated on the test.

Zina: You're angry.

Ron: No, I'm not at all *angry*. I'm *mad*. I told you. I'm mad at you.

As you can see, Ron's personal definition of the word *mad* was different from his definition of *angry*. Thus, when reflecting what a person feels, it is important to use precisely the same words. For example:

Ron: I am so mad that you told my mother that I cheated on the test.

Zina: You're mad.

Ron: Yes, I'm so mad that I don't know what to do. I can't even look my mother in the eyes anymore. I'm so sad.

People can also reflect body language. Acting like mirrors, they can imitate the posture of other people. Just as with reflecting feelings, reflecting body language can help the other people clarify their feelings and thoughts. It can also comfort them. For example, suppose an angry girl leans back in her chair and yells at her boyfriend. He could reflect her body language by leaning back in his chair, which could subtly signal to the girl her feelings and behavior.

---

* Reflective listening deals with emotions, while paraphrasing, another skill, deals with factual information. For the purpose of simplification, both will be grouped together under the name of reflective listening.

MATERIALS

"The Mirror" activity sheet, pencils

TEACHER TIPS

It may take students a while to fully understand how to reflect information. To make sure that students apply this skill in their own lives, you could have them role play using reflective listening skills at least once a week.

The exception to using exact words in reflective listening is when racial, ethnic, religious, or gender slurs, profanity, put-downs, or other derogatory comments are used. These should be left out in reflective listening. This is often called *laundering language*, which is discussed more in Part II—School Mediation.

ACTIVITY

1. Divide the class into pairs.
2. Have each pair stand and face each other.
3. One of the students in each pair pretends to be standing in front of a full-length mirror. This student moves his/her body in any way possible. The other student in each group pretends to be the reflection, trying to imitate all movements as quickly and accurately as possible.
4. After a few minutes, the two students in each pair reverse roles.
5. Have students sit down.
6. Discuss reflective listening. Explain that reflecting the exact words people say helps them talk more. All you have to do is reflect back the "feeling words" they say or some of the information they share.
7. In pairs, have students complete the activity sheet.
8. Ask for pairs to volunteer to act out their story to the class.

DISCUSSION QUESTIONS

1. What is reflective listening?
2. How is reflective listening like a mirror?
3. Why is it important to reflect exactly what a person says?
4. Suppose you are in a fight with a friend. How can it be helpful to reflect his/her feelings?

ADDITIONAL ACTIVITY

Divide students into pairs. Have them role play a conflict in which one student is angry at the other. Students should take turns reflecting their partner's body language.

ACTIVITY SHEET
The Mirror

Finish the story. Make sure that every time Mitko talks, he reflects either the feelings or information that Melissa has said. As an example, Mitko's first reflective statement is done for you.

Melissa: I am so angry with you, Mitko. I can't believe you did that! You were supposed to meet me yesterday.

Mitko: It sounds like you are angry.

Melissa: Yes, I am angry. You were supposed to meet me yesterday so we could do our homework together. But you weren't there. I was so sad.

Mitko:

Melissa:

Mitko:

2004 © Open Society Institute

The Publisher grants permission for the reproduction of this worksheet for non-profit educational purposes only.
Activity sheets may be downloaded from www.idebate.org/conflictandcommunication.htm

THE FEELING LIST

OBJECTIVES
Upon completing this lesson, students will be able to:
1. List feeling vocabulary words.
2. Describe ways in which emotions are expressed.
3. Recognize the variety of ways that different people express the same emotion.

KEY CONCEPTS
appreciating diversity
feelings
nonverbal communication
self-esteem
verbal communication

BACKGROUND
It is sometimes difficult for people to communicate their emotions because they cannot seem to find the right word to describe how they feel. Students can express themselves more clearly by expanding their awareness of "feeling words." This awareness is especially useful in conflict situations, when people need to express their feelings accurately.

MATERIALS
chalkboard and chalk (or a large piece of paper and a pen)

TEACHER TIPS
If students find it difficult to think of "feeling words," offer scenarios. For example, you could ask how a person feels if he/she has to make a very difficult decision.

ACTIVITY
1. Write "feeling words" in the middle of the board or paper. Ask students to name as many different "feeling words" as they can. Tell them that you think they can name more than twenty-five different words.

2. After the students have exhausted their ideas, tell them they will now play a game. A volunteer walks to the front of the room, chooses a "feeling word" (without telling anyone which word), and acts out that feeling. The class attempts to guess the word. Whoever correctly guesses comes to the front of the room and acts out another word.

3. After the students have acted out many of the words, have the class stand in a circle. Have a volunteer call out one of the "feeling words." Everyone in the class acts out that feeling. Tell everyone to observe everyone else's expressions. Ask for a few more students to call out different words, one at a time. Each time, everyone in the class acts out the feeling and observes each other.

NOTE: The first volunteer who calls out a "feeling word": could choose the next person, and so on.

DISCUSSION QUESTIONS

1. Was it easy or hard to think of so many "feeling words"? Why? Which words were more difficult to think up? Why?

2. Which were hardest to act out? When everyone acted out the feelings, did everyone's expressions look the same? (No.) Why not? (Because not everyone expresses himself/herself the same way.)

3. Can two people have entirely different expressions on their faces but still feel the same? What is an example of when this can happen?

4. If two people are in a fight and only one person looks angry, does this mean that the other person is definitely not angry?

5. Have a volunteer come to the front of the room and circle all words on the feeling list that are positive (e.g., happy, excited, etc.). Classes usually offer more negative than positive "feeling words." If this is so with your class, ask why. Emphasize that it is important to become aware of words that describe our emotions when we feel bad, as well as when we feel good.

MY EMOTIONAL PROPERTY

OBJECTIVES

Upon completing this lesson, students will be able to:

1. Describe "I Statements."
2. Clearly state feelings in a non-accusatory way using "I Statements."

KEY CONCEPTS

behavior
conflict analysis
feelings
verbal communication

BACKGROUND

Imagine that you are in a big argument with a friend. Read the following two sentences and decide which helps facilitate discussion between you and your friend.

1. "You never listen to me anymore, and you are a terrible friend!"
2. "I feel sad when you don't listen to me, because I feel you don't care about me."

Notice that the first sentence may make your friend feel resentful and defensive. Thus, communication may break down. In the second sentence, you take responsibility for your own feelings. Because of the way the second sentence is phrased, it is called an "I Statement."

An "I Statement" is a way we can show that we own our feelings and thoughts. When using "I Statements," not only do we take responsibility for ourselves, but we also present ourselves in a way that does not offend or accuse others.

"I Statements" are a very useful communication skill in conflict situations. By taking responsibility for our own lives, we can sometimes prevent conflicts either from occurring or escalating. When using "I Statements" in a conflict situation, we can express our thoughts and feelings while not causing the other disputants to become defensive.

"I Statements" are also useful for teachers. You can communicate to students what you feel and think in a non-threatening manner.

How do you use "I Statements?" You simply state what you feel and explain why. A normal format for saying "I Statements" is:

I feel [an emotion] when you [do something] because [of this reason].

The following are some examples contrasting statements with and without "I Statements":

Without: You are such a mean teacher!

With: I feel mad because you yelled at me in front of all of my friends.

Without: Why do you talk to everyone except me?

With: When you talk to other people, I feel sad because you exclude me from the conversations.

MATERIALS

"I Feel" activity sheet, pencils

TEACHER TIPS

The skill taught in this activity may be difficult for students to understand and apply, depending on their intellectual capabilities. However, it is very useful in teaching students how to express their emotions in a non-defensive manner. It may be worth the extra effort to teach this skill to your students.

Point out to the students that the words *never* and *always* sometimes make conflict situations worse. They become blaming words and block communication of the real problem. Two sample sentences are, "You never listen to me" and "You always say things like that."

ACTIVITY

1. Explain to the class what "I Statements" are and when they are helpful.

2. Hand out the activity sheet and have students complete it.

3. Divide students into pairs and have them share answers with each other.

4. Go over the sheet with the class, having students volunteer changes that they made in the dialogue.

5. Divide students into new pairs. Have them role play a common conflict situation in their lives using "I Statements" to help de-escalate the conflict.

DISCUSSION QUESTIONS

1. What is an "I Statement?"

2. How are "I Statements" useful when people are in conflicts?

3. While role playing, how did it feel when "I Statements" were used?

4. Why should the words *never* and *always* be avoided in arguments?

ACTIVITY SHEET
I FEEL

The way you say an "I Statement" is:
"I feel [an emotion] when you [do something] because [of this reason]."

Directions: While reading the following story, change every sentence in bold into an "I Statement." Write the "I Statement" in the parentheses. The first one is done for you.

Violeta and Sonia are sitting outside. It is a sunny day. "Let's go to the lake today," says Violeta.

"We always go there, and the lake is so dirty! I hate it there," says Sonia.
("I feel <u>frustrated</u> when you say <u>where we should go</u> because <u>I would like to choose where we go</u> sometimes.")

"You don't have to be so mean. I think that you are just jealous that I have so much fun at the lake," says Violeta.
("I feel __ when you _____ because _____.")

"The only reason you have fun at the lake is because you think the guys there are cute! I hate how they all smile at you and talk with you. No one ever looks at me," says Sonia.
("I feel __ when you _____ because _____.")

"I hate when you say that! It's not true at all! I saw a few guys looking at you. Actually, I think they all look at you," says Violeta.
("I feel __ when you _____ because _____.")

"You hate when I tell you my true feelings? I thought you were my friend, Violeta, but I guess not. Go to the lake by yourself. Goodbye!" yells Nicole.
("I feel __ when you _____ because _____.")

2004 © Open Society Institute

The Publisher grants permission for the reproduction of this worksheet for non-profit educational purposes only.
Activity sheets may be downloaded from www.idebate.org/conflictandcommunication.htm

SUSAN SAYS

OBJECTIVES

Upon completing this lesson, students will be able to:

1. Describe the risks of giving advice.
2. Explain the importance of making their own decisions.
3. Describe actions that identify different ways to behave in a discrimination situation.
4. Describe what power is.
5. State ways of balancing power.

KEY CONCEPTS

decision-making
personal responsibility
power/authority
self-empowerment

BACKGROUND

When students are in conflict situations, they often seek the advice of others. This exercise is designed to help students realize that most of the time they have the answers to their conflicts. They merely need a patient person who will listen to their problems.

Think of the conflicts you have faced in your life. You may have asked others for advice about how to handle your situations, but ultimately, the decisions were yours. By teaching students not to give advice, we help them become more responsible for the decisions in their lives.

But why should we not give advice? We've done it all our lives! Think about what happens when you or a student offers advice to classmates. If they take the advice, one of two things could happen: 1) If the advice is good, the students come back to you again and again whenever they need to make a life decision. They become dependent on you and feel less responsible for their choices. 2) If the advice is bad, the students take little or no responsibility for their decisions because you offered the advice. The students can blame you for their problems. In either case, allowing students to analyze the positive and negative consequences of their options helps them become more responsible for their behavior.

MATERIALS

"Muscles" resource sheet

TEACHER TIPS

Although this activity is designed to teach the risks of advice giving, make sure that students understand that it is not always bad to seek or offer advice. You could ask students to suggest some circumstances in which advice may be useful. Who would they seek advice from and why?

ACTIVITY I

1. Have student volunteers, one at a time, be Susan.

2. Susan stands in front of the class, facing everyone, and states commands (such as "touch your nose").

3. These commands either begin with "Susan says" or they do not.

4. If the command begins with "Susan says," the class must comply with the command. If the command does not begin with "Susan says," the students should not comply with the command. If someone makes a mistake, he/she can try again. The faster the game is played, the more difficult it is.

5. Once a few students have been Susan, you become Susan.

6. After issuing a few commands, you point to a chair and say, "Susan says to eat this chair." Of course no one in the class will attempt to eat the chair (and if anyone attempts to, stop them and tell them that you were only kidding).

7. When the class is confused and curious by your statement, start the discussion.

DISCUSSION QUESTIONS

1. Why didn't you eat the chair?

2. Why did you do what Susan said?

3. Why should you listen to Susan?

4. Are leaders always right, or can some leaders give bad advice?

5. Why do we listen to our parents? teachers? friends? government?

6. When someone comes to you and wants to talk about a conflict, is it better to listen to that person or to give them advice?

7. What could happen if you give a person bad advice?

8. It is very easy to listen to other people and accept what they say as true. But why is it important to make decisions on your own?

9. What if Susan told you to do something mean to other people? What would you do?

ACTIVITY II

NOTE: "Susan Says" can lead to this discussion about power.

1. Ask the students why they followed Susan's orders (in Activity I). Ask them if they always follow their parents' orders. What would they do if they wanted to play with their friends after school, but their parents demanded that they stay home?

2. Discuss with the class what power is, how someone acquires it, and why people follow powerful people's orders. (Power can be defined as the ability to have others listen and comply with one's requests.)

3. Ask what kind of power parents, students, teachers, politicians, religious leaders, and other groups have.

4. Hand out the "Muscles" resource sheet and read it with the class.

5. Divide students into pairs.

6. Instruct each pair to create a role play about a conflict in which a powerful person treats a less powerful person disrespectfully. Have the less powerful person balance power through at least one of the four methods described on the sheet.

7. Have a few of the pairs demonstrate their role plays to the rest of the class.

8. Have students offer specific ways that these four methods of balancing power could be useful if someone is bullying someone else.

Resource Sheet
Muscles

METHODS FOR BALANCING POWER

What can you do when someone has power over you? You could:

1. **Speak honestly about your thoughts and feelings.** Even if someone is more powerful, openly express your thoughts and feelings. Do not let the person's power awe you into silence. However, try not to lose your temper.

2. **Be a good listener.** Carefully listen to what the more powerful person says. Use positive body language.

3. **Ask! Ask! Ask!** If you want something from a high-powered person, continually and politely ask until the request is granted.

4. **Gain the support of a person with a lot of power.** For example, if a classmate continually steals your belongings, you could seek help from a teacher, parent, or police officer.

2004 © Open Society Institute

The Publisher grants permission for the reproduction of this worksheet for non-profit educational purposes only.
Activity sheets may be downloaded from www.idebate.org/conflictandcommunication.htm

Chapter Four:
ME vs. YOU

Conflicts are often fueled by differing perceptions and poor communication. Once we understand others' points of view and develop our communication skills, we are equipped to effectively manage conflicts.

This chapter's activities allow students to directly examine conflict, exploring its roots and consequences. They realize that nearly every conflict has positive potential and provides an opportunity for growth and learning. Important issues are raised, such as why people resort to violence during conflicts. Some of the activities encourage students to think about possible nonviolent resolutions to disputes.

This chapter's activities provide students with a basic understanding of the use and misuse of conflict. The next chapter then builds on this understanding and offers a specific strategy for managing conflicts.

MY PICTURE OF CONFLICT

OBJECTIVE
Upon completing this lesson, students will be able to illustrate their personal ideas of conflict.

KEY CONCEPTS
conflict analysis
empathy

BACKGROUND
This is one of the more popular activities used to help people explore how they view conflict. The directions for this activity are vague, allowing students to freely explore and express their feelings. This activity's importance lies in making students aware of their current (and usually limited) ideas of conflict. Usually conflict is envisioned and expressed as a bad, terrifying, or undesirable situation, not as a healthy opportunity for growth. Self-awareness of prejudices and stereotypes about conflict is the first step toward understanding and change.

MATERIALS
Paper, pencils

TEACHER TIPS
Although this activity seems simple, be prepared for the possibility that some of the students might become emotional. This is a natural response to dealing with conflict. If a student should become emotional, there are several options you could pursue:

1) You could try to soothe him/her with calming words. Having the student talk about conflict might be very helpful for him/her. Use your own judgment in assessing the situation.

2) You could invite the student to meet with you after class, at which time you could find out the details behind the emotional outburst. (With severely emotional children, you could refer them to a psychologist.)

ACTIVITY

1. Instruct students to draw conflict. Tell them that they can draw whatever they want to express their idea of conflict.

2. Have students sit in a circle. Each person shares his/her drawing and explains what it means. Students who feel uncomfortable should not be forced to share the drawing.

DISCUSSION QUESTIONS

1. What are some of the similarities among many of our pictures?

2. What are some of the differences?

3. How do most of us view conflict: positively or negatively? Why?

THE ROOTS OF CONFLICT

OBJECTIVES

Upon completing this lesson, students will be able to:

1. Explore their own ideas on conflict.
2. Identify and explain the basic sources of conflict.
3. Describe how conflicts are resolved in various contexts.

KEY CONCEPTS

community conflict
family conflict
peer conflict
school conflict
sources of conflict

BACKGROUND

A comedian once joked that there are probably more conflicts in the world than grains of sand. However, although conflicts are so abundant, there are surprisingly few sources of conflict. Most of our conflicts relate to the following six sources (explained on The Roots of Conflict activity sheet): basic needs, differing values, differing perceptions, differing interests, limited resources, and psychological needs.

How can such a wide variety of conflicts stem from such a small list of roots? To illuminate, let's look at two conflicts and find the similar source. Conflict One concerns a brother and sister who are yelling at each other; each wants the last piece of bread on the table and does not want to share it. Conflict Two concerns two countries at war with each other; each wants to own the same piece of land and doesn't want to share it. In both conflicts there is a similar root: a limited resource. This same type of analysis can be conducted with other conflicts and with other sources of conflict.

By analyzing and discovering the roots of a conflict, people can develop a method for dealing with the conflict itself. For instance, when the conflict's roots lie in differing values, they can try to respect and understand each other's perspectives of the situation. When the roots lie in differing perceptions, they can try to clarify their views and offer information to correct misunderstandings. When the conflict's roots lie in differing interests, they can try to share their interests and find a mutually satisfying solution.

MATERIALS

"What Do We Want?" activity sheet, pencils, chalkboard and chalk; paper, clear area in the classroom

TEACHER TIPS

To help your class understand that most conflicts have the same roots, you could have the students suggest conflicts that they face. The class could discuss the roots of each suggested.

ACTIVITIES

1. Write the word *conflict* in big letters on a piece of paper and place it on the floor in an open, clear area of the classroom where everyone can see it.

2. Hand out one sheet of paper to each student.

3. Instruct students to count the number of letters in their first name and to cut (or rip) their sheet of paper into that number of pieces.

4. Students then write a different word or idea that they associate with conflict on each small piece of paper.

5. One at a time, each student lays his/her words on the floor around the sheet of paper that says "Conflict." As each student puts his/her words on the floor, he/she should say them aloud. If students have words that are similar to other words already on the floor, they should place them close to one another. For example, if the word *fighting* is given, a word like hitting could be placed beside it. Students are permitted to explain their words if they would like to.

6. Discuss with students whether most ideas about conflict are good or bad. Ask them how conflict can be good. Make sure they give specific answers. Ask them to offer examples of times when conflict was useful or helpful.

7. Have students complete the activity sheet. (Note: This could be a homework assignment.)

8. In groups of four to six, students share their stories.

DISCUSSION QUESTIONS

1. Why do people have conflicts?

2. Should we avoid having conflicts? Why or why not? What are some examples of times in your life that you avoided having a conflict? How did you feel by avoiding the conflict?

4. How are conflicts resolved:

    a. within yourself?.

    b. within our class?

    c. within our school?

    d. within our community?

    e. within your family?

    f. among you and your friends?

ADDITIONAL ACTIVITY

The last discussion question is very useful and insightful. You could transform it into an ACTIVITY Divide the class into six groups. Read the question to the class. Each group is told to figure out ways in which conflicts can be resolved. One group thinks about how conflicts are resolved within oneself, another group discusses how conflicts are resolved within the class, and so on. After the groups have brainstormed how conflicts are resolved, each group shares its ideas with the rest of the class. (Each group could also think of how a specific conflict is resolved and create a role play.) You can follow the activity with a discussion of the similarities and differences between how different types of conflicts are resolved.

ACTIVITY SHEET
THE ROOTS OF CONFLICT

WHAT DO WE WANT?

What do we have conflicts about? There are six different sources of conflict. Most of our conflicts relate to these six sources:

1. Basic Needs are the things that we need in order to survive, such as food, water, and air.

2. Differing Values occur when people have different beliefs. For example, people of different religions may have differing values.

3. Differing Perceptions occur when people have different thoughts about something. For example, two people may argue about the color of a friend's shirt. They each may perceive the color of the shirt differently.

4. Differing Interests occur when people have different concerns. For example, two students may disagree about whether to go to a party or to the movies.

5. Limited Resources refers to a limited amount of something. Not every person in the world is rich, because money is a limited resource.

6. Psychological Needs are the things that we need in order to feel capable, responsible, accepted, important, and healthy. For example, we all have the need to be loved.

Now write a short story about a conflict. Use at least one of the six sources of conflict to help you write the story. Specify which source(s) you use. For instance, you could write a story about two brothers fighting over a book. They each want to read the book now, but there is only one book. The source of the conflict is a limited resource—there is only one book that they both want.

The Conflict Dictionary

OBJECTIVES

Upon completing this lesson, students will be able to:
1. Describe the word *conflict* based on their own definitions.
2. Achieve a general agreement about what constitutes a conflict.

KEY CONCEPTS

conflict analysis
conflict management

BACKGROUND

Conflict is such a natural, important, and inescapable part of society and our own lives that it is difficult to give it a single definition. After all, how can we reduce conflict to a single definition when there are so many different kinds of conflict?

The following three activities are designed to allow students to explore underlying similarities in conflict situations ranging from family arguments to international wars. Rather than imposing theoretical views of conflict on the students, these activities provide the students with the opportunity to develop an understanding of conflict on their own.

MATERIALS

"Is This A Conflict?" and "Most Conflicts" activity sheets, paper, pencils, chalkboard and chalk (or large paper and a pen)

TEACHER TIPS

To help students feel comfortable working in small groups, you may want to facilitate an icebreaker (see Appendix II) before this activity.

Encourage the students to make sure everyone in their group participates in the discussion.

These three activities offer an opportunity for you to ask students to share their successful, peaceful solutions to conflicts.

ACTIVITY I

1. Divide the class into groups of four to six.

2. Each group chooses a representative who will report back to the class highlights of the small group's discussion.

3. Give one copy of "Is This a Conflict?" to each group representative. Tell each group that it must decide whether or not each situation is a conflict. Stress that the groups must think of reasons to support their decisions.

4. Once the groups are finished, the representatives from each group report their conclusions and reasons to the whole class.

5. Record on the chalkboard or large paper the major points made by each group. Have the students discuss these points openly, telling them that it is okay to disagree.

ACTIVITY II

1. This activity is fun and easy. Divide the class into pairs.

2. Hand out a piece of paper to each pair.

3. Tell students that they are going to create definitions of conflict. Write the phrase "Conflict is..." on the chalkboard. Ask the students to complete the sentence and record all responses on their papers. To stimulate ideas, offer the students examples such as, "Conflict is terror," "Conflict is something I deal with every day," and "Conflict is fun." Encourage each pair to think of at least ten ideas.

4. Once the students have exhausted their ideas, ask them to think about which ones can be grouped together as positive and which can be grouped together as negative.

5. One of the students in each pair draws a circle around every idea that seems positive. The other draws a square around every idea that seems negative.

6. The pairs will find that some of the definitions could be either positive or negative.

7. The pairs use their definitions to help them create a definition of conflict. Their definitions can be more than one sentence. For example, a pair might decide that conflict is: "Something that people do every day. People in conflict fight, hurt each other, and also get what they want. Not all conflicts are bad."

8. Each pair shares its definitions of conflict with the whole class.

9. Discuss the following questions.

    a. Which definition seems like the clearest definition of conflict for us?

    b. Did you find that you thought of more positive or negative definitions of conflict? Why? What are some of the positive definitions of conflict?

10. Tell the students that you would like to share with them dictionary definitions of conflict. Have them compare their definitions of conflict with the dictionary ones.

11. Have students note that the dictionary definitions are not the perfect, only definitions of conflict.

    * The word conflict comes from the Latin language. The Latin word *conflictus* means "to strike together."

    * A simple definition of conflict is: a disagreement between two or more persons or ideas.

ACTIVITY III

1. Hand out The Roots of Conflict activity sheet and ask students to complete it.

2. Divide the students into groups of five or six.

3. Through a shared group discussion, each group must decide which five ideas on the sheet are most helpful in managing conflicts.

DISCUSSION QUESTIONS

1. What images do you think of when someone says the word *conflict*?

2. What are some of the underlying similarities among different types of conflicts? Be specific.

3. How do you feel about conflicts? Do you think they are harmful or helpful for people? Why? Are conflicts harmful or helpful for you? Why?

4. Ask students to describe a specific conflict they experienced and one helpful thing they learned from it.

FOLLOW-UP ACTIVITY

Have the students go back over the situations discussed in Activity 1 and try to reconsider them.

ACTIVITY SHEET
IS THIS A CONFLICT?

Directions: Read and decide whether or not each of these situations is a conflict. Write down reasons to explain your decisions.

1. Andreea, Veronika, and Irena talk during their biology class. They whisper and write notes to each other. The biology teacher gets angry with them one day, yells at them, and sends them out of the classroom. He tells them to clean the blackboard every day for one month.

2. Jelena and Eva are good friends. Last week they both took a history test and received good grades. Jelena thinks that Eva received her good grade because she is the teacher's favorite student. Eva says that she studied and honestly deserved the grade. The two girls now argue and shout with one another.

3. Andris loves a nighttime radio show. It is on now, and he wants to listen to it. But his father wants him to go to sleep. Andris refuses to turn off the radio. His father becomes very angry, unplugs the radio, and tells him he is not allowed to listen to the radio all weekend.

4. A lot of kids like to play games in the schoolyard at night, but recently, a few stray dogs bit three kids there. Now many parents do not allow their children to play in the schoolyard at night.

5. Students divide into two separate groups at a school party. Marius is the leader of one of the groups, and Donna is the leader of the other. Each group laughs and has a lot of fun but ignores the students in the other group.

2004 © Open Society Institute

The Publisher grants permission for the reproduction of this worksheet for non-profit educational purposes only.
Activity sheets may be downloaded from www.idebate.org/conflictandcommunication.htm

ACTIVITY SHEET
MOST CONFLICTS

Directions: Place a check by every statement that you agree with. When there is a conflict, most people:

__argue
__try to understand each other
__help one another
__yell at one another
__cooperate
__trick one another
__listen carefully to each other
__are suspicious of each other
__try to win
__forgive each other
__try to help both people win
__fight
__trust one another
__lie to each other
__smile
__compete with one another
__hit each other
__work together to resolve the conflict
__try to understand how the other person is feeling
__blame one another
__ask other people for help
__try to end the conversation
__get angry at each other

CONFLICT IN THE NEWS

OBJECTIVES

Upon completing this lesson, students will be able to:

1. Distinguish between what is and what is not a conflict.
2. Explain how conflicts are depicted in newspapers and magazines.
3. Distinguish between positive and negative ways of handling conflict.

KEY CONCEPTS

conflict analysis
media

BACKGROUND

We are all unique, differing in our ages, our genders, our religious beliefs, and so on. We also differ in how we see the world. What seems like acceptable behavior to one person may seem like unacceptable behavior to another person. At what point do disagreements over different views transform into conflict?

More generally, how do we recognize conflicts? Conflicts that are associated with physical violence, such as when someone shoves someone else, are simple to recognize. However, it is more difficult to identify conflicts regarding differences in attitudes. For instance, when two people of different religions start arguing over religious concepts, at some point the discussion may become a conflict.

This activity allows students to understand how newspapers and magazines may unintentionally promote conflicts. While a picture may appear totally acceptable to you, someone else may perceive the same picture negatively.

MATERIALS

pictures from magazines and newspapers. Make sure that:
* Most of the pictures show people interacting in obvious conflict situations.
* A few of the pictures show people interacting in less obvious conflicts. In these pictures, it may be ambiguous as to whether there truly is a conflict. For example, a picture might consist of representatives of a few different ethnic minorities talking at a dinner table or interacting in some other way.
* A few of the pictures show no conflict at all. These pictures could show cooperation, caring, etc.

NOTE: Make sure that the pictures represent a wide variety of conflict situations. Also, instead of finding the pictures yourself, the students could bring in newspapers and magazines and find pictures. Simply tell the students what types of pictures to search for.

TEACHER TIPS

The Additional Activity introduces the concept of conflict resolution. Help students understand that cooperation is a way of resolving conflicts. You can also encourage them to watch for examples of conflicts that are peacefully resolved. This heightened awareness will help them with later activities.

ACTIVITY

1. Divide the students into groups of four to six.
2. Give each group some of the pictures from the magazines and newspapers.
3. Instruct each group to analyze each picture, deciding whether the picture contains a conflict situation. Each group should lay the pictures on the floor, side-by-side. It should order the pictures from the one it feels most obviously represents conflict to the one it feels least depicts conflict. If members disagree with most of their group's decision, they should explain why.
4. After all of the groups have analyzed and ordered their pictures, each group presents its pictures to the class and explains why it ordered the pictures as such.

DISCUSSION QUESTIONS

1. What were some difficulties in deciding whether the pictures showed conflict situations?
2. How did you decide whether a picture showed a conflict situation?
3. Who would like to share an argument they had when trying to agree? How did you handle the argument?
4. How did it feel when you didn't agree with the decision of most of the group?
5. How did it feel when you agreed with the decision of most of the group, but someone else didn't agree?

ADDITIONAL ACTIVITY

Ask students to collect pictures showing cooperation. The students can create a scrapbook of pictures or can compile the pictures in a folder. Underneath each picture the students explain how that picture relates to cooperation. Have students share their scrapbooks with the class orally or by exchanging books.

DISCUSSION QUESTIONS

1. How is cooperation related to conflict?
2. How do you use cooperation in your everyday life?

AN EYE FOR AN EYE

OBJECTIVES
Upon completing this lesson, students will be able to:
1. Explain how many of their attitudes and values originate from family, friends, school, community, and society.
2. Identify how their own values affect the way they resolve conflicts.
3. List the strengths and weaknesses of messages they receive from different sources.

KEY CONCEPTS
attitudes
behavior
conflict analysis
feelings
values

BACKGROUND
Why do so many people view conflicts so negatively? First of all, conflicts generate emotions and remind us of unpleasant experiences. When we think of conflict, we think of anger, frustration, and other disagreeable emotions. Secondly, society affects our view of conflict. Throughout our lives, parents, teachers, friends, and people in our community send us various messages about how to view the world. From these messages, we build a system of values, principles, and beliefs that influence how we behave in conflict situations.

This activity explores how different people in our lives send us conflicting messages, leaving us confused about how to act. Becoming aware of these messages allows us to make more knowledgeable decisions.

MATERIALS
chalkboard and chalk (or large paper and pen); list of sayings to help you facilitate Activity 1

TEACHER TIPS
Activity 1 of this lesson can function as an icebreaker, helping students to feel more comfortable during Activity II.

ACTIVITY I

1. Ask the students to think up as many different sayings as they can about how to act in a conflict situation. If students have a difficult time thinking of examples, you could offer them suggestions such as "An eye for an eye, a tooth for a tooth" or "You asked for trouble."

2. Write the sayings on the chalkboard.

DISCUSSION QUESTIONS

1. While pointing to specific sayings on the chalkboard, ask the students:
    a. Where did you learn this saying?
    b. How does this saying suggest that you handle conflict?

2. Tell the students that the sayings suggest how we should resolve conflicts. Ask them to think of conflicts that they have seen at school, at home, and elsewhere. They should describe a time in which they saw someone solve the conflict in the way the saying asserts. (You may want to offer the students an example first. For instance, you could tell them that if they saw one person yell at another person and the other person yell back, that is similar to the saying "An eye for an eye, a tooth for a tooth." In other words, I yell at you, you yell at me.)

ACTIVITY II

1. Explain to the class that we receive messages about how to behave and what to value from many different sources (see the background information for details). Sometimes these different messages conflict with one another.

2. Tell the class that we are now going to explore what messages people tell us.

3. Divide the class into six groups.

4. Each group makes a list of messages that are sent to us. Explain that the messages can be spoken, such as when our parents tell us not to stay out past a certain hour; or they can be less obvious, such as when we dress to look like rock stars. Assign each group as follows:
    - Group 1 makes a list of messages we receive from family.
    - Group 2 makes a list of messages we receive from school.
    - Group 3 makes a list of messages we receive from our friends.
    - Group 4 makes a list of messages we receive from books, newspapers, and magazines.
    - Group 5 makes a list of messages we receive from our community.
    - Group 6 makes a list of messages we receive from television.

5. Have students compare the different messages sent from the various sources.

DISCUSSION QUESTIONS

1. What happens when we receive messages that conflict with one another? For instance, when your parents tell you to come home by a certain hour, do you come home by that time?

2. What if friends persuade you to stay out later? What message do you follow? Why?

FOLLOW-UP ACTIVITY

1. In this activity, which is an extension of Activity II, the students apply the messages they learned (from family, friends, community, and so on). Read the following situation to the class:

Last week you had a math exam. You studied and were confident that you did well on it. Yesterday, the teacher handed you your exam. In front of the whole class, the teacher said, "You failed this test because you cheated."

2. Have each group think of different possible ways that the student might react to the teacher's accusation. Have each group develop a role play in which the student reacts to the accusation consistently with the messages of that group. For instance, the group that listed ways we receive messages from our family might develop a role play in which the student calmly denies the accusation; the group that listed ways we receive messages from television might develop a role play in which the student yells and screams at the teacher.

DISCUSSION QUESTIONS

1. What are the strengths and weaknesses of listening to the messages sent to us by:
    a. family?
    b. school?
    c. friends?
    d. books, newspapers, and magazines?
    e. community?
    f. television?

2. If we have conflicting messages, how do we decide which one to follow? For instance, should the student scream back at the teacher who wrongly accuses him of cheating, or should he calmly tell the teacher that he didn't cheat?

Faces of Violence

OBJECTIVES

Upon completing this lesson, students will be able to:

1. Identify subtypes of violence.
2. Describe subtypes of violence.

KEY CONCEPTS

conflict analysis
violence

BACKGROUND

Many people think that conflict and violence are the same thing. The two concepts are often related, but they are not identical. For example, many people use violent means to manage conflicts. However, violence is only one of many possible ways of managing conflict.

There are three main categories of violence. For most people, the word *violence* is associated with physical violence. But two other types of violence, psychological and systemic violence, can be just as destructive. What exactly are these types of violence?

1. **Physical violence:** When physical force is used to hurt someone else. This type of violence is usually intentional. An example of this is a student punching someone else.

2. **Psychological violence:** When someone damages someone else's sense of self-worth. An example of this would be parents continually telling their child that the child is stupid and worthless.

3. **Institutional violence:** When an institution denies basic rights to certain members. An example of this is a government not permitting certain citizens to work. When violence becomes institutionalized, it becomes acceptable and part of the culture.

Keep in mind that discussing issues of institutional violence in the schools may not be easy, especially since you and the students may think about situations within your school.

It is noteworthy to explain the difference between another subdivision of violence: hostile violence and instrumental violence. **Hostile violence** occurs when violence is committed with the intent to hurt. If I am angry with you and I punch you, I have committed an act of hostile violence. On the other hand, **instrumental violence** occurs when violence is committed as a means for attaining some other goal. For instance, a student may start a fight to prove his/her strength to others. In this case, violence is used as an instrument so that the student can attain a goal: proof of strength.

MATERIALS
two pieces of paper and a pencil for every student

TEACHER TIPS
Violence is a part of all of our lives. Because some of us have witnessed or experienced more intensive acts of violence than others, facilitate this activity with sensitivity. If you notice students becoming distressed, approach them after class and ask them why they looked so distressed. If many students appear distressed, it may be wise to discuss with the class reasons why violence can be upsetting. Also, it may be helpful to teach the class a stress-relieving activity (see Appendix I).

It may be useful for students to think of problems they have seen in their school that have been resolved in a violent manner and to role play nonviolent alternatives.

ACTIVITY
1. Divide students into groups of four to six, making sure that each student has a pencil and paper. Each group should make a small circle.
2. Instruct students to write the word *violence* on the top of their papers.
3. Students individually write down what they think violence is.
4. Each student shares his/her definition of violence with the group.
5. Going clockwise around each group circle, each student calls out words that come to mind when he/she thinks of violence. Some of the words may describe actual examples of violence. Other words may describe the meaning of violence. Everyone in each group should write down every idea called out. Each group must think of at least twenty words.

NOTE: If a person does not feel comfortable calling out a word, he/she does not have to do so.

6. Have students get out a clean piece of paper and divide it into three separate sections.
7. Tell students to write down the words *physical violence* at the top of the first section. Discuss with the students what physical violence is.
8. Tell the students to write down the words *psychological violence* at the top of the second section. Discuss with the student what psychological violence is. Help students understand the difference between physical and psychological violence.
9. Tell students to write down the words *institutional violence* at the top of the third section,. Discuss with the students what institutional violence is. Help them understand the differences between the three types of violence listed on their papers.
10. Instruct the groups to decide in which of the three sections to place each of the words that they called out earlier (in step 5). Members of each group work together to categorize the words.
11. Next, the students in each group discuss a possible way to stop each of the three types of violence. If this task proves too difficult, have the students discuss a possible way to end a specific example of violence listed on their sheets..
12. Students in each group share their examples of violence with the group. They also tell the group their ideas on how to stop the different types of violence.

DISCUSSION QUESTIONS

1. Why was it difficult to categorize some of the examples of violence into just one heading?

2. What is violence? Why do people's definitions of violence differ?

3. Ask students to describe some times when people used violence to try to manage conflict. Why did the people use violence? In what other ways might the conflicts have been managed?

4. Tell the class to listen to the following two scenarios, which include acts of violence. Ask them to think about what is different between the violence used in each situation. Then have a discussion about the difference between instrumental and hostile violence (discussed in the background section of this lesson). Ask the students to share examples of real-life situations in which hostile or instrumental violence was used.

    Scenario 1: Two students are arguing with one another. One student is so furious and enraged at the other student that he/she punches him/her in the face.

    Scenario 2: A student starts a fight to prove his/her strength to the class.

NOTE: Explain that it is important not to confuse hostile and instrumental violence. Sometimes when students are violently attacked, they view themselves negatively, thinking that the attack is a result of personal inadequacies. However, violence is often due to the hidden agenda of the attacker.

WHERE IS VIOLENCE?

OBJECTIVES
Upon completing this lesson, students will be able to:
1. Define and describe what violence is.
2. Identify the large number of violent activities they are exposed to every day.
3. Offer multiple nonviolent ways of resolving actual violent situations.
4. Explain why exposure to violence makes it seem like a healthy, useful conflict management strategy.

KEY CONCEPTS
conflict analysis
violence

BACKGROUND
Violence is everywhere. Pick up the newspaper and you read about wars in the world. Turn on the television and you see people yelling or shooting each other. Watch children play and you notice that they play violent games.

In our world, violence is accepted as a way to resolve conflict. This is problematic, because children learn from their environment. If their environment emphasizes violence, they will become accustomed to violence as a practical and healthy way of resolving conflicts. To change this mentality, children must learn to: 1) recognize violence, and 2) manage conflicts using means other than violence.

The prior activity "Faces of Violence" helped students recognize different kinds of violence. The present activity takes a deeper look at issues of violence.

MATERIALS
"Where is Violence?" and "Spotting Violence" activity sheets; chalkboard and chalk (or large paper and a pen), pencils

TEACHER TIPS
Students who have either experienced or witnessed physical or psychological violence can slowly heal by talking about their problems. By using the communication skills from Chapter Three,

you can help this difficult healing process along. Students should feel that they can talk about personal situations during the activities; they can also choose not to share their feelings.

After the students complete this activity, you could discuss whether the situations on the activity sheets describe examples of physical, psychological, or institutional violence (described in the previous lesson).

ACTIVITY

1. Write the word violence on the chalkboard.
2. Divide the class into groups of four.
3. Instruct each group to complete the "Where is Violence" activity sheet, discussing each question before writing an answer.
4. Once the activity sheet is completed, have the whole class form a large circle.
5. Have each group share its definition of violence.

DISCUSSION QUESTIONS

1. What would our society be like if there were no violence?
2. Is there a lot of violence in our society?
3. Because there is so much violence surrounding us, it makes us think that violence is okay. What are some of the difficulties with solving a problem by using violence?

FOLLOW-UP ACTIVITY

Hand out "Spotting Violence" and have students carry the sheet around with them for two days. Tell them to document any violence they think they witness on the left side of the sheet. Explain that they might see violence at school, at home, on television, on the playground, or anywhere else. Tell students that when they write down violent instances, they should not use people's real names. On the right side of the sheet, students should write down a possible way of managing each situation without using violence.

Offer the students the following example to clarify the assignment:

On your way home from school, you notice a young child crying. The mother slaps her child. On the left side of the paper, you record that you saw a mother slap her child. On the right side, write down a nonviolent solution the mother could have used to stop the crying. For instance, the mother could calmly ask the child to be quiet instead of slapping her.

Ask the students to complete the sheet and bring it to class. Everyone who wants to can share what they witnessed. They should also describe their nonviolent alternative to handling the problem.

DISCUSSION QUESTIONS

1. How many violent acts did you notice?

2. Why do you think there is so much violence surrounding us?

NOTE: If you tell the students not to write their names on the sheets, you can collect them and use them for discussion and role play.

ACTIVITY SHEET

WHERE IS VIOLENCE ?

Directions: Answer the following questions with the help of everyone in your small group.

1. What do you think violence is?

2. Is it violence when someone punches and hurts someone else?
   Yes___No___

   Why or why not?

3. Is it violence when someone calls someone else mean names?
   Yes___No___

   Why or why not?

4. What if the other person's feelings are hurt?

5. Is it violence if someone accidentally hurts someone else? For instance, if you accidentally step on someone else's foot and break the bones, did you commit a violent act?
   Yes___No___

   Why or Why not?

6. Name at least four places where violence can be seen or heard. (For example, violence can be seen on television when people shoot each other.)

2004 © Open Society Institute

The Publisher grants permission for the reproduction of this worksheet for non-profit educational purposes only.
Activity sheets may be downloaded from www.idebate.org/conflictandcommunication.htm

Activity Sheet
Spotting Violence

INSTRUCTIONS: Carry this sheet with you everywhere you go. Every time you witness any kind of violence, write it in the column titled *Violence Seen*. You could see violence at home, at school, on television, on the playground, or anywhere else. In the column titled *The Person/Circumstance*, describe what the reasons for the violence appeared to be and how the person seemed to be feeling. In the column titled *How the Situation Was Managed*, describe how the violence affected the conflict situation. In the column titled *Other Ways of Handling the Situation*, write other ways the situation could have been managed without the use of violence. When describing other people's violent acts, do NOT write their real names. Change the names or refer to them as a man, a woman, or a child.

Violence Seen	The Person/Circumstance	How The Situation Was Managed	Other Ways of Handling The Situation

2004 © Open Society Institute

The Publisher grants permission for the reproduction of this worksheet for non-profit educational purposes only.
Activity sheets may be downloaded from www.idebate.org/conflictandcommunication.htm

Chapter Five:
ME WITH YOU

Conflicts are a natural, inevitable part of everyone's social life. Most people view conflicts as irreconcilable, destructive clashes, in which one side wins at the expense of the other. However, the scientific field of conflict management has developed models and strategies for effectively and constructively dealing with conflicts. New models present the process of conflict resolution not as a competitive battle, but rather as an opportunity for learning new information, building relationships, and cooperatively resolving conflicts.

In this chapter, we present Climbing the Ladder, a simple five-step strategy for resolving conflicts effectively. Here, in a specific order, is a format that we recommend for you to teach the strategy:

1. Hand out the "Climbing the Ladder" activity sheet located on page 171. Read the sheet with the students. Briefly explain that conflicts are not always bad things. In fact, conflicts can be times when we grow, learn, and develop understanding about one another. Tell the students that they will be learning how to "climb the ladder" and deal with conflicts more effectively. By following the steps, two students in conflict will communicate clearly and get what both want.* Instruct students to bring the activity sheet to every lesson on conflict.
2. Facilitate at least one lesson about each of the five steps of the conflict resolution strategy. This chapter contains lessons that clarify and demonstrate each of the steps. Beside the titles is a brief description of the steps the lessons highlight. Choose lessons that would work most effectively in your classroom.
3. Facilitate the lesson "Climbing the Ladder."
4. Have the students practice the five-step strategy at least once a week, if possible. Students must practice these skills if they are to successfully incorporate them into their lives. For example, once a week you could have students think of conflicts and role play how to manage them using the strategy. (The activities in this chapter after the lesson "Climbing the Ladder" also allow students to practice the five-step strategy.)

---

* The background section of "Climbing the Ladder," located on page 168, contains a more complete description of the strategy..

MY POUNDING HEART
(STEP I OF "CLIMBING THE LADDER")

OBJECTIVES
Upon completing this lesson, students will be able to:
1. Recognize their own physical responses to conflict.
2. Describe their own physical responses to conflict.
3. Describe how physical responses to conflict affect behaviors.

KEY CONCEPTS
recognizing conflict

BACKGROUND
Conflicts are often considered to be times of tension, stress, and attack. While many of the activities so far have focused on understanding the mental aspects of conflict, this activity examines our physical reactions during conflicts.

During conflicts, we physically react in tense, stressful ways: we raise our voices, our hearts pound quickly, we tremble in anger, we grow pale, and so on. Our responses in a conflict situation also affect the other person in the conflict. For example, if I raise my voice, you raise your voice. Once you raise your voice, I raise my voice even more! Our physical responses create fiercer and fiercer conflict situations.

Sometimes, we knowingly use our own physical responses to influence others. A student might raise his/her voice to scare and influence classmates, or a parent arguing with a child might suddenly become very quiet, threatening the child with merely a look of the eyes.

At other times, we conceal our true feelings. In these circumstances, although our hearts might be beating quickly and our hands shaking, we pretend not to be afraid: we try to appear strong and not weak.

Here is a list of some examples of how we respond physically in conflict situations:

- our voices get louder
- we sweat
- we tremble
- we run away
- we talk faster
- we breathe faster
- we clench our hands into fists
- our faces flush or grow pale
- we tap our fingers or feet
- our hearts beat quicker
- we cry

- we talk very calmly
- we don't talk at all
- we clench our teeth
- we grimace

MATERIALS

"My Pounding Heart" and "Don't Say That to Me" activity sheets; paper, pencils, chalkboard and chalk (or large paper and a pen)

TEACHER TIPS

This activity requires students to imagine physical reactions to conflict. A quick icebreaker (see Appendix II) before this activity may help students be more imaginative, realistic, and comfortable.

Explain to students that physical responses in conflict situations include both physiological responses, such as sweating, and conscious physical responses, such as running away.

Make sure students clearly understand how to complete the "My Pounding Heart" activity sheet.

ACTIVITY

1. Divide students into groups of six.
2. Explain that during conflict situations we act, talk, and feel differently than we normally do. For instance, we might yell at a friend instead of just talking at a normal volume.
3. Tell the groups that they will have 10 minutes to write down as many physical responses to conflict as they can. If they are having difficulty, tell them to think of different conflicts that they have recently been in, and ask them how their bodies reacted during those incidents.
4. The students in each group share their physical responses to conflict with the rest of the class. A student writes all of the suggestions on the chalkboard. You can also suggest some of the examples listed in the background section of this activity.
5. Hand out "My Pounding Heart." Students should write the list of physical responses to conflict on their activity sheet (in the first column).
6. Now hand out "Don't Say That to Me!" and have students complete it. (To help students feel comfortable answering the questions, you may want to tell them not to put their names on the sheet. In this case, they would not need to share their answers with anyone.)
7. Have a discussion with the students (see the discussion questions provided).
8. "My Pounding Heart" can be used as either a classroom or homework activity. Have the students ask four of their classmates how they respond physically in a conflict situation. Do they yell? Do they use foul language? Do they become very quiet? The students should put a check mark in the appropriate block for each response.

9. After "My Pounding Heart" has been completed, facilitate a discussion about the variety of ways that people respond to conflicts. Also, discuss ways in which students' physical reactions intensify conflicts. For example, if one student yells, the other student yells louder. Escalating conflicts often lead to violence.

DISCUSSION QUESTIONS

1. How do your feelings affect the way you act?

2. Imagine two students, Julius and Frances, arguing in a neighborhood park. Julius wants to leave the park to buy ice cream, but Frances wants to stay in the park and play football. Julius yells and stares angrily at Frances. How might Frances react? How might Julius react to Frances?

3. When boys are in conflict situations, how do they react? When girls are in conflict situations, how do they react?

4. Why do you think differences in the way boys and girls react to conflict situations do/do not exist?

5. Do you think there is a difference in the reactions of mothers and fathers in conflicts? Why or why not?

6. Is anger or patience more useful in resolving most conflicts? Why? (It should be understood that anger is OK and must be acknowledged. It is how we use anger that determines its role in a conflict.)

ACTIVITY SHEET
MY POUNDING HEART

DIRECTIONS: List physical responses to conflict in Column l. Ask four classmates how they respond physically in a conflict situation. Put a checkmark in the appropriate box for each response.

Physical Response to Conflict	Student 1	Student 2	Student 3	Student 4
1				
2				
3				
4				
5				
6				
7				
8				
9				
10				

2004 © Open Society Institute

The Publisher grants permission for the reproduction of this worksheet for non-profit educational purposes only.
Activity sheets may be downloaded from www.idebate.org/conflictandcommunication.htm

ACTIVITY SHEET
Don't Say That to Me

Directions: Answer the following questions honestly and completely.

1. Write down three things that someone might say to you that would get you angry enough to start an argument.
   A.)
   B.)
   C.)

2. Write down three things that someone might do to you that would get you angry enough to start an argument.
   A.)
   B.)
   C.)

3. How do I act when I am very, very angry?

4. Write down three things that you might say to someone that could get him/her angry enough to start an argument.
   A.)
   B.)
   C.)

5. Write down three things that you might do to someone that would get him/her angry enough to start an argument.
   A.)
   B.)
   C.)

6. How do you feel when someone you are arguing with is very, very angry?

2004 © Open Society Institute

The Publisher grants permission for the reproduction of this worksheet for non-profit educational purposes only.
Activity sheets may be downloaded from www.idebate.org/conflictandcommunication.htm

MIND AND HEART
(STEP 2 OF "CLIMBING THE LADDER")

OBJECTIVE
Upon completing this lesson, students will be able to distinguish between their attitudes, feelings, and behaviors.

KEY CONCEPTS
attitudes
behavior
conflict analysis
feelings

BACKGROUND
Think about the last argument you had. How did you handle the conflict? What emotions did you feel? What were you thinking?

The way we act is largely a product of what we think and how we feel. Therefore, if we are involved in a conflict and want to successfully resolve it, we should become aware of our feelings and our thoughts. Figuratively speaking, we should attempt to distinguish between what is in our hearts and minds.

Becoming more aware of what is in our own hearts and minds forces us to become more aware of what is in other people's. A mutual understanding of each other's thoughts and feelings often promote a mutual acceptance of each other: Once we can understand how the different people in a conflict feel and think, it is easier to understand why they behave the way they do. People act differently depending on what they think and how they feel.

Here's an example to illustrate the power of becoming aware of how we think and feel:

> Lara was mad at her mother. Lara wanted to play outside, but her mother would not let her until she cleaned her room. Normally Lara would yell at her mother when she got mad at her. But today, before starting to yell, she tried to distinguish between feelings and thoughts. Her feelings were that she was extremely angry and frustrated with her mother. Her thoughts were that she wanted to play outside. And how was her mother feeling? She realized that her mother loved her and wanted her to live in a clean, orderly room. Instead of yelling at her mother, she decided to calmly express how she was feeling. Her mother empathized with her. Proud that Lara did not yell back, the mother helped her clean her room, and Lara then went out to play.

In the story about Lara, it becomes clear how one can use what is in the heart and the mind to constructively resolve conflicts.

MATERIALS

"What Would You Do?" and "Think And Feel" activity sheets; pencils

TEACHER TIPS

To help students feel comfortable working in small groups, you may want to facilitate an icebreaker (see Appendix II) before facilitating this lesson.

If you describe the story of Lara, you might point out that this is an example of someone deciding that the relationship is important to preserve. Lara's relationship with her mother was more important to her than getting her way.

ACTIVITY

1. Divide the class into groups of four to six, giving each group the activity sheets.
2. One person in each group reads aloud the first situation on "What Would You Do?" Everyone imagines what it would be like to be in that situation.
3. Each group discusses: a) what the difficult situation is, b) what the main character might be thinking, and c) what the main character might be feeling.
4. One person in each group writes everyone's thoughts on "Think And Feel."
5. The groups repeat the same process (steps 2–4) with the other three situations.
6. Once everyone has completed "Think And Feel," each group shares its answers.

DISCUSSION QUESTIONS

1. In real life, do you think that everyone in our class would act the same way in each of the situations on the activity sheet? Why not?
2. We all have unique thoughts and feelings. Depending on how we feel and what we think, we act differently. For instance, if someone kicked a boy during a football game, how might he act if he thought that the person kicked him intentionally? How might the boy act if he thought that the kick was accidental?
3. Some students think that every time people hurt them, such as when the boy was kicked, it is intentional. Is this true? Why not? What are some examples of times when you thought someone hurt you on purpose, but you later realized it was an accident?
4. What is the difference between a feeling and a thought?
5. When children argue with their parents, which affects how they act more: their feelings or their thoughts? Why?
6. When you are in a conflict situation, what kinds of emotions do you experience?
7. What kinds of thoughts do you have when you are in a conflict situation?
8. Why is it important to become aware of your feelings and thoughts?

ADDITIONAL ACTIVITY

Students could role play the different situations and act out successful resolutions to the conflicts.

Activity Sheet
What Would You Do?

Directions: Read the following situations one at a time. Then discuss each situation with the others in your group. Write your group's thoughts in the space provided or on a separate sheet.

1. The older students often tease Pedje for no reason at all. Occasionally, they even yell at him. Pedje can't understand why they always tease him and not anyone else. In the school hallways, if another student even looks at him, he starts to shake, sweat, and feel angry. Today, an older student walked up to him and teased him. Pedje felt more angry and bitter than ever before. **Imagine some ways in which Pedje might react to the older student today.**

2. A group of children was playing handball. Immediately after Madelyn scored a goal, Stuart kicked her in the leg. **What might Madelyn have felt and thought the moment after she was kicked?**

3. Emil and Tomas do not like each other because they are both in love with Solvita. Today the science teacher assigned the two boys to work together on a project, forcing them to spend a lot of time with each other. **What are some of the ways that the two boys might act?**

4. Maja is a good student, but today the teacher yelled at her in class. **What could have influenced the teacher to act that way? What might the teacher have been thinking and feeling? What are some of the thoughts and feelings Maja had in reaction to the teacher's actions?**

2004 © Open Society Institute

The Publisher grants permission for the reproduction of this worksheet for non-profit educational purposes only.
Activity sheets may be downloaded from www.idebate.org/conflictandcommunication.htm

ACTIVITY SHEET
THINK AND FEEL

Situation	What you think	What you feel
1		
4		
7		
10		

2004 © Open Society Institute

The Publisher grants permission for the reproduction of this worksheet for non-profit educational purposes only.
Activity sheets may be downloaded from www.idebate.org/conflictandcommunication.htm

COLORING IN THE OUTLINES OF PEOPLE (STEP 2 OF "CLIMBING THE LADDER")

OBJECTIVES

Upon completing this lesson, students will be able to:

1. Recognize the role of feelings in a conflict situation.
2. Describe the connection between feelings and behavior.
3. Identify people's feelings in a conflict situation.

KEY CONCEPTS

behavior
conflict analysis
feelings

BACKGROUND

When we are in conflict situations, we often feel very powerful emotions, such as anger, fear, relief, satisfaction, and frustration. However, we hardly ever try to identify or express those feelings. Instead, we keep them locked within ourselves.

It is also difficult to identify what others in a conflict are feeling. In fact, we sometimes forget that the other person is having emotional reactions. Consequently, both people in a conflict often feel misunderstood and are unaware of each other's feelings.

This activity helps students identify feelings that may arise in conflict situations.

MATERIALS

articles from newspapers or magazines. The articles must be about conflict situations, ranging from family to foreign conflicts. The articles should be cut out so that students can individually read them and pass them around. Either you or the students can find the articles and bring them into school.

NOTE: If articles are not available, think about a book with conflict situations in its plot. You will find directions on how to facilitate the activity without articles at the end of the activity description.

TEACHER TIPS

It may be helpful for students you facilitate "The Feeling List" (page 101) prior to this lesson. However, if this lesson is completed first, "I Feel" can reinforce this lesson's objectives.

ACTIVITY

1. Either you or the students bring in newspaper and magazine articles. Cut out articles that describe conflicts. If possible, try to obtain articles showing a diversity of conflict situations, ranging from family conflicts to political conflicts.

2. Divide the class into groups of three or more, making sure that each group has an article on conflict.

3. Have one student in each group read the group's article aloud.

4. Instruct each group to decide what the conflict in its article is about.

5. Next, instruct each group to try and identify the feelings of the characters in the conflict situation. For example, if the conflict describes a mother and father yelling at one another, the students might identify feelings such as anger and frustration.

6. Have each group stand in front of the class and show its article. Each group should explain the conflict shown and the feelings of the people in the conflict.

7. Here's what to do if newspaper and magazine articles are not available:

Describe to the students a conflict situation from a literary work. Explain how the different characters in the story act. Divide the students into small groups and have them analyze and identify some of the feelings of the characters in the story. Finally, have each group stand in front of the class and explain a) what feelings they identified and b) why they assumed that the characters would have those feelings.

DISCUSSION QUESTIONS

1. How do we know when another person is mad at us? How do we know when another person likes us? How can we tell what another person is feeling toward us?

2. Do all people act out their feelings in the same way? For example, when you get mad, do you behave the same way your friends do when they get mad? Why or why not?

3. Is it always possible to control our feelings in a conflict situation? If we can't control our feelings, what should we do?

4. Have students think of a specific conflict in their lives during which they lost or almost lost control of their feelings. If that situation occurred again, how could they control their feelings more effectively?

WHOSE SHOES?
(STEP 2 OF "CLIMBING THE LADDER")

OBJECTIVES
Upon completing this lesson, students will be able to:
1. Explain what empathy is.
2. Describe the importance of empathy in conflict situations.

KEY CONCEPTS
empathy
feelings

BACKGROUND
In a conflict situation, it is important for us to address our emotions. We must ask ourselves how we feel and why. However, it is also important to ask ourselves how the other person feels and why. In other words, we need to empathize with the other person, metaphorically stepping into their shoes and trying to understand how she feels in the conflict situation.

MATERIALS
clear area in the room

TEACHER TIPS
This is a fun activity with an important objective. When doing the activity, make sure students choose two different people's shoes.

During the discussion, emphasize the importance of confidentiality. This activity connects very well with "The Mirror" (page 98), which emphasizes the importance of "feeling words."

ACTIVITY
1. Have students stand in a large circle.
2. Instruct students to take off their shoes and place them in a pile in the center of the circle.
3. Have students get two shoes (one left shoe and one right shoe) that are not their own.

4. Tell the students to put on the two shoes, being careful not to damage them. (It is usually very funny to attempt to put on different people's shoes, especially since students' shoe sizes vary widely.)

5. Instruct students to find the two students wearing the same shoes they are wearing. Students should stand side-by-side, with each left shoe directly beside its matching right shoe forming a circle. In the end, there should be one circle of matching shoes. Some students may have to stretch their legs to match shoes, but the activity is usually possible! Occasionally, two or more circles are formed.

6. Have everyone put his or her shoes on again.

7. Explain to students that in conflict situations, we must be aware of not only our feelings, but also the other person's feelings. We must be empathetic, stepping into the other person's shoes (like we did in the activity) and trying understand how they feel.

DISCUSSION QUESTIONS

1. What is empathy? How is it helpful in a conflict situation?

2. Ask students to describe common conflict situations that they or friends of theirs have experienced. Have them describe how each person involved in the conflict may have felt.

THE MILK BOTTLE
(STEP 3 OF "CLIMBING THE LADDER")

OBJECTIVES

Upon completing this lesson, students will be able to:

1. Explain what positional argumentation is.
2. Describe what underlying interests are.
3. Clarify people's underlying interests in conflict situations.

KEY CONCEPTS

conflict analysis
positional arguments
sibling conflict
underlying interests

BACKGROUND

This lesson is important in helping students realize how to manage conflicts in a manner that meets their underlying needs.

In most conflicts, people take different positions. Usually, positional arguments are difficult to resolve because neither person in the conflict is willing to budge from his/her position. And usually, both people's positions cannot be equally satisfied. Furthermore, if either person does compromise, he/she often feels embarrassed, ashamed, or not as strong-willed as the other person.

A more efficient way to resolve conflicts is to have the disputants look for underlying interests. In most conflicts, people's positions are incompatible. But usually, they have underlying interests that can be satisfied. Therefore, when trying to resolve conflicts, those involved should think about each others' underlying interests. Working as a team, they should think about ways in which both of their underlying interests can be met.

The following activity clearly demonstrates the utility of investigating underlying interests.

MATERIALS

"Milk Bottle" activity sheet, pencils

TEACHER TIPS

This activity presents one of the most important ideas behind conflict management. Be sure that students clearly understand the difference between positional argumentation and looking for underlying interests. It may be necessary to spend a few lessons role playing different conflicts and how they can be resolved by looking for underlying interests. Students could role play a conflict in front of the class and then you and the class could discuss what each person's position and underlying interests were.

ACTIVITY

1. Hand out the activity sheet and read it with the class.
2. Discuss what positions and underlying interests (wants) are.
3. Have students individually complete the questions at the bottom of the activity sheet.
4. Discuss their answers, clarifying the difference between positional arguments and looking for underlying interests. For example, in the story, the girl's position was that she wanted the milk bottle. Her underlying interest was the empty bottle for her hiking trip.
5. Have students divide into pairs.
6. Each pair creates a role play about a common conflict and how the conflict can be resolved if the people involved look at underlying interests.
7. Have volunteers present their role plays to the class. After each role play, discuss what each person's position was and what his/her underlying interests were.

DISCUSSION QUESTIONS

1. What is a position? What is an example of an argument in which students each hold a position?
2. What is an underlying interest? Describe a conflict in which students resolve a conflict by investigating underlying interests.

ACTIVITY SHEET
MILK BOTTLE

MILK

A brother and sister were sitting at the kitchen table. A milk bottle rested at the center of the table.

> "I want the milk bottle!" yelled the boy. He picked up the bottle.
> "I want the milk bottle!" screamed the girl. She grabbed the bottle from her brother.
> "Hey, give that back to me!" he yelled.
> "No, I want it!" hollered the girl.

The children's mother walked into the kitchen. "I am tired of the two of you fighting all the time," the mother said. She took the bottle from the girl, got out two glasses, and poured milk for each of them. She placed the empty milk bottle outside for the milkman to take in the morning.

The brother and sister looked at each other. Neither of them was satisfied, because neither of them got what he or she really wanted. The brother wanted the milk to feed the neighbor's cats. And the sister wanted the empty bottle: she was going on a hike with her friends and she wanted to fill the bottle with water.

Both of them drank their milk unhappily.

QUESTIONS:
1. What was the girl's position during the argument?
2. What did she really want?
3. What was the boy's position during the argument?
4. What did he really want?
5. How did the mother resolve the children's conflict?
6. What could the mother have asked the children so that both of their underlying interests would have been met?
7. How could the brother and sister have resolved the conflict without their mother's help?

2004 © Open Society Institute

The Publisher grants permission for the reproduction of this worksheet for non-profit educational purposes only.
Activity sheets may be downloaded from www.idebate.org/conflictandcommunication.htm

WHAT DO I NEED?
(STEP 3 OF "CLIMBING THE LADDER")

OBJECTIVE

Upon completing this lesson, students will be able to prioritize needs and wants.

KEY CONCEPTS

conflict analysis
needs/wants
values

BACKGROUND

We all have needs and wants. Our needs are the things that we cannot live without. For example, we cannot live without air, shelter, food, water, and clothing. We also have psychological needs, such as the need to socialize, to be loved, and to have fun. Although our wants also seem necessary for survival, they typically deal more with our quality of life. For example, someone may want to live in a large apartment. But does one need a large apartment in order to survive? Probably not.

Conflicts can arise when students have difficulty distinguishing between wants and needs,. Often, these are conflicts over values, ways of acting, or priorities. For example, a student may be unsure whether to steal money to buy food or whether to uphold religious values of morality (which may claim that stealing is wrong). This activity and "The Roots of Conflict" (page 114) will help to clarify the differences between needs and wants.

MATERIALS

paper, pencils, chalkboard and chalk (or large paper and a pen); large space in which to move around

TEACHER TIPS

It may be difficult for some students to think of ten important things. Encourage them to think about all aspects of their lives. To help them think of ideas, you could ask them what they need in order to live, to be happy, to feel good, and so on.

There may be strong disagreement during this activity,. For example, some may define money as a want and others as a need; some may even define it as both. Emphasize that it is okay to disagree as long as students respect all opinions.

ACTIVITY

1. Tell the students that we make decisions about what is important to us daily. Some of these decisions are simple to make, such as what clothing to wear to school. Other decisions are more complex and serious, such as whether to skip school for the day without telling anyone.

2. Instruct the students to take out a paper and pencil and make a list of all the things that are important to them. Tell them that they should write at least ten things. To clarify the directions, you could offer the students a personal example. For instance, you could say that your family is important in your life. You could add that money is also important.

3. After the students have completed their lists, have each student share one of the things that is important to him/her. Stress that everybody's thoughts are important and valuable. Write each person's idea on the chalkboard.

4. Explain what needs and wants are.

5. Instruct the students to stand in a circle. Tell them that you are going to read the list of things on the chalkboard, one idea at a time. If students think the item is a need, they should move to the right side of the room. If they think it is a want, they should move to the left side of the room.

6. Students might have opposing opinions as to whether certain things are needs or wants. You can facilitate a discussion by asking the students on each side of the room why they think the items are either wants or needs.

7. After you have read all the items on the chalkboard, tell the students to resume their seats.

DISCUSSION QUESTIONS

1. What is the difference between a need and a want?
2. Why is it important to pay attention to other people's needs during conflicts?
3. Have students describe conflicts over needs and conflicts over wants.
4. Let's talk about a specific important item: money. Is money a need or a want? Why?
5. What do needs and wants have to do with violence?

THE SPACESHIP
(STEP 3 OF "CLIMBING THE LADDER")

OBJECTIVES

Upon completing this lesson, students will be able to:

1. Prioritize needs.
2. Evaluate options.
3. Identify five things they value most in life.

KEY CONCEPTS

decision-making
needs/wants
self-understanding
values

BACKGROUND

Students in conflicts face many decisions: They have to think about what they actually need and what they merely want. Learning how to prioritize needs and wants can aid students in making wise decisions. When they know what they want and need, students often can manage conflict successfully.

MATERIALS

"The Spaceship" activity sheet

TEACHER TIPS

Do not require students who feel uncomfortable to share their lists. This activity could lead to a discussion about war refugees. Refugees leave their homes, often with nothing more than the clothes they are wearing. You could ask students what it would be like to leave their home—or even their country—forever.

ACTIVITY

Have students read and fill out "The Spaceship" activity sheet. Ask them to fold the sheet in half once they have completed it.

2. Now tell the students that the spaceship has room for only one of their possessions and ask them to determine what they want to take.
3. Have each student tell the class what he/she brought onto the spaceship.

DISCUSSION QUESTIONS

1. How did you decide which five things to take?
2. What did you think when you heard that you could only take one thing with you?
3. What process did you go through in deciding which one thing you should take?
4. Sometimes it is difficult to make decisions during conflicts. How can you decide what you value most?

ACTIVITY SHEET
THE SPACESHIP

Read the following story and answer the question afterward.

The Spaceship

The year is 2100. School has ended for the day. You have a lot of homework and you are tired. You walk home, go to your room, and lie down. You turn on the radio and listen to the music. The soft guitar and the slow rhythm cause your eyelids to slowly close. You are almost asleep. Suddenly the music stops. You hear someone on the radio screaming something. You sit up and listen.

The voice on the radio says, "There is going to be a very bad tornado in 15 minutes. The tornado is going to be so bad that it will destroy everything on the land. Everyone must leave their homes now and fly toward the Moon. Hurry!"

Your father runs into your room. He is very nervous because he wants to save you and the rest of the family. He tells you that your family is going to take a spaceship to the Moon.

Your father says that you can only take five things with you (besides your family members). It doesn't matter how big or small the five things are, but everything else will be destroyed. What five things would you bring onto the spaceship with you?

1.
2.
3.
4.
5.

2004 © Open Society Institute

The Publisher grants permission for the reproduction of this worksheet for non-profit educational purposes only.
Activity sheets may be downloaded from www.idebate.org/conflictandcommunication.htm

CONFUSING DECISIONS
(STEP 3 OF "CLIMBING THE LADDER")

OBJECTIVES

Upon completing this lesson, students will be able to:

1. Explain what a moral dilemma is.
2. Identify factors that influence their behavior in conflict situations.
3. Explain how their actions are affected by their wants, needs, and values.
4. Recognize the many choices we can make when deciding how to act in a conflict situation.

KEY CONCEPTS

attitudes
behavior
conflict analysis
decision-making
self-understanding
values

BACKGROUND

Many factors influence how we behave in a conflict situation. To resolve conflicts successfully so that relationships are preserved or improved (and not destroyed), it is important that we become aware of how our needs and values relate to our behavior. For instance, sometimes friends get into very large arguments about trivial things. But the more the friends argue, the angrier they get. By the time the argument ends, they no longer regard each other as friends. They forget how much they value their friendship and let their emotions control their actions.

Society affects how we act, too. Our friends, relatives, and other people around us all influence how we interact with other people.

Making decisions during conflicts can be confusing. Because we are influenced by so many different factors—society, values, needs, feelings, and thoughts—we are often faced with moral dilemmas. Often our minds tell us to do one thing, while our hearts, values, and needs, tell us to do other things. Although there is no way to teach children how to make perfect life decisions, self-understanding allows them the opportunity to make more informed decisions.

MATERIALS

"Decisions, Decisions, Decisions" activity sheet; pencils

TEACHER TIPS

Stress that if anyone feels uncomfortable sharing his/her responses, he/she does not have to.

ACTIVITY

1. Hand out the activity sheet and explain the concept of a moral dilemma.
2. Have students read each moral dilemma on the activity sheet and write down what they would do in that circumstance.
3. Divide students into groups of five and have them share their answers to the dilemmas.
4. After everyone has shared their answers, hold a class discussion.

DISCUSSION QUESTIONS

1. Go through the different situations with the students. Ask them how they decided to act in each situation. (Try to focus the discussion on what values the students think most important.)
2. Is there only one correct solution to each situation? Why not?
3. Do people always act the way they want to? Why not?
4. Tell the students the following: Imagine yourself in an argument with your best friend. What kinds of questions can you ask to discover how your friend feels? What kinds of questions can you ask to discover how you are feeling? How are you feeling now?
5. What do you value in your life? When you get into a conflict, why is it important to think about what you value?
6. Look at your list from the previous lesson, "The Spaceship." Are these the things you value most?

ACTIVITY SHEET
DECISIONS, DECISIONS, DECISIONS

Directions: A moral dilemma occurs when you face a difficult decision. Read each of the following moral dilemmas and write exactly what you would do in these circumstances.

1. You are at the market buying fruit for your family. The saleswoman puts the fruit on the scale to see how much it costs. You notice that she presses her finger on the scale, making the fruit cost more than it should. You are not sure whether she is trying to cheat you. I would...

2. A classmate receives a new cell phone case as a birthday present. You witness another student take the cell phone case and put it in his bag. You are not sure whether the student stole the case or took it as a joke. I would...

3. Your family always warned you not to talk to the family across the street. They said that the people were very mean. As you walk home from school today, the son of the family across the street approaches you. He has tears in his eyes and asks if you would mind helping him with his family problems. He says that he has no one else to talk to. I would...

4. You and your friends are playing football in the schoolyard. A friend kicks the ball very hard and breaks a school window. The teacher asks who broke the window. I would...

2004 © Open Society Institute

The Publisher grants permission for the reproduction of this worksheet for non-profit educational purposes only.
Activity sheets may be downloaded from www.idebate.org/conflictandcommunication.htm

BOTTLE CAPS
(STEP 4 OF "CLIMBING THE LADDER")

OBJECTIVES

Upon completing this lesson, students will be able to:

1. State the four rules of brainstorming.
2. Brainstorm.
3. Apply the brainstorming method during conflict situations.

KEY CONCEPTS

brainstorming
conflict analysis

BACKGROUND

Brainstorming is a simple, effective method for generating ideas. Often we think that we cannot resolve our conflicts. We may feel locked into specific ways of thinking, but by brainstorming a list of solutions, we can find creative, mutually satisfying resolutions.

In a broader sense, brainstorming is a useful technique for generating ideas about almost any problem. For example, you can brainstorm different ways of dealing with a difficult decision in your life.

The specific guidelines for brainstorming are described in this activity.

MATERIALS

"Bottle Caps" resource sheet; pencils

TEACHER TIPS

Encourage students to think of all ideas, no matter how silly they may seem. Create a supportive classroom atmosphere by emphasizing that all ideas are good ideas.

ACTIVITY

1. Hand out the resource sheet.
2. Explain brainstorming and go over the four guidelines written on the activity sheet.

3. Tell the class the following story:

   Today, the principal informed me that our school received a very unusual gift. A soda company gave us one million bottle caps. The principal asked me what we should do with them, and I responded that I was not sure. So, in small groups, we are going to brainstorm as many different uses for the bottle caps as possible. Our school needs your help.

4. Divide the class into groups of four to six.

5. Instruct students to follow the brainstorming guidelines and to think of ideas about what to do with the bottle caps. One student in each group records all ideas.

6. After 10 minutes, each group shares its ideas with the rest of the class.

7. Tell the class that the school did not really receive bottle caps. The activity was important for learning how to brainstorm.

8. Each group brainstorms solutions to a typical conflict. One student in each group records all ideas.

9. After 10 minutes, each group shares its ideas with the rest of the class.

DISCUSSION QUESTIONS

1. What is brainstorming?
2. When can you use brainstorming?
3. How can you use brainstorming during a conflict situation?

FOLLOW-UP ACTIVITY

Have students think of a conflict in their own lives and brainstorm possible resolutions.

Resource Sheet
Bottle Caps

Brainstorming is a simple way of generating ideas. There are four rules to brainstorming:

1. **Write down every idea you can think of.** Some ideas may sound impossible or silly, but that's okay. Sometimes the most outrageous ideas cause us to think of other, good ideas.

2. **Think of as many ideas as possible.** The more ideas you think of, the greater the chance you have of finding good ideas.

3. **Don't judge any idea as good or bad.**

4. **Don't talk or think about the ideas.** Just write them down.

2004 © Open Society Institute

The Publisher grants permission for the reproduction of this worksheet for non-profit educational purposes only.
Activity sheets may be downloaded from www.idebate.org/conflictandcommunication.htm

THE RIGHT CHOICE
(STEP 5 OF "CLIMBING THE LADDER")

OBJECTIVES

Upon completing this lesson, students will be able to:

1. Describe a conflict.
2. Analyze the feelings and wants of disputants.
3. Identify mutually satisfying resolutions to conflicts.

KEY CONCEPTS

brainstorming
conflict analysis
conflict resolution

BACKGROUND

The final step in resolving a conflict is to choose and act on a solution that meets the needs of the disputants. Specifically, after the disputants brainstorm ideas that meet each of their needs, they discuss and decide which option is the most feasible and realistic. If an option seems mutually satisfying, they can act on that solution.

MATERIALS

"The Right Choice" activity sheet, pencils

TEACHER TIPS

Conflict resolution is a process of communication. Not all conflicts can be resolved, but there is positive potential in every conflict. No matter whether a solution is found, communication helps each of the people in the conflict grow, learn, and understand each other more clearly. Stress this point to the students.

ACTIVITY

1. Divide students into pairs and give each pair an activity sheet.
2. Tell each pair to think about a common conflict and fill out the activity sheet.
3. Have each pair describe its conflict and share its analysis with another pair.

DISCUSSION QUESTIONS

1. How did you decide which solution to choose?

2. Almost every conflict has positive potential. We can learn a lot from almost any conflict. But what can you learn if you and the other person in the conflict cannot agree on a solution? (See the Teacher Tips for a possible answer.)

ACTIVITY SHEET
THE RIGHT CHOICE

Directions: Answer all questions on this sheet. Be specific.

1. What is the conflict about?

2. Who is involved in the conflict?

3. How does each person in the conflict feel?

4. What does each person want to get from the conflict?

5. Brainstorm possible resolutions to the conflict and write all your ideas here:

6. Which solution(s) will make both people in the conflict feel good?

2004 © Open Society Institute

The Publisher grants permission for the reproduction of this worksheet for non-profit educational purposes only.
Activity sheets may be downloaded from www.idebate.org/conflictandcommunication.htm

Climbing The Ladder

OBJECTIVES

Upon completing this lesson, students will be able to:

1. Apply an explicit, simple strategy for recognizing and managing interpersonal conflicts in a nonviolent manner.
2. Describe factors involved in family conflicts.
3. Describe strategies for dealing with family conflict.

KEY CONCEPTS

conflict resolution
family conflicts

BACKGROUND

We all have patterns in the way we deal with conflicts: some people act aggressively and scream and holler, while others retreat and are quiet. But how do we recognize when we are about to become involved in a pattern of conflict? And once involved, what are some useful techniques for managing the conflict constructively? That is, how can we use the conflict dynamics to satisfy our needs and not destroy friendships and partnerships?

The following strategy includes five simple steps for dealing with conflicts:

1. **Conflicts must be recognized.** We can recognize them by recalling how we felt when in past conflict situations: our hearts pounded faster, our muscles tightened, and we started to feel anger, hurt, or other emotions.
2. **We must think about feelings.** We will have difficulty resolving the conflict if we don't address our feelings.
3. **We discover what our underlying interests and the underlying interests of the other person in the conflict are.**
4. **We brainstorm different solutions to the conflict.** We think about any possible ways that all the people involved can get what they want. We don't care how ridiculous or stupid the ideas are; we simply state every possible idea that comes to mind.
5. **We identify and act on the solution that most satisfactorily satisfies the conflicting people's underlying interests.**

The five steps to conflict resolution are easy to remember and easy to use. The following activity teaches students the strategy and helps them learn how to use it in daily conflicts.

NOTE: If you want students to use this strategy, you must use it in your classroom behavior with your students. Also, remember that learning the strategy takes time. If you do not notice immediate changes in the behaviors of your students, be patient and don't lose hope. In the beginning, students may think the five steps mechanical, but with continued practice, the steps will become an established part of their behavior patterns during conflict situations.

MATERIALS
"Climbing the Ladder" resource sheet

TEACHER TIPS
This is one of the most important activities in this curriculum.

To help students incorporate the strategy into their normal conflict behavior patterns, have them create role plays as often as possible. The role plays should show how they can resolve typical student conflicts using the strategy. The more often you expose students to the five-step strategy, the more likely they will be able to recall and utilize it.

Remind students about the importance of keeping personal statements confidential.

ACTIVITY
1. Hand out the resource sheet and read it aloud with the students, explaining each step of the conflict resolution strategy.
2. Divide students into pairs.
3. One of the students in each pair pretends to be a parent; the other pretends to be the child.
4. Tell everyone in the class to listen carefully. Explain:

The parent and the child are in the midst of a conflict. It is a Friday afternoon. The parent feels that the child has not studied as much as he/she should. Therefore, the parent wants the child to stay home and do homework. But the child is tired of sitting through classes all day. The child's friends are all playing at the park, and he/she wants to go to the park and play with them. The parent and the child are in a conflict."

5. Reread the scenario in step 4 so that everyone clearly understands what the family conflict is about.
6. Have the pairs act out the conflict. They should follow the steps outlined on the activity sheet to resolve the conflict.
7. Once each pair has resolved the conflict, the students switch roles and repeat the exercise.
8. The students can think of other conflicts that have occurred in their lives (or in other children's lives) and role play them. Remind the students to incorporate the five-step strategy for conflict resolution into their role plays.

DISCUSSION QUESTIONS

1. What are some feelings someone might have that would help him/her recognize that he/she is in a conflict situation with a parent or loved one?

2. When you are in a conflict situation, you want to satisfy your own needs. You want to get what you want. But why should you want to satisfy the other person's needs as well?

NOTE: This is a difficult question to answer. You could explain that: a) Helping others makes us more caring people, and b) a conflict is an opportunity for students to express themselves and get what they want. If everyone were greedy, no one would ever get what they want.

3. What types of conflicts do children have with their parents?

4. What are some of the feelings that children have when they fight with their parents?

5. What are some of the feelings that parents have when they fight with their children?

6. Why do parents argue with their children? What do they want from their children?

7. Why do children argue with their parents? What do they want from their parents?

8. What are some ways in which parents and children can satisfy each other's needs and wants?

NOTE: Be cautious when facilitating this discussion: powerful emotions may emerge. For instance, children may express anger and resentment toward parents. Allow the students to express themselves freely. However, make the students aware of their feelings. Help the students to acknowledge, accept, and take responsibility for their own feelings, but also stress that learning and using the conflict resolution strategy with may help strengthen or heal relationships. If the discussion seems very tense (or too light), you could ask the students questions about the importance of family and other relationships.

RESOURCE SHEET
CLIMBING THE LADDER

Think about how it feels when you are in a conflict with someone else. Your heart pounds, your hands are sweaty, your muscles are tight. When you are in a conflict situation, you may feel as if you are stuck at the bottom of a deep hole. You want to get out of the hole. You want to breathe the fresh, calm air outside. But the only way you can do that is by climbing up a ladder. Each step you take in resolving a conflict gets you and the others in the conflict one step closer to the fresh air outside. The good news is that there are not hundreds of steps to climb. There are only five. Here they are:

THE FIVE STEPS FOR CLIMBING OUT OF A CONFLICT:

1. RECOGNIZE CONFLICT

You may think to yourself, "Hey, something doesn't feel right!" Recognize when you feel hurt, anger, shame, or some other uncomfortable feelings and ask yourself, "Does this have to do with a conflict?"

2. OUR FEELINGS

If you think you are in a conflict, ask yourself:
"How do I feel? (Name the feeling.) Why?"
"How does the other person feel? Why?"

3. WHAT WE WANT

Recognize what you and the other person want from the conflict by asking yourself:
"Why is there a conflict? What do I want from this?"
"What does the other person want from this?"
"How is the other person stopping me from getting what I want?"

4. OUR IDEAS

Think of ideas so that you both can get what you want at the same time.

5. OUR PLAN

Find the solution that makes you both feel good. Act on that solution. Take time to talk with the other person and strengthen your relationship.

2004 © Open Society Institute

The Publisher grants permission for the reproduction of this worksheet for non-profit educational purposes only.
Activity sheets may be downloaded from www.idebate.org/conflictandcommunication.htm

THE SOAP OPERA
(PRACTICING THE 5 STEPS OF "CLIMBING THE LADDER")

OBJECTIVES
Upon completing this lesson, students will be able to:
1. Identify family conflicts.
2. List strategies for resolving family conflicts.
3. Role play solutions to family conflicts.
4. Utilize the five-step strategy ("Climbing The Ladder") to help them resolve family conflicts.

KEY CONCEPTS
conflict resolution
family conflicts
sibling conflicts

BACKGROUND
Every family is a small society with its own unique structure, relationships, strengths, modes of communication, and conflicts. In most families, arguments are a frequently occurring type of conflict.

Family arguments differ from arguments with non-family members. Because family members feel close to one another, they feel more comfortable and less restricted in expressing their true feelings. On the other hand, during social conflicts outside of the family, people are less free to express their emotions because the relationships are usually more structured.

Family conflicts often involve generational differences. For instance, grandparents may hold an entirely different set of values than their grandchildren. However, the generation gap is not only a source of conflict: the people of each generation can offer valuable insight about the different ways the world can be viewed.

MATERIALS
"Climbing the Ladder" resource sheet (page 171), books, radio shows, newspaper stories, films, or TV shows depicting a common family conflict.

TEACHER TIPS
A discussion of family conflicts can be a very intimate experience. If students reveal personal issues, remind the class that: 1) everything said is confidential; 2) students should respect one another; and 3) they should not tease each other because of family conflicts.

If someone appears seriously disturbed by a family conflict or reveals that he/she is involved in a life-threatening family conflict (such as child abuse), you should seek out the proper psychiatric and/or legal help.

ACTIVITY

1. Have the students acquaint themselves with a family conflict situation in the media (television, radio, newspaper, etc.).
2. After watching, listening, or reading about the conflict, have each student write a description of the conflict and list possible strategies for resolving it. They can refer to the five-step conflict resolution strategy from the "Climbing the Ladder" resource sheet.
3. Divide the students into groups of four to six.
4. Have the groups role play the conflict situation, acting out how it can be resolved.
5. Compare the students' resolutions with later episodes of the television show (or news article, radio program, etc.).

FOLLOW-UP ACTIVITY

Have students list some of their family conflicts and brainstorm solutions. (Family conflicts include sibling conflicts.) If the students feel comfortable, they could share their conflicts and solutions. Be very careful, though, because discussing family conflicts can be a very intimate experience. Remind students that everything said is strictly confidential. Also, reiterate that students must respect each other.

A less personal variation of this activity is to have students generate a list of common family problems and create role plays demonstrating how they could constructively manage them.

THE FACTORY
(PRACTICING THE 5 STEPS OF "CLIMBING THE LADDER")

OBJECTIVES

Upon completing this lesson, students will be able to:

1. Identify the positions and underlying interests of disputants involved in environmental conflicts.
2. Describe the complexity of environmental problems.
3. Utilize the five-step strategy "Climbing the Ladder" to help them resolve environmental conflicts.

KEY CONCEPTS

conflict resolution
decision-making
environmental conflicts

BACKGROUND

All people share a common interest in environmental problems. But if everyone has an interest in resolving environmental problems, why are they not solved? One reason is that it is very difficult and tedious to reach an agreement among competing groups. Industry representatives, local authorities, scientific institutions, governmental agencies, and non-governmental organizations often have different views about how environmental problems should be solved. But if environmental conflicts cannot be resolved, human lives may be lost. The present activity deals with the difficulty of trying to resolve environmental conflicts.

MATERIALS

"Climbing the Ladder" resource sheet (page 171)

TEACHER TIPS

You can substitute local environmental concerns for those in the activity.

ACTIVITY

1. Divide students into pairs.

2. Tell half of the pairs that they are no longer students. They are now representatives of a large factory. The factory produces many useful things for the community. The factory employs many people, and if it ever closed down, many families would no longer have enough money to buy food.

3. Tell the other half of the pairs that they are now residents of a town called Dingleberry. They believe that the factory should be closed because it creates great amounts of pollution. It dumps its trash into the nearby river where the Dingleberry residents get their fresh drinking water. Polluted water could kill the residents.

4. Tell each pair of Dingleberry residents to find a pair of factory representatives and discuss whether to close the factory or not. Tell the students that they must make a decision within the next 10 minutes.

5. Have the class reassemble in a large circle and share their experiences about the negotiation process.

DISCUSSION QUESTIONS

1. Was it easy or hard to decide on a solution to the conflict? Why?

2. What was each group's position? That is, what did the Dingleberry residents want? What did the factory representatives want?

3. What were the underlying interests of both groups? What interests did both groups share?

4. What was the hardest part of the negotiation process?

5. How was a decision eventually reached? If no decision was made, what problems occurred that prevented the decision from being made?

6. Why are real environmental conflicts so difficult to resolve?

FOLLOW-UP ACTIVITY

Once again, divide students into pairs, telling half the pairs that they are factory representatives and the other half that they are Dingleberry residents. Tell each pair of Dingleberry residents to find a pair of factory representatives and work together to resolve the problems the factory creates. They should use the steps listed on the "Climbing the Ladder" resource sheet to help them find a mutually beneficial solution to the conflict.

Chapter Six:

US

This chapter focuses on defining and understanding basic human rights and their connection to conflict. The lessons in this chapter will help students become more aware of their rights and, therefore, more capable of protecting themselves from human rights violations. Students will also learn how to stand up for their basic rights.

Studying human rights involves integrating the main points of the previous chapters. For example, human rights violations often involve prejudice and discrimination.

Why are basic human rights often violated during conflicts?

There are many answers to this question. We will discuss one of the possible answers that holds true in many circumstances.

Many people act as if conflicts were battles between opposing viewpoints, ideas, needs, or values. Normally, during times when there is no conflict, people obey the rules, norms, and laws of their society. However, during times of battle, there are few rules. People do whatever they want to obtain their goals.

Think about how battles usually evolve between countries. At first, a country feels that it has the right to act in a certain manner in support of specific values, ideas, needs, or viewpoints. The country begins to devalue, dehumanize, or develop prejudices against the other country. Consequently, communication between it and other countries breaks down. Eventually, at least one side takes the law into its own hands, creating its own rules to reach its goals. The top priority of at least one side is to win.

Similarly, think about how conflicts evolve between individuals. Suppose Matej and Nela are conversing. At first, he says something with which she disagrees. The two start arguing. Slowly, she begins thinking that his opinion is stupid because he is a male. Nela begins to dehumanize and devalue Matej's human worth. In other words, she develops a prejudice against him because of his gender, and she no longer respects his opinion. The two get angrier, expressing their opinions more and more hostilely. Communication breaks down. Eventually, she becomes so angry that she slaps him and runs away. Nations, and people, often use violence to resolve conflict, and in so doing, inevitably violate human rights.

MY PROTECTIVE SHIELD

OBJECTIVES
Upon completing this lesson, students will be able to:
1. Describe what basic human rights are.
2. State the rights they believe are human rights.
3. List the rights that children deserve.
4. Compare human rights they defined with what the United Nations considers them to be.

KEY CONCEPTS
conflict analysis
human rights

BACKGROUND
The United Nations has developed charters listing basic human rights that we all deserve and should respect. Because of the United Nations' involvement in issues of human rights, human relations within and between countries are much more regulated. Yet, human rights violations still occur.

Human rights violations can be prevented by ensuring that:

1. People are aware of their own and others' basic human rights.
2. People discuss their basic human rights.
3. People consciously stand up for their basic human rights and the rights of others. In this way, basic human rights become guidelines to follow in conflict situations. People become actively aware of their basic rights, and resolve conflicts with the tacit agreement that human rights will be respected.

MATERIALS
Universal Declaration of Human Rights, Convention on the Rights of the Child, chalkboard and chalk (or large sheet of paper and a pen), paper, pencils

TEACHER TIPS
Make sure that students understand the difference between basic human rights and human wants. Also, you may want to discuss what to do if they feel their human rights have been violated.

You may decide to design other activities that explore the Universal Declaration. For example, if your country is a signatory to the charter, you might locate news articles about the vote or signing to show your students how seriously your country feels about basic human rights.

ACTIVITY

1. Write the following phrase on the board: "Because I am human, I deserve... "

2. Have each student brainstorm at least five different ways to complete the phrase. If students are having difficulty completing the phrase, offer them an example such as "Because I am human, I deserve love" or "Because I am human, I deserve food."

3. Have each student tell the class two (or more) of his/her suggestions. Write all suggestions on the chalkboard.

4. Tell the students that they will explore how often they deserve each suggestion. Say each suggestion listed on the board, asking the students how often they deserve it:

    Do we deserve [the suggestion on the board]:
    a. sometimes
    b. most of the time
    c. all the time
    Circle all suggestions the students agreed that we deserve all the time.

5. Tell the students that the suggestions circled are basic human rights (according to them).

6. Ask students what basic human rights are.

7. Present the Universal Declaration on Human Rights. Ask students to compare the rights they feel humans deserve with those the United Nations established.

8. Divide students into groups of four to six.

9. Each group creates a list of rights that children deserve. To help the students create their lists, ask them what rights students deserve all of the time.

10. Once students have completed their lists, have the class form a large circle.

11. Each group presents its list to the class.

12. Present the United Nations' Convention on the Rights of the Child. Students compare the rights they feel they deserve with those the United Nations established.

DISCUSSION QUESTIONS

1. What are basic human rights?

2. Suppose you want this great new toy, but your parents won't give you the money to buy it. Do you have a basic human right to buy the toy? Why or why not?

3. If two people are arguing and yelling at each other, what human rights might they eventually violate? How can you and your friends resolve your arguments without violating human rights?

4. Why do you think the United Nations wrote a special convention of rights for children?

FOLLOW-UP ACTIVITY

Have the class brainstorm possible ways to inform others of their basic rights. For instance, your class could create posters and advertisements listing basic human rights (possibly under the theme of respecting others) and display them in the school's hallways or classrooms. Or students could create role plays demonstrating conflicts solved in ways that do not violate basic human rights. The students could present their role plays in classrooms with younger students.

Universal Declaration of Human Rights

In 1948, the United Nations created a list (declaration) of human rights, a standard of achievement for all peoples and all nations. Here are some of the rights they created:

1. All human beings are born free and equal in dignity and rights. They are endowed with reason and conscience and should act towards one another in a spirit of brotherhood.

2. Everyone is entitled to the rights and freedoms set forth in this Declaration, without distinction of any kind, such as race, color, sex, language, religion, political or other opinion, national or social origin, property, birth, or other status.

3. Everyone has the right to life, liberty, and the security of person.

4. No one shall be held in slavery.

5. No one shall be subjected to torture or to cruel, inhumane or degrading treatment or punishment.

6. All are equal before the law and are entitled without any discrimination to equal protection of the law.

7. No one shall be subjected to arbitrary arrest, detention or exile.

8. Everyone is entitled in full equality to a fair and public hearing by an independent and impartial tribunal, in the determination of his [or her] rights and obligations and of any criminal charge against him [or her].

9. Everyone charged with a penal offence has the right to be presumed innocent until proven guilty according to law in a public trial at which he [or she] has had all guarantees necessary for his [or her] defense.

10. No one shall be subjected to arbitrary interference with his [or her] privacy, family, home or correspondence, nor to attacks on his [or her] honor and reputation.

11. Everyone has the right to freedom of movement and residence within the borders of each State. Everyone has the right to leave any country, including his [or her] own, and to return to his [or her] country.

12. Everyone has the right to seek and to enjoy in other countries asylum from persecution.

13. Everyone has the right to a nationality.

14. Men and women of full age, without any limitation due to race, nationality or religion, have the right to marry and to found a family.

15. Everyone has the right to own property alone as well as in association with others.

16. Everyone has the right to freedom of thought, conscience and religion; this right includes freedom to change his [or her] religion or belief, and freedom, either alone or in community with others and in public and private, to manifest his [or her] religion or belief in teaching, practice, worship and observance.

17. Everyone has the right to freedom of opinion and expression; this right includes freedom to hold opinions without interference and to seek, receive and impart information and ideas through any media and regardless of frontiers.

18. Everyone has the right of peaceful assembly and association. No one may be compelled to belong to an association.

19. Everyone has the right to take part in the government of his [or her] country, directly or through freely chosen representatives. Everyone has the right of equal access to public service in his [or her] country. The will of the people shall be the basis of authority of government; this shall be expressed in periodic and genuine elections which shall be by universal and equal suffrage and shall be held by secret vote or by equivalent free voting procedures.

20. Everyone, as a member of society, has the right to social security.

21. Everyone has the right to work, to free choice of employment, to just and favorable conditions of work and to protection against unemployment.

22. Everyone has the right to rest and leisure.

23. Everyone has the right to a standard of living adequate for the health and well-being of himself [or herself] and of his [or her] family, including food, clothing, housing and medical care.

24. Everyone has the right to education. Education shall be free, at least in the elementary and fundamental stages. Education shall be directed to the full development of the human personality and to the strengthening of respect for human rights and fundamental freedoms. It shall promote understanding, tolerance and friendship among all nations, racial and/or religious groups.

25. Everyone has a right to participate in the cultural life of the community, to enjoy the arts and to share in scientific advancement and its benefits. Everyone has the right to the protection of the moral and material interests resulting from any scientific, literary or artistic production of which he [or she] is the author.

26. Everyone has duties to the community in which alone, the free and full development of his personality is possible.

All United Nations Rights Reserved.

Convention on the Rights of the Child

The "United Nations Convention on the Rights of the Child" is the first legal document which establishes standards of protection to one of the most vulnerable groups in society–children. The document has sometimes been a "bill of rights" for children. Here are some of the highlights of the document:

1. Every child has the inherent right to life, and States shall ensure, to the maximum, child survival and development.

2. Every child has the right to a name and nationality from birth.

3. When courts, welfare institutions or administrative authorities deal with children, the child's best interests shall be a primary consideration. The child's opinions shall be given careful consideration.

4. States shall ensure that each child enjoys full rights without discrimination or distinctions of any kind.

5. Children should not be separated from their parents, unless by competent authorities for their well-being.

6. States shall protect children from physical or mental harm and neglect, including sexual abuse or exploitation.

7. States shall provide parentless children with suitable alternative care.

8. Disabled children shall have the right to special treatment, education and care.

9. The child is entitled to the highest attainable standard of health. States shall ensure that health care is provided to all children, placing emphasis on prevention measures, health education and reduction of infant mortality.

10. Primary education shall be free and compulsory; discipline in schools should respect the child's dignity. Education should prepare the child for life in a spirit of understanding, peace and tolerance.

11. Children shall have time to rest and play and equal opportunities for cultural and artistic activities.

12. States shall protect the child from economic exploitation and work that may interfere with education or be harmful to health or well-being.

13. Children in detention should be separated from adults; they must not be tortured or suffer cruel and degrading treatment.

14. No child under 15 should take part in hostilities; children exposed to armed conflict shall receive special protection.

15. Children of minority and indigenous populations shall freely enjoy their own culture, religion and language.

16. Children who have suffered maltreatment, neglect or detention should receive appropriate treatment or training for recovery and rehabilitation.

17. Children involved in infringements of the penal law shall be treated in a way that promotes their sense of dignity and worth and that aims at integrating them into society.

All United Nations Rights Reserved.

STEPPING ACROSS THE LINE

OBJECTIVES

Upon completing this lesson, students will be able to:

1. Identify human rights.
2. Identify which human rights are violated in various situations.
3. Explain how teasing can violate human rights.
4. Describe a conflict that relates to one human right.
5. List three ways people in a conflict might behave if there were no human rights violation.
6. List three ways people in a conflict might behave if there were human rights violation.
7. Role play a conflict situation that relates to human rights.

KEY CONCEPTS

attitudes
behavior
conflict analysis
feelings
human rights

BACKGROUND

We can use our knowledge of human rights constructively in conflict situations. This knowledge makes us more respectful of others, and others become more respectful of us.

While facilitating the following activity, emphasize the importance of three ideas.

1. People should respect each other, being careful not to violate others' human rights.
2. Because we are human, we all equally share basic rights.
3. We have freedom in choosing how to act.

Respecting others' human rights is a choice. Ultimately, students may choose not to respect others; but they must be given the opportunity to explore how respecting other people helps others, society, and themselves develop and grow.

For example, it is very difficult for students to work together to complete a class project if they do not respect each other's human rights. Suppose that every time one student disagreed with another, she hit him. They would accomplish nothing, because human rights are violated (the student has no right to hit the other student in the face). The student conduct affects everyone in the group, for the project cannot be finished and everyone in the group suffers the consequences. Just as in society at large, the group cannot grow and develop if its members violate human rights.

A dilemma arises, though. Suppose that a group of students is working together to complete a task. The group constantly teases one of the students so much that he/she feels completely distressed and depressed. Even without the help of the one individual, the group might still be able to complete its task. So, in this case, why should the group not tease the individual? What could influence the group to stop teasing the individual?

Research has shown that if children consider the consequences of their behavior, they are less likely to violate human rights. Students must understand that one of the consequences of teasing or hurting someone else is that they themselves become less caring people. For instance, the students in the group might stop teasing the individual if they think about possible harmful consequences of teasing:

1. by teasing, the students in the group are uncaring people,
2. the student being teased could have otherwise contributed a lot to the group,
3. the student being teased is becoming distressed and depressed, and so on.

MATERIALS

"Stepping Across the Line" activity sheet

TEACHER TIPS

Students may have difficulty understanding how human rights violations limit the ways conflicts can be resolved. It is a mature, complex idea. To help students understand the concept, you might start the activity with a role play: students could act out situations in which basic human rights are violated. For example, suppose that one of the basic human rights identified is the right to equality. A role play might be developed about a group of friends not allowing a new student to play their ball game.

ACTIVITY

1. Complete steps 2 and 3 of the activity in the previous lesson "My Protective Shield," having the class identify as many human rights as they can.
2. Count how many human rights the class listed. Divide the class into that number of groups and hand each group a copy of the activity sheet.
3. Assign each group a different human right from the list.
4. Have each group think of a conflict situation that relates to the human right it was assigned.
5. Ask each group to discuss and write answers to the questions on the activity sheet.
6. Have the class form a large circle and ask the students to share their answers to the questions. Make sure the students tell the class which human rights violation they are discussing.

DISCUSSION QUESTIONS

1. Students are humans and therefore have basic human rights (just like all other humans). What could someone do to students that would greatly endanger one or more of their basic human rights?

2. Look at the list of basic human rights. Which ones are most easily violated in a conflict situation?

3. What is teasing? What is an example of someone teasing someone else? How can teasing violate human rights? What can you do if someone teases you?

4. Teachers are humans and therefore have basic human rights (just like all other humans). Can teachers' human rights ever be violated? What are some common situations in which teachers' rights are violated at school?

FOLLOW-UP ACTIVITY

Hand out a piece of paper to every student. Have students draw a line down the center of the paper. For one week, students should record every conflict that they see in school on the left side of the paper. On the right side of the paper, they should note what human rights they think were violated during the conflict.

After the students have completed the assignment, have the whole class generate a list of the most common situations in which students' rights were violated. Write the list on the chalkboard.

Facilitate a discussion about ways to resolve the conflicts without violating human rights.

ADDITIONAL ACTIVITY

The following activity is not only fun, but also very educational. The students must make difficult decisions concerning where the line should be drawn between what is and is not a human rights violation.

Divide students into groups. Read each group one of the scenarios listed under "Do I Have a Right to Say That?" Give the groups approximately 15 minutes to prepare a role play of their scenario. Each group then performs its role play for the class. After each role play, the class discusses whether the situation depicted a violation of human rights, and if so, what rights were violated. Tell the students to think of ways to have the characters stand up for their rights. If time remains, students could create new role plays in which the characters stand up for their human rights.

This activity may make you and your students feel somewhat vulnerable. Try to encourage your students (and yourself) not to be defensive. It sometimes takes a great deal of courage to create changes in society, but you can do it!

DO I HAVE A RIGHT TO SAY THAT?

1. A brother and sister argue, yell, and hit one another.

2. The teacher returns students' tests. One student, jealous that another student received a better grade, lends the other student math notes with incorrect formulas.

3. A child has a birthday party, and all of her friends attend. In the middle of the party, the mother yells at the child in front of all the friends.

4. A student worked very hard on a school project, and the teacher is supposed to meet with him to discuss it. At a designated time, the student waits for the teacher, but he never arrives.

5. Students tease a classmate and tell him that he looks funny.

6. A student is very sad because she has serious family problems. In the back of the classroom she tells a friend about the problems. The teacher hears the students talking and asks them to leave the room because they cannot keep quiet.

7. A student misbehaves. The teacher orders him to stand in the corner for two hours.

8. Before class begins, a student in the hallway says something rude about a teacher. A few students laugh. The teacher and the rest of the class overhear the student's remarks.

ACTIVITY SHEET
STEPPING ACROSS THE LINE

Directions: Discuss and answer the following questions.

1. Describe the human right your group is discussing.

2. What is a conflict situation that relates to that human right?

3. List three ways the people in the conflict might behave if there were no human rights violation. Be specific.

   A.

   B.

   C.

4. List three ways the people in the conflict might behave if there were the human rights violation you described above. Be specific.

   A.

   B.

   C.

5. How are the people's choices limited by the human rights violation?

6. How can the people in the conflict express their feelings and resolve the conflict without violating human rights?

2004 © Open Society Institute

The Publisher grants permission for the reproduction of this worksheet for non-profit educational purposes only.
Activity sheets may be downloaded from www.idebate.org/conflictandcommunication.htm

Same Script, Different Play

OBJECTIVES

Upon completing this lesson, students will be able to:

1. Describe the relationship between rights and responsibilities in conflict situations.
2. Set up a code of responsible behavior for resolving conflicts.

KEY CONCEPTS

conflict resolution
human rights
social norms

BACKGROUND

When we are in public, we often notice people struggling to resolve their conflicts. We see or hear people arguing in the mall, at the park, by the river. Most of the time, people have difficulty resolving conflicts because they lack conflict resolution skills. Sometimes, though, conflicts are difficult to resolve because one person (or group) in the conflict deliberately attempts to embarrass or hurt the other person (or group).

There are different behavioral norms that govern our behavior in conflict situations. That is, the way we act in a conflict situation is different from the way we normally act. For instance, under normal circumstances, it is not socially appropriate to yell loudly and hit someone. But the social norms are different in conflict situations. It would not be surprising to see two people in a conflict situation yelling and hitting each other. Basically, the social norms that exist in conflict situations often make violent methods of conflict resolution appear socially acceptable and tolerable. Usually, though, violent methods of conflict resolution are nothing more than violations of human rights.

There are different social norms that affect us in various circumstances. For example, the way we act in conflict situations differs depending on our location. If we have a conflict in a public place, we may not yell as loudly or act as aggressively as when we are in a private place (such as in a house).

Creating new norms for how to deal with conflict is not easy, but it is one of the long-term goals of conflict management programs. We want to help students realize that there are many ways to solve conflicts besides using aggressive means (the norm). The following activity allows students to look at how social norms influence behavior. For instance, if they have the same conflict in different locations, they may act differently. In one location, they may argue with a friend quietly; in another location, they may violate human rights by hitting the other person without justification.

What is a viable option for how students can react in conflict situations? To effectively resolve conflicts while not violating human rights, students can: 1) avoid hurting other people in conflicts and 2) protect themselves as well.

MATERIALS

"Different Stages, Same Play" activity sheet, pencils

TEACHER TIPS

After facilitating this lesson, you could have students look at the Universal Declaration on Human Rights (p. 181) and, in small groups, decide which rights are more often violated in private. Ask students what things can be done to protect these rights.

ACTIVITY

1. Hand out the activity sheet and have students complete it.
2. Divide students into pairs and have them compare their answers.

DISCUSSION QUESTIONS

1. How many people decided to act differently in the various conditions? Why?
2. In what conditions did you decide to violate human rights and hurt your friend (either physically or mentally)? Why did you decide to hurt your friend in certain conditions and not in other conditions?
3. What is respect? Why is it important to respect other people's human rights?
4. If we hurt other people, what kind of people does that make us?
5. What are some of the rights we have when we are in conflict?

SAMPLE ANSWERS:

A. We have the right to try and resolve the problem.

B. We have the right to forgive the other person or to be forgiven.

C. We have the right to learn from our mistakes by changing our views.

ACTIVITY SHEET

DIFFERENT STAGES, SAME PLAY

Imagine the following: Last week, you had an exam. You were very nervous about it because you wanted to do well. The night before the exam, you reached in your book bag to get the book to study. The book wasn't there! You became very nervous. You searched your room for the book. You couldn't find it anywhere. You searched your book bag again and found a note from one of your friends. The note said: "I lost my book, so I borrowed yours. I'll return it tomorrow." Your friend took the book without asking you. Now you cannot study for your exam!

The following day you see your friend. Describe what you would say and how you would act if you approached your friend in each of the following locations:

1. An empty classroom?

2. At the park with a police officer nearby?

3. Alone on the street that evening?

4. While he/she was talking to your parents?

2004 © Open Society Institute

The Publisher grants permission for the reproduction of this worksheet for non-profit educational purposes only.
Activity sheets may be downloaded from www.idebate.org/conflictandcommunication.htm

DON'T PUSH ME

OBJECTIVES

Upon completing this lesson, students will be able to:

1. Identify and discuss human rights violations that occur at school.
2. Identify and discuss possible remedies for some of the human rights violations at school.

KEY CONCEPTS

human rights
school conflicts

BACKGROUND

Human rights are often systematically violated in schools. Teachers, students, and parents all complain about violations of human rights. However, only a small amount of research has examined and tried to identify basic problem areas concerning human rights in schools. Schools need structures for spreading the ideas of human rights and assuring that these ideas are respected.

The present activity allows students to analyze what type of human rights violations occur in their school. Students also create a system for reducing the number of human rights violations.

MATERIALS

paper, pencils

TEACHER TIPS

This activity is very important for students, for it allows them to think about how human rights are violated daily in their own environment. When facilitating and participating in this activity, both you and the students may feel vulnerable. Try to encourage the students (and yourself) to be open and not defensive.

Note that it may take a few minutes for students to talk about human rights violations involving teachers. For this activity to work effectively, you may have to ask students for examples of violations of human rights by teachers. (Remind the class not to use people's real names.) This may not be easy for you, but it takes courage to create a more peaceful world.

ACTIVITY

1. Explain to students that human rights violations occur in your school. Students, teachers, and parents have all had their rights violated.

2. Ask students to share any human rights violations that occur at school. Remind students not to use real names. This should take approximately 10 minutes.

3. Discuss the different violations with the students. (You can combine similar violations.) Ask the students what types of conflicts were generated before or during each violation.

4. Ask the students to group different violations into main ideas. (You may need to help the students group them. For example, suppose some of the violations were: students hitting students, teachers hitting students, and students hitting teachers. These violations could be grouped under the main idea of "The Right to Safety of One's Body.")

5. Once all the suggestions are categorized, divide the students into groups (the same number as the number of main ideas). Each group is assigned a different idea.

6. Ask each group to think of ways to end human rights violations within its main idea.

7. Have each group write down its suggestions and share them with the rest of the class.

9. Ask the class to compile the recommendations into a small booklet, which they can give to other teachers, students, the principal, members of the school board, parents, and so on.

DISCUSSION QUESTIONS

1. What are some examples of school conflicts in which human rights are violated? What are some ways the conflicts could be resolved without hurting other people or violating their basic human rights?

2. Do teachers and students have the same basic human rights? Why or why not?

3. What does it mean to respect someone's basic human rights? What are some ways that we can let other people know how important it is to respect everyone's basic human rights?

ADDITIONAL ACTIVITY

Background:

There are at least four sources of conflict in schools:

1. Schools have systematic, rigid ways of handling conflicts. Although this rigidity protects the students' rights, it can block more creative thinking about conflicts. The students are often accustomed to less formal ways of handling conflict within the family

2. The hierarchy of schools (between teachers and students) distances teachers from students and creates conflict.

3. Students' relationships with other students often create conflicts over values, resources, interests, and personalities.

4. Schools require students to follow specific rules (such as arriving on time for classes). These rules can promote conflict if students do not understand why they should follow them.

Activity:

Students make a list of three of their most upsetting school conflicts. Tell the students to list only conflicts that they feel comfortable sharing with others. Divide the students into pairs and ask them to brainstorm suitable strategies for resolving the conflicts without violating basic human rights. Students could share their solutions with the class.

NOTE: If the school already has methods and procedures in place for addressing human rights violations, share them with the students. They need to see that the school is making an effort. Students may also gain insights into why certain procedures are part of school policy.

CREATING A CONFLICT MANAGEMENT ACTIVITY

OBJECTIVES

Upon completing this lesson, students will be able to:

1. Identify the most important concepts in conflict management.
2. Evaluate their own progress in handling conflicts.
3. Demonstrate their leadership skills.

KEY CONCEPTS

communication
conflict analysis
conflict resolution
leadership skills
self-esteem

BACKGROUND

This activity provides students with the opportunity to process the different conflict resolution skills they have learned. It is important because it allows students to think about how the different elements of conflict management relate to one another. For example, students can consider how communication skills are important in their lives and in improving their conflict management skills.

MATERIALS

"Reflections of Myself" activity sheet, paper, pencils

TEACHER TIPS

This is an excellent activity for increasing students' sense of self-confidence and empowerment. However, students need a great deal of support from you and their classmates to stand in front of the class and teach. Specific ways of creating a "safe atmosphere" for students are included within this activity.

The activities the students write could be the basis for their own book on conflict management. They could present the book to the school for all teachers to use.

ACTIVITY

1. Tell the class that it is going to design a conflict management program.

2. Explain that each student is going to design his/her own conflict management activity. One of the first steps is to think about what he/she wants the program to emphasize: What are the most important parts of a conflict management program?

3. Have each student list three of the most important points for a conflict management program. For example, a student might write that his/her program emphasizes no fighting, effective communication skills, and tolerance of others.

4. Next, give each student a piece of paper. Students should design an advertisement for their program. Tell the students to be creative while drawing their pictures.

5. Collect the drawings. One by one, display the drawings and have the class guess who drew each picture.

6. If there is more time (possibly on another day), you could continue the activity. Divide the class into groups of four to six.

7. Have each group think of an activity to teach the ideas it feels are important for conflict management. If the students find the task difficult, explain that they can modify one of the activities in which they have already participated.

8. Have the groups teach their activities to the class.

NOTE: Be aware that many children may be nervous or lack the confidence to stand in front of the class and teach. Therefore, it is important to create a safe atmosphere for the students. Tell the class that you understand that some people get nervous or feel uncomfortable when leading or speaking in front of others. It is a very natural experience to get nervous when speaking in front of others. Explain that while a group leads an activity, the entire class must follow certain rules:

    a. Everyone should listen to the group leading the discussion.
    b. No one should be disruptive or make fun of the group leading the discussion.
    c. Everyone should be respectful of the group leading the discussion.

Do not force anyone to lead the class.

Below are some discussion questions you can discuss if groups have created their own conflict management activities. You can ask these questions after each or all of the groups have led their activities.

DISCUSSION QUESTIONS

1. How did it feel to lead the class in an activity?

2. What was difficult about creating your own conflict management activity?

3. What are the most important points to emphasize when teaching conflict management?

ADDITIONAL ACTIVITY I

The class can compile the group activities into a conflict management program. The students can design a plan for teaching their conflict management program to students in other classes.

ADDITIONAL ACTIVITY II

Hand out the activity sheet. Have students fill in the table. They should try to define:

1) their most serious conflicts,
2) some positive things that they have always done to try and solve conflicts,
3) some positive things that they have recently changed due to the conflict management lessons, *and*
4) some ways they can make improvements in their management of conflict situations in the future.

ACTIVITY SHEET
REFLECTIONS OF MYSELF

My most serious conflicts are...

Some positive things that I have always done to try and solve my conflicts are...

Some positive things that I have recently changed due to the lessons are...

I can resolve conflicts more successfully in the future if I...

PART II
Student Mediation: Training and Implementation

(This section is self-contained. It can be used either in conjunction with Part I or as a completely separate program.)

Student Mediation: Introduction

Every day, people encounter many internal and interpersonal conflicts. Internal conflicts occur in your head and in your heart, such as when you are deciding whether it is okay to share a secret. Interpersonal conflicts are between you and other individuals or groups. For example, you and a family member might argue about whose turn it is to do the dishes. Now stop reading for a moment and think about how many internal and interpersonal conflicts you and your students must deal with every day. If people had to develop a new strategy for handling every conflict they ever had, they would never get anything accomplished!

Fortunately, you and your students are usually able to resolve conflicts by the appropriate use of conflict management skills (such as active listening, communicating with respect, and empathy). Most people have developed personal strategies for dealing with conflict situations, which are usually resolved without much hassle. But what happens when two students are so angry or frustrated with one another that they can't resolve their conflict on their own?

Student mediators are students trained in facilitating discussion between disputing students or groups as they search for a solution. Their goal is to provide the disputing parties with a forum for better communication and understanding, which often leads to a mutually satisfying resolution to the conflict. By learning how to manage conflict at a young age, students are equipped with valuable skills that they can use for the rest of their lives.

Student Mediation: Purpose

STUDENT MEDIATION SERVES MANY FUNCTIONS:

1. It creates an alternative route toward the resolution of conflicts.

In many schools, disputing students think they have only three possible ways to resolve their problems: appeal to authority, fight, or escape the situation, Student mediation offers students access to a fourth route: mediation. Because students are active participants in helping their peers work through conflict, the process empowers students in a way that appealing to authority does not.

2. It establishes conflict as a positive, constructive process.

Student mediators function as role models, conveying the message that the disputants themselves can resolve conflicts without violence or shouting. Students become more attuned to the positive potential in conflict and deal with conflicts more fairly because conflicts are seen as opportunities. Research in the United States has also suggested that student mediation reduces school absenteeism, vandalism, and suspensions.[1] Students in schools with mediation programs develop more tolerance for other people, cultures, and ethnicities.

In many conflicts, people will not budge from their positions. They state that the other party must comply or else there will be no agreement. This type of argument is called an *all-or-nothing argument* or *positional argument*. Because student mediation provides students with a framework for cooperation, there are more shared (win/win) decisions and fewer all-or-nothing (win/lose) decisions than if school officials become involved in the process.

3. It improves relationships.

Because mediation is a systematic process, the disputing students each have the opportunity to talk and listen to one another. The tensions and hostilities of conflict are eased by the presence of mediators and by the knowledge that mediation is a process during which the disputants are equally respected. The confidentiality of mediation also gives students a sense of confidence in expressing themselves honestly. Improved communication leads to improved relationships.

Mediation can improve the post-dispute climate, too. The process is effective not only in addressing the immediate conflict, but also in improving long-term relationships between the disputing parties.[2] Mediation also improves communication between students, parents, school faculty, and administration.

4. It reduces the burden of discipline.

Since students mediate, teachers, counselors, school psychologists, and other staff tend to spend less time dealing with disputing students. Mediation usually occurs before actual violence begins, so this early intervention means fewer suspensions and expulsions. Also, as the program gains respect, peer pressure makes it likely that the disputing students stick to their agreed-on resolutions.

5. It teaches the process behind resolving conflicts.

Students involved in both the mediation training and process learn the skills of problem solving and active listening, which are useful throughout their lives. Students also refine their leadership skills.

6. It encourages democratic ideals.

Students learn to solve their own problems. They realize what it means to have freedom of choice and a sense of responsibility, and they learn from the consequences of their decisions. Student mediators feel helpful because they contribute to the community. They are valued both in and out of school.

HOW DO YOU SET UP A STUDENT MEDIATION PROGRAM?

Following the ten sessions, there is a very detailed outline to guide you and your students in setting up and maintaining a student mediation program.

You can enhance the effectiveness of the student mediation program by participating in the activities with your students. In this way, students will perceive you not only as an adviser, but also as a confidant, and more readily accept the information and skills you present.

---

1. Jacobsen, Michael G. et al. Effective School Climate: Roles for Peers, Practitioners, and Principals. Rural Research Report, Vol. 3(4), Spring 1992.
2. Kressel and Pruitt. "Themes in the Mediation of Social Conflict." *Journal of Social Issues,* Vol. 41(2), 1985.

Student Mediation: The Ten Sessions

OBJECTIVES OF THE TEN MEDIATION SESSIONS

The following ten sessions are designed to teach students mediation skills. This training is very effective when done in large blocks of time (for example, in four or five full school days of training). However, you can use shorter sessions over a longer period of time. The mediation program is presented in a different format than the activities in Part I of the curriculum, since student mediation training requires systematic training to properly prepare students for the responsibility. But you can adapt the lessons and activities to suit the needs of the trainees.

Each session should take approximately 2 to 4 hours, depending on how thoroughly you want to explore the concepts. Because some sessions cover more material than others, they may take more time. Consequently, you may need to cover the material in some of the sessions during two or more training meetings. Use your judgment about giving short breaks when the students need them. Also if students become restless or tense during sessions, we recommend that you: 1) complete the activity being facilitated and then 2) facilitate an icebreaker (see Appendix II). Most skills and concepts are taught through games and experiential learning strategies. In this way, the students learn while they have fun, thus developing a more positive outlook on school and learning.

Since many of the skills involved in student mediation are basic conflict management skills, some of the following sessions include lessons from Part I of this curriculum. If your group has already experienced the lessons, you still have many viable options. You could:

1. Facilitate the activities again to refresh, reinforce, or refine the skills. Students always need to practice these skills.

2. Facilitate role plays using the skills learned.

3. Have student volunteers lead the activities. This reinforces their skills and develops leadership.

4. Be creative and design new activities that emphasize the skills presented.

5. Have students form small groups and think of new activities to teach the skills. Students can present their activities to the group and facilitate discussion.

To introduce students to student mediation, you may want to act out the play "The Three Lovely Little Pigs," in Appendix III. In a very amusing way, it allows the audience to grasp the concepts of mediation. Once students are trained in mediation, they could perform the play for others, thus advertising or explaining student mediation.

STUDENT MEDIATION - SESSION ONE

OBJECTIVES

Upon completing this session, students will be able to:

1. Create a working definition of mediation.
2. Identify conflict situations.
3. State whether they agree to become student mediators.

MATERIALS

"The Party, Before We Fight," and "Did You See That?" activity sheets
Student Mediation Commitment Sheet
paper, pencils
chalkboard and chalk (or large pieces of white paper and a pen)
a small ball, rolled up sock, or crumpled piece of paper

SESSION

I. WELCOME/ ICEBREAKER

After all interested students have arrived, have everyone (including yourself) sit in a large circle.

Welcome everyone to the student mediation training session. Explain that before you begin, you would like to play a game so that everyone starts to feel comfortable with one another.

Tell the students that they will have 10 seconds to think of a movement that describes themselves. The more creative, the better! For example, an energetic, athletic student could jump up and down.

Introduce yourself and show your movement. Now, going around the circle, have each person say his/her name and show a movement, as well as the name and movement of each person that already presented.

II. ACTIVITIES

Step 1: Getting to Know More About Each Other

Have students (and you) fill out "The Party" activity sheet.

Now tell all the students that they have each magically turned into the person they wrote down in Statement 6 on their activity sheet (one of the people they love most). Tell them to act like that person.

One at a time, students should describe themselves to the class through the eyes of the person they love. Remind them they should look, act, and talk like that person while describing themselves. They can use their answers to the other questions on the activity sheet to help their description.

You can first give an example. You could pretend to act very old and say:

Hello. My name is Andrea. I am 86 years old. I am Monika's Grandmother. I love her. Her favorite hobby is reading. After school, she likes to play outside. Her favorite food is pizza. The funniest thing that ever happened to her was when she couldn't stop sneezing while taking a test. I love her very much.

Make sure that every student has the opportunity to pretend to be someone else.

Step 2: Introduction to Mediation

Ask if anybody can explain what mediation is. Explain that when two people cannot resolve a problem on their own, a mediator sometimes can help them out.

Explain that a mediator:

a. Listens to both sides of the story, but does not judge who is right or wrong.
b. Creates an atmosphere in which the people in the conflict can express their feelings and interests.
c. Facilitates communication between the people in conflict as they work together and try to solve their problem.

Step 3: I Think That Conflict Is...

Hand out the "Before We Fight" activity sheet. Have students complete the form. Once completed, divide students into groups of four to six.

Tell them to share their answers to question 1 ("I think that conflict is"). Ask the groups to discuss how their answers are similar and different. Have each group report its findings to the class. Note whether any of the groups expressed conflict positively. If not, discuss why most people view conflict negatively.

Ask students how conflicts can be positive experiences. Possible answers are that during conflict situations people can grow, learn new things about each other, and preserve or enhance their relationship.

Read aloud question 5 from the activity sheet. Ask for volunteers to contribute their answers. List their answers on the chalkboard. If a student does not say so, explain that you could also go to student mediation with your best friend. The mediators could help you both deal with your problem.

Step 4: The Magic Ball of Wisdom

Have everyone sit in one small, tight circle.

Get out one of the following objects: a small ball, a rolled up sock, or a tightly crumpled piece of paper. Tell everyone that the object is the Magic Ball of Wisdom. Whenever people hold it, they know everything there is to know in the whole world. Explain that any time you ask a question and then throw the ball to one of the students, that student must attempt to answer the question. If he/she has too much knowledge about other important things that obscures the answer to the question, he/she may throw the ball to another student. When a student answers the question appropriately, he/she throws the ball back to the teacher, who asks students another question and throws the ball again.

Here are a few sample questions you can ask:
 a. What is conflict?
 b. What does a mediator do?
 c. What are some feelings people experience when in a conflict?
 d. When you are in a conflict, what different things can you do to resolve the conflict?

Step 5: The Big Fun Commitment

Make sure the students understand that while becoming a student mediator is fun, it is also a big commitment:

 a. There are eight training sessions (each session should take 2 to 4 hours, depending on how thoroughly you cover the material).
 b. Upon completion of training, students must pledge to work regularly as student mediators and to attend weekly meetings with other mediators and the adviser to discuss the mediation sessions and support each other.
 c. Mediators maintain strict rules of privacy. They discuss the content of mediation sessions only during mediation support group meetings. Even then, they do not use people's real names. Everyone has the right to privacy in his or her personal life.
 d. Mediators follow rules of confidentiality. Everything said in the group stays in the group. During mediation training sessions, discussions may become personal. People feel more comfortable sharing if they know that everything discussed remains confidential within the group.

Step 6: Student Mediation Commitment Sheet

Put the Student Mediation Commitment Sheet on a table, telling students that those who would like to become student mediators should sign their names by a specific date and time; this shows that they agree to commit themselves to the program, attending all sessions and participating in session activities. You can skip this step if you are teaching mediation to your entire class.

Explain to students that occasionally a student may not like mediation or mediation training. If so, he should speak with you. Listen to the student's complaints, and if he truly no longer wants to be a mediator, let him drop the course. Be sure to explain to the mediation group that although the student is no longer a part of the group, everyone should still remain friendly with him. Offer the group positive feedback, explaining that even though the group has lost a member, it still has a very important school function.

III. REVIEW

Tell all the students to think back to today's activity (when students acted like someone they loved). Ask for a volunteer to try saying who every classmate pretended to be.

IV. HOMEWORK

Hand out the "Did You See That?" activity sheet. Tell students that their homework assignment for this week is fun and easy: write down every conflict they see or are involved in during the week. Ask them to bring the activity sheet back next week. Also tell students to be aware of and to write down any "trigger words" they hear. "Trigger words" are words that arouse people's emotions and cause them to lose touch with their rational thoughts. For example, if one student says to another, "You're stupid," that might trigger an angry outburst from the other student.

V. CLOSING

Be encouraging. Thank all the students for their participation; tell them that even if they decided not to sign up to become mediators now, perhaps later they may change their minds. Tell everyone who signed up that they will become good mediators and that you will see them at the next session. (Also make sure that everyone who wants to become a mediator signs the Student Mediation Commitment Sheet.)

ACTIVITY SHEET

THE PARTY

1. My name is:

2. My hobbies are:

3. After school, I:

4. My favorite food is:

5. The funniest thing that ever happened to me was:

6. One of the people I love most in the world is:

ACTIVITY SHEET

BEFORE WE FIGHT

1. I think that conflict is

2. Everyone encounters many conflicts daily. List three conflicts you have experienced. Put a star (*) next to each conflict that you feel you have resolved successfully.
    A.
    B.
    C.

3. When I argue with someone, I feel:

4. When I can't decide whether to read a book in the house or to play outside, I feel:

5. You are in a fight with your best friend. Your best friend shouts and calls you rude names. What are some things you could do or say in response?
    A.
    B.
    C.
    D.
    E.

2004 © Open Society Institute

The Publisher grants permission for the reproduction of this worksheet for non-profit educational purposes only.
Activity sheets may be downloaded from www.idebate.org/conflictandcommunication.htm

ACTIVITY SHEET
DID YOU SEE THAT?

Carry this paper with you everywhere you go this week. Write down every conflict you see or are involved in. Make sure to write who was involved and what the conflict was about. Also write any "trigger words" you hear. Don't write people's names, though. Instead, use words like *boy, girl, man*, or *woman* to describe people. If you describe your family, you can use *sister, brother*, etc.

Who was involved ?	What was the conflict about :
Example: my sister and I	I argued with my sister about who can ride the bike faster. She used "trigger words," calling me a grouchy, mean brother.
1	
2	
3	
4	
5	
6	
7	
8	
9	
10	

2004 © Open Society Institute

The Publisher grants permission for the reproduction of this worksheet for non-profit educational purposes only.
Activity sheets may be downloaded from www.idebate.org/conflictandcommunication.htm

Student Mediation Commitment Sheet

I fully understand that by training and becoming a school mediator, I am volunteering to commit time, energy, and excitement to learning and applying mediation skills.

Sign your name here:
1.
2.
3.
4.
5.
6.
7.
8.
9.
10.
11.
12.
13.
14.
15.
16.
17.
18.
19.
20.
21.
22.
23.
24.
25.
26.
27.
28.
29.
30.

2004 © Open Society Institute

The Publisher grants permission for the reproduction of this worksheet for non-profit educational purposes only.
Activity sheets may be downloaded from www.idebate.org/conflictandcommunication.htm

STUDENT MEDIATION - SESSION TWO

OBJECTIVES

Upon completing this session, students will be able to:

1. Describe the reasons mediators should be nonjudgmental and not give advice.
2. Explain how to be empathetic.
3. Explain the necessity of keeping mediation sessions confidential.
4. Describe why mediators should care about the mediation process and the people involved.

MATERIALS

"The Five Keys" and "An Exchange" activity sheets
Magic Ball of Wisdom
cup or glass filled with water

SESSION

I. WELCOME/ ICEBREAKER

After all students have arrived, have everyone (including yourself) sit in a large circle. Welcome everyone back to the student mediation training session. Tell them that you will begin this session with a quick game. Choose a fun icebreaker from Appendix II. After the icebreaker, have the students return to the circle.

II. REVIEW PAST SESSION

Ask students what they learned from last week's mediation training session.

For example:

- What is conflict?
- How can conflict be a positive experience?
- When do people use mediation?

III. ACTIVITIES

Step 1: Rules for mediators

Explain that there are certain rules that mediators and those training must follow:

a. Anytime anyone in the group shares a personal experience, it remains confidential and is not discussed outside of the group.

b. Name-calling is not allowed.

   c. Because each person will have a turn to speak, interrupting is not allowed.

   d. A mediator's role is to facilitate communication. It is not the mediator's responsibility to resolve the conflict.

   e. If mediators need help from their adult coordinator, it is both okay and important to ask for it.

Post these rules during training and mediation sessions.

Step 2: Getting to Know Our Conflicts

Tell everyone to get out their homework sheets from Session One (Did You See That?), which lists the conflicts they experienced or saw during the week).

Get out the Magic Ball of Wisdom, reminding students that if they hold the ball, they are very wise.

Randomly throw the ball to a student, asking her to read one of her conflicts. After she reads one, tell her to throw the ball to someone else in the class. The student with the ball now reads one of his/her conflicts, throws the ball to someone else, and so on, until everyone in the group has had a chance to read a conflict. If students did not do the assignment, ask them to name a feeling people experience during conflict.

TEACHER TIPS: Be aware that some of the students might share personal conflicts with the group. If this becomes a deep, stressful activity, follow it up with a stress-relieving activity from Appendix I.

Step 3: The Five Keys

Hand out "The Five Keys" resource sheet and have a volunteer read it aloud.

Tell students that by the end of the session, they will understand each of the five aspects clearly and will know how to apply them to the mediation process.

Step 4: Do Not Judge And Do Not Give Advice (Keys One and Two)

Have students study the design on the bottom of the activity sheet. Tell them that they will have 10 minutes to write as many different words that they can think of that describe the design. Stress that they should be unique and creative: they should not compare ideas with anyone else.

After 10 minutes, have students read their favorite one or two ideas.

DISCUSSION QUESTIONS

(Ask them in the order given.)

1. Did everyone have the same answers? Why not?

2. Does everyone think the same? (Perceive the same?) Why should we not judge other people involved in conflict situations?

3. If I have a conflict and I ask every student in this room how to resolve it, will each person's solution be the same? Why not?

4. What is advice?

5. If two students are fighting and ask you to help them, should you give them advice? (No.) Why not?

(Answer: Because everybody has his or her own way of thinking. We can guide people without giving advice. For instance, not everyone described the random design the same way. By not giving advice, students learn how to make their own decisions and take responsibility for them.)

NOTE: To make the discussion livelier, you could ask a question, and then throw the Magic Ball of Wisdom to a student who should answer it.

Step 5: Empathy (Key Three)

Hand out "An Exchange" activity sheet. While still in the circle, separate the class into two groups, Group A and Group B. Choose two volunteers to come to the center of the circle and act out the parts of Roxandra and Lily.

Tell Group A that during the role play it should focus on the reasons Lily is more considerate; Group B should focus on the reasons Roxandra is more considerate. Following the role play, have the two groups move to opposite sides of the room.

DISCUSSION QUESTIONS

1. Ask Group A for the reasons it thought Lily acted more considerately.

2. Ask Group B for the reasons it thought Roxandra acted more considerately.

3. Tell everyone that Roxandra and Lily stayed mad at each other. They went to school mediators to help them resolve their conflict. What would happen if the mediators in their conflict were allowed to judge who is right and who is wrong? What would Group A say to Lily and Roxandra during the mediation? What would Group B say to them during the mediation?

4. Why is it important not to judge who is right and wrong in mediation? Explain that student mediators need to know how to empathize equally with all disputants.

Tell Group A to empathize with Roxandra and Group B to empathize with Lily. This requires students to take both girls' points of view seriously. Ask a member of Group A to explain Roxandra's point of view, how she felt, and the reasons why she acted the way she did. Then ask a member of Group B to explain Lily's point of view, how she felt, and why she acted the way she did.

DISCUSSION QUESTIONS

1. What is empathizing?

2. Why is it important?

TEACHER NOTE: In an actual mediation session, thee is a step in which disputants explain the position and feelings of the other person.

Step 6: Confidentiality (Key Four)

Facilitate "Can You Keep a Secret" (page 87). Discuss with students the importance of keeping mediation confidential. Ask students why it is important to keep confidentiality.

(Answer: It makes the disputants feel more comfortable in talking honestly and lets them know they can trust the mediators; they might reveal personal, private thoughts and feelings; they might talk about things that could hurt other people's feelings; and so on).

Ask the students if they can think of any times when it might be necessary to break confidentiality. Stress that although mediators must keep the mediation sessions confidential, there are two conditions in which they can break confidentiality by talking with the adult coordinator:

    a. During a mediation session, if either disputant harms or threatens to harm themselves or someone else, immediately stop the mediation and tell the coordinator.

b. If mediators have questions about how to handle a conflict mediation session, or if they need to talk about a past session, they should talk with the coordinator (the teacher keeps the session confidential).

NOTE: During later sessions, it may be useful for students to role play mediation sessions in which disputants threaten to injure themselves or others.

Step 7: Show That You Care (Key Five)

Re-assemble the students in a large circle. Ask students why they should care about mediation and the people that come for mediation. Explain that student mediators do not play favorites: they do not give one disputant more attention than the other. Mediators have equal respect for both people, so they follow the guidelines of mediation. Student mediators care about the process of mediation.

IV. REVIEW

Review with the students what they learned today:

    A. What are reasons a mediator should be nonjudgmental? Why should a mediator be neutral?
    B. Why should a mediator not give advice?
    C. What is empathy? How is it important in mediation?
    D. What are the two times you can break confidentiality?
    E. Why do we care about the mediation process and the people who come for mediation?

End the session by asking if anyone can still remember each classmate's movement from the last session (when students introduced themselves).

V. CLOSING

Compliment the students on something positive they accomplished during the session. Tell them you will see them at the next session.

Resource Sheet
The Five Keys

It is very difficult—almost impossible—to open a locked door (unless you are very, very strong). But if you have a key, you just fit it into the keyhole, turn the key, and the door swings open. Sometimes when friends fight, they are very similar to locked doors: they won't listen to anybody and they won't open up. If you have keys to your friends' thinking, you might be able to help them unlock their problems. Luckily, there are keys to help you help your friends. You cannot touch these keys, but you can learn them and use them. They are very helpful in allowing your friends and classmates to feel comfortable in talking about their conflicts. The five keys are:

1. **Do not judge.** Mediators are unbiased. They do not take sides, even when they think that one disputant is right and the other is wrong.
2. **Do not give advice.** Sometimes mediators might think of solutions to the disputants' conflicts, but they should not suggest them. This is the disputants' conflict: let them resolve it themselves; only then will they feel responsible for the solution.
3. **Be equally empathetic.** An empathetic mediator attempts to understand what the disputants feel by imagining what it would be like to be in their shoes—to experience conflict from their perspective. Avoid taking sides, but try to understand how each person views the conflict.
4. **Keep confidentiality.** Disputants feel more comfortable honestly expressing their feelings and problems when they know that the mediators will not tell anyone about their conflict.
5. **Show that you care.** Mediators care about the process of mediation and about the people. They try their hardest to help the disputants reach their goal of understanding each other and resolving the conflict. If the mediators respect the mediation process, the disputants will trust that mediation can help them solve their problem.

2004 © Open Society Institute

The Publisher grants permission for the reproduction of this worksheet for non-profit educational purposes only.
Activity sheets may be downloaded from www.idebate.org/conflictandcommunication.htm

ACTIVITY SHEET
AN EXCHANGE

Roxandra and Lily are sitting across from each other. They just finished eating lunch.

Rox: That meal was so good!

Lily: Yeah, and the fish tasted so fresh I'd bet they just caught it today.

Rox: Hey! I heard you're going fishing this weekend.

Lily: Yeah, with my family. We're going to the lake.

Rox: I heard that you invited Vikki to go also. Is it true?

Lily: Well...yes.

Rox: I thought that I was your best friend. Why did you invite her instead of me?

Lily: Vikki always invites me to her house. I thought it would be nice of me to invite her somewhere for once.

Rox: But I always invite you to my house. I thought we were best friends.

Lily: Well, I can have more than one friend, can't I?

Rox: But don't favor them over me. I'm your best friend.

Lily: Well if that's the way you want to treat things, you're a jerk!

Rox: You're a jerk! I don't need a friend like you.

Lily: I hate you and am glad I didn't invite you to go fishing!

Rox: I hate you more!!!

STUDENT MEDIATION - SESSION THREE

OBJECTIVES
Upon completing this session, students will be able to:
1. Describe and illustrate verbal and nonverbal means of communication.
2. Prepare a mediation area.
3. Welcome people to the mediation area.

MATERIALS
Student Mediation Guide

SESSION

I. WELCOME/ ICEBREAKER
After students have arrived, have everyone sit in a large circle. Facilitate an icebreaker from Appendix II. Following the icebreaker, ask the students to return to the circle.

II. REVIEW PAST SESSION
Ask for volunteers to explain the five keys (the five essential aspects) of a student mediator. If they have trouble remembering, refer them to "The Five Keys" resource sheet (page 217).

III. ACTIVITIES

Step 1: The Student Mediation Guide
Hand out the Student Mediation Guide. Tell the students that by the end of the ten sessions, they will have a firm understanding of each of the ten steps of student mediation explained on the sheet. They should bring this guide to every mediation session. As they learn each step, they should use the third column of the guide to keep notes about important things to remember. These notes will be especially helpful when they begin mediating. By the end of today's session, they will have an understanding of steps 1 and 2 of the guide.

Step 2: Why Students in Conflict Should Face Each Other During the Mediation Session
Tell the students to find a partner, someone in the group that they do not know very well. The pairs sit on the floor, back to back. One of the partners pretends that he/she is very, very sad because of a recent fight with his/her best friend. The other partner listens and asks questions, trying to make the partner feel better. Then the two reverse roles and repeat the process.

Next, repeat the entire process, only instead of having partners sit back to back on the floor, ask them to stand on opposite sides of the room. They will need to raise their voices in order to converse. Reverse roles and repeat.

Last, repeat the entire process again, but this time have the partners sit face to face on the floor. Partners should sit close to each other. Reverse roles and repeat.

Discussion Questions

1. Which way of communicating helps you feel most confident that the other person is listening? Why?

2. Which way of communicating is the most comfortable and easy? Why?

3. Suppose two students are arguing. They ask you to mediate their argument. Should the students face each other, be far away from each other, or be back to back? Why?

(Answer: Facing each other communicates interest and the desire to solve the argument together. This is due mainly to body language, such as the use of eye contact.)

Step 3: Quiet, Private, Neutral Place for Mediation

Explain to the students that mediation session must take place in a quiet, private, neutral setting. Ask the class why. You can give them a hint by reminding them to think about one of the five essential characteristics of a good student mediator. (Possible answer: Mediation sessions are confidential. In a quiet, private area, there is no one to cause distractions and there is no one to overhear the mediation session.)

Tell the class that before they mediate, they should find a quiet, private place and set up the area. Once the disputants arrive, ask them to sit down. Welcome them to the mediation session and have everyone, including the mediators, introduce themselves.

Step 4: Preparing the Area

Explain to the class how to prepare the seats. The arguing students should sit on opposite sides of the table, facing one another. The mediators sit at the head of the table, on the same side. Have four students (two mediators and two students in conflict) demonstrate the proper seating arrangement.

Divide students into groups of four. In each group, have two students decide on a common conflict that children their age encounter. Ask them to pretend to have that conflict with one another. The other two students in each group should act as mediators and set up the mediation area. Students should make sure the desks are arranged properly. Each group should act out the first two steps of the mediation session. Tell the mediators to refer to the Student Mediation Guide if they can't remember what to do. Have students switch roles so that everyone has the opportunity to be a mediator.

NOTE: In some schools, mediation is done in a mediation room, while in other schools it takes place in corners of the classroom, on the playground, and so on. Adapt this activity to suit the facilities and needs of your school or classroom.

Step 5: Paying Attention to Body Language, Behavior, and Speech

Tell each group to stand in a small circle. They should spend approximately one minute inspecting each other's appearances. Two of the members, the mediators, turn so their backs are toward the circle. The other two group members, the disputants, now change three things about their appearance. For instance, one of the disputants could mess up his/her hair, take off a watch, etc. After the disputants have changed their appearance, the mediators turn around and guess how the disputants changed their appearance. Once they have guessed, the mediators and disputants reverse roles and repeat the activity.

After groups finish, have them discuss what this activity teaches them: How does this activity relate to mediation? What should mediators observe during mediation sessions? Explain that mediators must be observant and pay close attention to the disputants' body language, behavior, and speech. Body language is explained in detail in the next step.

Step 6: Facilitate "Body Talk," located on page 91.

Additional Discussion Questions For "Body Talk":

1. Why is it important for mediators to have positive body language?
2. Why should mediators always be aware of both their body language and the disputants' body language?
3. What can someone's body language communicate?

Step 7: Feelings

Have the students sit in a large circle.

Explain that feelings can often be communicated by one's body language. Therefore, mediators should always pay attention to disputants' body language because it provides hints about how students are feeling. Tell everyone in the class to sit in a position that expresses a specific feeling. (Each student chooses a feeling; different students will be expressing different feelings simultaneously.) For example, a student could pretend to be mad by crossing his/her arms and having an angry look on his/her face. Put a chair in the center of the group's circle. Have a volunteer, the imitator, sit on the chair and imitate one of the students. Each student around the circle gets one guess about who the imitator is imitating. Once someone guesses correctly, the students in the circle then have to guess what feeling the body language illustrates. The student who guesses the feeling becomes the imitator. The process repeats.

Discussion Questions

1. What can body language tell us about feelings?
2. When people are angry or sad, do they always tell us immediately how they feel? How can we attempt to figure out how they feel if they don't tell us?
3. How does reading body language help a mediator understand how the arguing students feel? (You may want to warn students that while reading body language can help them determine how people feel, it can also backfire; it can give them an inaccurate perception because different people react differently.

IV. REVIEW

V. CLOSING

Compliment the students on something positive they accomplished during the session. Tell them you will see them at the next session.

STUDENT MEDIATION GUIDE
THE 10 STEPS OF STUDENT MEDIATION

The 10 Steps of Student Mediation	Brief Description of Each Step	Your Notes and Things to Remember
1. Prepare the Area	1. Find a quiet place. 2. Make sure the area is private so no one can overhear the conversation. 3. Set up the room.	
2. Welcome	1. Welcome everyone to the mediation session. 2. Have everyone introduce themselves.	
3. Explain the Rules	1. Say, "Mediation will give both of you the opportunity to work together and understand more about each other. Through this process, you can try to find a solution that improves your situation. Mediation can make it possible for both of you to win." 2. Explain ground rules. Say, "Before we start, we want to tell you about a few rules that will be followed during the mediation. Two rules that we, as mediators, will follow are: a. We don't take sides or judge either of you; b. Everything said here is confidential. Now there are ground rules we would like you to agree to: a. No name-calling, insults, or blaming; b. No interrupting; c. Be honest and respectful; d. Work hard to solve the problem; e. Everything said here is confidential." 3. Ask each student, "Do you agree to the rules?"	
4. Listen To the Conflict	1. One mediator asks one of the students to explain what happened and how he/she feels. The mediator summarizes what was said and asks the student if the summary was accurate. If anything is still confusing, the mediator should ask questions to clarify details. 2. The other mediator repeats this process with the second student. 3. If new information is revealed by either of the students, ask them how it affects their view of the conflict. 4. Say, "In this part of mediation, we want you to talk with each other." 5. Say to each student in turn, "Please describe to the other student what he/she said." Ask the other student if the description was accurate. If he/she says yes, continue on. Otherwise, have the student repeat or clarify what he/she said.	

222 | Conflict and Communication

The 10 Steps of Student Mediation	Brief Description of Each Step	Your Notes and Things to Remember
5. Discover Shared Interests	Ask questions like: a. If you were the other student, how would you feel right now? b. What do you want to get out of this conflict? c. What are some things you both agree on?	
6. Think of Possible Solutions	1. Say, "We are now going to see how we understand things differently than at the beginning of the session. Let's think of possible solutions to the conflict." 2. Explain guidelines: Things to do: * Say every idea that you can think of. * Think of as many ideas as possible. Things to avoid: * Don't judge any idea as good or bad. * Don't talk about the ideas yet. Just say them. 3. One of the mediators writes all ideas on the Ideas Sheet (page 248).	
7. Find a Resolution	1. Have students evaluate possible solutions. Ask: * What are the positive and negative consequences of choosing each solution? * What solutions address both of your interests? 2. Have them choose one that they both agree on. Make sure the solution is: * realistic and possible * specific 3. If students cannot agree on a solution, you can: * Encourage each person to think of more ideas and variations. * Ask them to list what new information they have learned about the conflict and about each other.	
8. Put It All on Paper	1. If there was an agreement, summarize it aloud and write it down on the Mediation Resolution Form (page 252) 2. With the students, always fill out the What Disputants Learned Mediation Form (page 253). Have each student sign it. 3. Congratulate them! 4. Give each student a Mediator Evaluation Form (page 254) Ask them to fill it out and return it to the adviser. They do not have to put their names on the form.	
9. Do the Office Work	1. File the agreement in the proper place. 2. Fill out a How Did the Mediation Go? form (page 255). 3. Talk with your group adviser about the mediation (positive and negative points of your performance).	
10. Give Yourself a Hug.	1. Congratulate yourselves on doing a great job in the mediation! 2. If you feel tense, you can do a stress-relieving activity.	

Part Two - Student Mediation / **TEN SESSIONS** |223

STUDENT MEDIATION - SESSION FOUR

OBJECTIVES

On completing this session, students will be able to:

1. Explain the rules of mediation.
2. Explain the difference between cooperation and competition.
3. Describe the usefulness of cooperation during mediation sessions.
4. Describe reflective listening.
5. Define language laundering.
6. Reflect feelings and body language.
7. Describe how to role play in a structured manner.

MATERIALS

Student Mediation Guide (page 222)
"The Mirror" activity sheet (page 98)
Observation Sheet, and the "Rules of the Game" and "Mediation Role Plays" activity sheets (for all participants) "Apples" activity sheet (for half the class}
"Oranges" activity sheet (for half the class)
four copies of "The Push" activity sheet
sturdy book
two small objects (such as two small balls)
scissors

SESSION

I. WELCOME/ ICEBREAKER

Welcome students and have them sit in a large circle. Facilitate an icebreaker from Appendix II, then have students return to the circle.

II. REVIEW PAST SESSION

Have student volunteers:

    a. Explain the five essential characteristics of a good mediator.
    b. Explain how being observant of body language helps a mediator.
    c. Demonstrate how to prepare a mediation area.

III. ACTIVITIES

Step 1: Explain the rules

Have students get out their Student Mediation Guides. Tell them that after preparing the area and welcoming the disputants, the mediators explain the rules of mediation. Ask for a volunteer to read the description of step 3 (Explaining the Rules).

Hand out the "Rules of the Game" activity sheet and have students complete it. Once they have finished, divide students into pairs and have them compare answers.

Have students act out the roles of the mediator, Laura, and Florin; the mediator should concentrate on how to respond when someone interrupts. Open a class discussion about mediator's answers.

Step 2: The importance of cooperation

Hand out the "Apples" activity sheet to half the class and the "Oranges" activity sheet to the other half. Tell students to note which fruit is drawn on their sheets. Students carefully cut out the four shapes on their papers.

Instruct students to divide into pairs: Those with oranges must pair up with those with apples. Draw a circle on the chalkboard. Announce that the students have 5 minutes to create a circle.

NOTE: Initially, students may assume that this activity is competitive. However, to solve this puzzle, each pair must share shapes. Once 5 minutes have passed, tell the class to stop working. Instruct those who created a circle to raise their hands. Ask them how they were able to create the circle. (Answer: They had to work with their partners and share pieces.) Ask the class what cooperation is. (Answer: Cooperation is working together to complete a goal.) Ask the class if the two students in a pair did not cooperate, could they have completed their circles? (No.) Could either one have completed the circle? (No.) Why not?

Have the class sit in a large circle again. Explain that cooperation is when people work together to complete a goal. With cooperation, everyone can win. How did everyone feel after finishing this game?

Ask the students to share times when cooperation is important. Offer the students the following example: When students compete with one another, one student wins and the other loses. With cooperation, everyone can win. For instance, suppose two students are studying for an exam. If they compete with each other, they may only get average marks on the exam. However, if they cooperate and study together, they may both get excellent marks

Ask: In mediation, why do we want the people in conflict to cooperate? Explain to the students that instead of competing with one another, the disputants work together to try and solve their problem. They become a team, wasting no time or energy blaming or insulting each other. Together, they have a great amount of creative energy. They also feel jointly and equally responsible for trying to solve the conflict.

Step 3: Cooperating in Conflict

Ask for volunteers to summarize what they have learned about cooperation. Explain that with competition, when one person wins, another person loses. With cooperation, both people can win.

In many conflicts students have positions from which they will not budge. They think that people in conflict must compete: If they are right, then the other person must be wrong; if they win the argument, then the other person must lose. But if students cooperate with each other, they can work together and try to resolve their conflicts. And by cooperating, both students can win the conflict. Even if no solution is found, by cooperating, their relationship grows, and they learn about each other.

What if disputants don't cooperate?

Explain that after mediators describe the rules, they ask each disputant if he/she agrees to them. Ask the students: What should the mediators do if a disputant does not agree to the rules? (Answer: Mediation cannot take place. Mediation is a cooperative effort.)

Step 4: Listening to the Conflict

Facilitate the lesson "The Mirror," located on page 98.

Explain to the students that reflective statements are one of the most important parts of mediation. After a disputant tells what happened, the mediator reflects what he/she has said.

Also, explain that in reflective statements it is important to neutralize any harsh language. This is called language laundering. For example, the statement "Cynthia is always gossiping about me and lying" could be restated "You feel that Cynthia talks about you and may not always tell the truth."

Optional: Divide students into groups of four. Have them role play a mediation session, practicing reflective listening that is laundered.

Step 5: Mediation Role Play of Steps 1-4

Have the group get back into a circle. Hand out the "Mediation Role Plays" activity sheets to everyone. Four volunteers come to the center of the circle. Give each volunteer a copy of "The Push" activity sheet. Tell two of the students that they are mediators; the other two are disputants. The mediators prepare the area in the center of the circle for a mediation session. The four volunteers role play "The Push." The group should use the "Mediation Role Plays" activity sheet to guide them through the process of role playing. Inform the class that this role play is an example of steps 1–4 of student mediation (excluding each disputants' description of what the other disputant said).

NOTE: Before students observe the role play, you can give them a copy of the Observation Sheet to help them note how mediators use body language. After the role play, stress the importance of reflective statements. Ask the class for an example of a reflective statement within the role play. Also, ask the class what it thought about each volunteer's body language.

IV. REVIEW

V. CLOSING

Compliment the students on something positive they accomplished during the session. Tell them you will see them at the next session.

ACTIVITY SHEET
RULES OF THE GAME

1. After you welcome the disputants, you need to explain the rules of mediation to them. What is the purpose of having rules in mediation?

2. When someone calls someone else names, how does the other person feel?

3. Imagine that you are mediating a fight between two students, Laura and Florin. Laura is trying to tell you her side of the story, but Florin keeps interrupting. You have already explained that interrupting is against the rules. Fill in the mediator's lines by writing what you could say to Florin after he interrupts.
Laura: Well, I was sitting in the park yesterday. It was quiet and I was doing my homework. I was concentrating very hard and…
Florin: THAT'S NOT TRUE! You weren't doing your homework. You were. . .

Mediator: _____

Laura: So, anyway, I was at the park doing my mathematics homework. Florin appears out of nowhere, grabs my homework, and runs off with it. I couldn't believe he would do that!

Florin: I ASKED YOU FOR IT!

Mediator: _____

Laura: You didn't ask me for my homework, Florin! You just took it and ran off. It's your fault that I was tired in school today. I stayed up so late last night working on the homework that I had already done. But the problem is that. . .

Florin: You had hardly completed any of your homework!

Mediator: _____

4. Why is it important that no one blames anyone else in mediation?

5. Circle one sentence in both Laura and Florin's arguments in which someone blames someone else.

2004 © Open Society Institute

The Publisher grants permission for the reproduction of this worksheet for non-profit educational purposes only.
Activity sheets may be downloaded from www.idebate.org/conflictandcommunication.htm

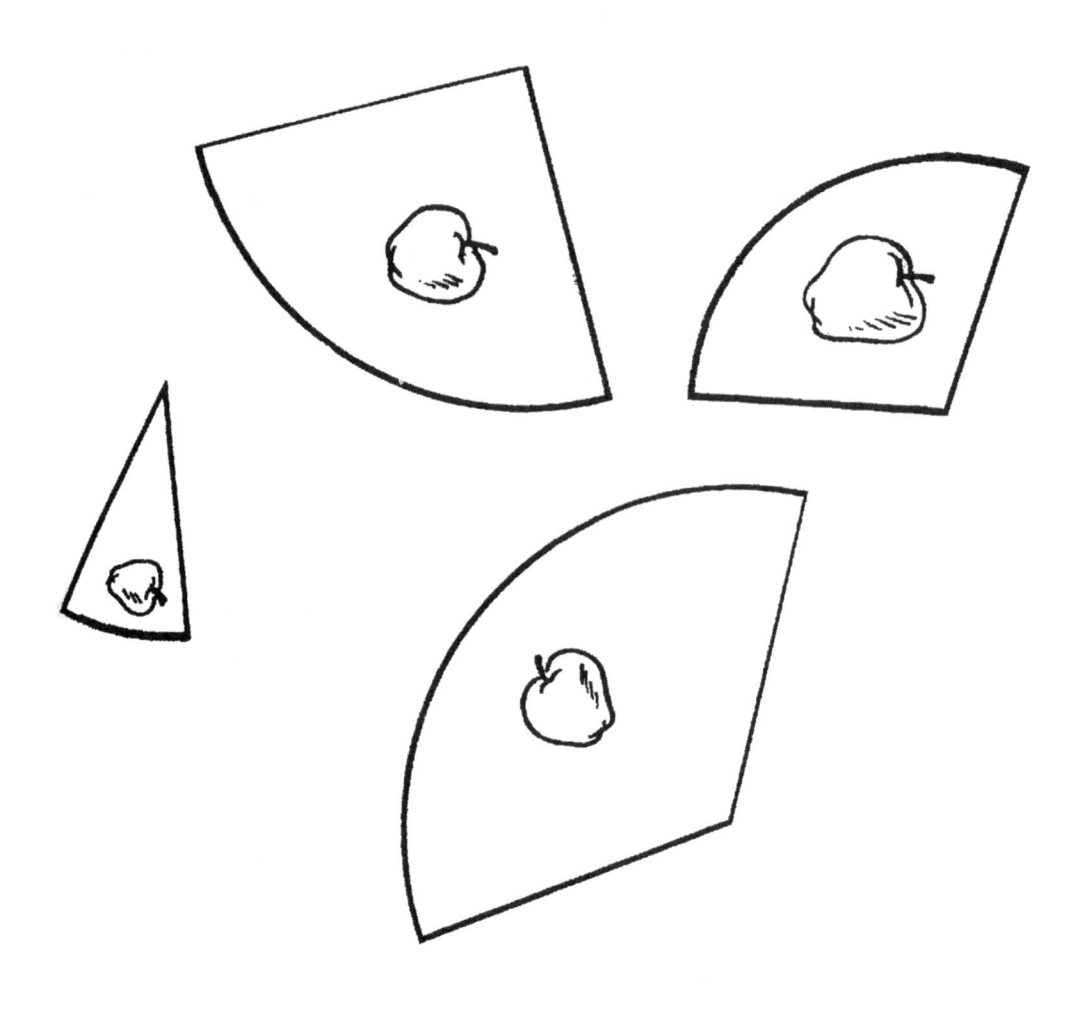

ACTIVITY SHEET
APPLES

228| Conflict and Communication

ACTIVITY SHEET
ORANGES

2004 © Open Society Institute

The Publisher grants permission for the reproduction of this worksheet for non-profit educational purposes only.
Activity sheets may be downloaded from www.idebate.org/conflictandcommunication.htm

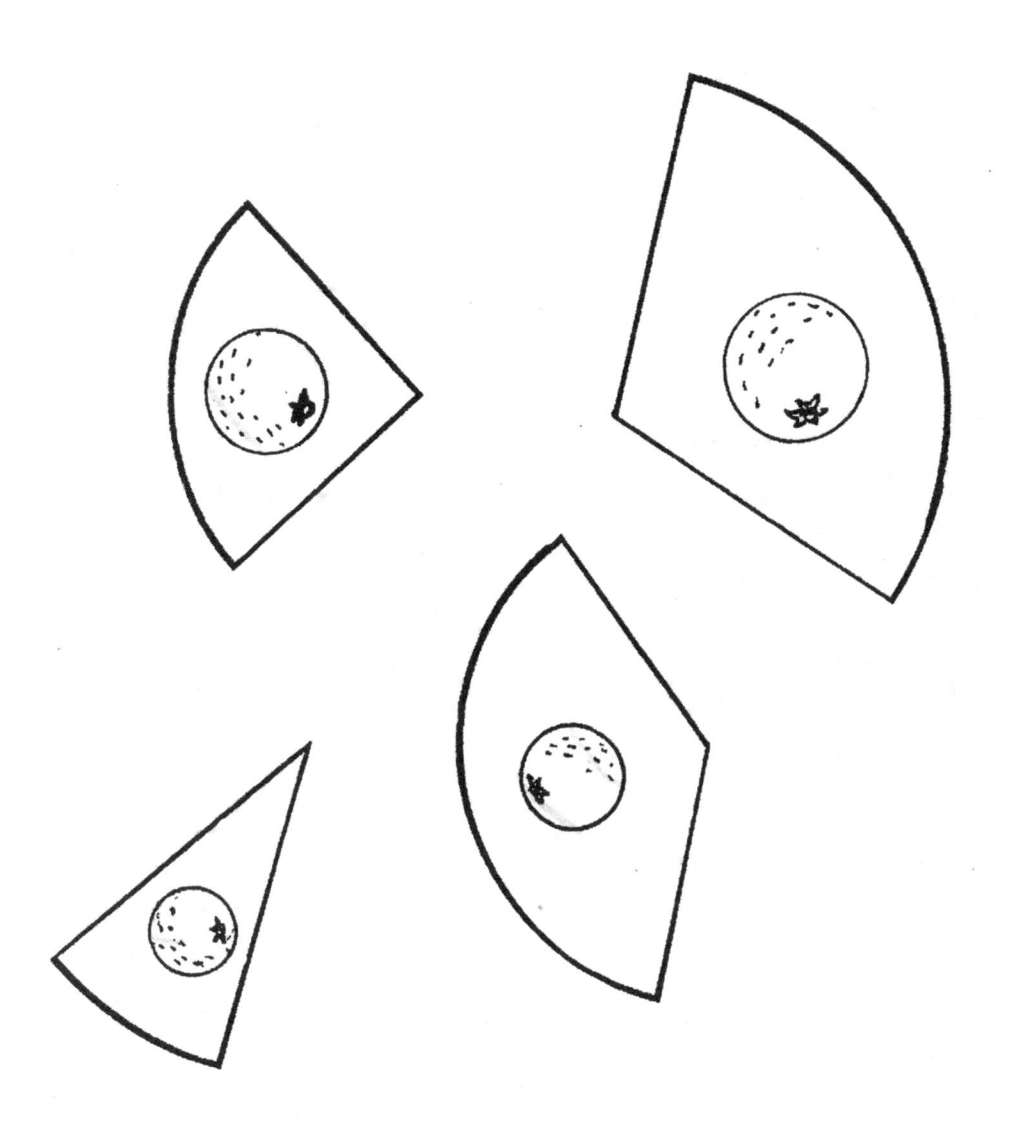

ACTIVITY SHEET
THE PUSH

The disputants walk to the center of the circle.

Mediator 1: Hello and welcome to this mediation session. Please sit down.

Anthony: Okay.

Zina: Thanks

Mediator 2: Welcome. Let's introduce ourselves. My name is Jerry.

Mediator 1: I'm Samantha.

Anthony: Hi. I'm Anthony.

Zina: Zina.

Mediator 1: Now, before we begin, I would like to explain a few things. Mediation will give both of you the opportunity to work together and understand more about each other. Through this process, you can try to find a solution that improves your situation. Mediation can make it possible for both of you to win.

Mediator 2: Before we start, we want to tell you about a few rules that will be followed during the mediation. Two rules that we, as mediators, will follow are:

* We don't take sides or judge either of you.

* Everything said here is confidential.

Now there are ground rules we would like you to agree to:

* No name-calling, insults, or blaming

* No interrupting

* Be honest

* Work hard to solve the problem

* Everything said here is confidential

Anthony, do you agree to follow the rules?

Anthony: Yes.

Mediator 2: Do you agree to follow the rules, Zina?

Zina: Well...yes.

Mediator 1: Good. Then let's begin. Zina, can you tell us what happened and how you feel?

2004 © Open Society Institute

The Publisher grants permission for the reproduction of this worksheet for non-profit educational purposes only.
Activity sheets may be downloaded from www.idebate.org/conflictandcommunication.htm

Zina: Sure. This morning I was walking to class. I was in the hallway, and I was in a hurry. There weren't many kids in the hallway. I thought I was going to be late for class. I had a lot of books in my hands. So I'm running down the hallway now. Then Anthony bumps into me! And I could tell he did it on purpose!

Anthony: THAT'S NOT TRUE!

Mediator 2 (turning to look at Anthony): Remember that we all agreed not to interrupt.

Anthony: Sorry.

Mediator 2: Okay. Continue telling us your story, Zina.

Zina: Well, after Anthony bumped into me, all my books fell on the floor. I was so late for class then because I had to pick them all up. I was so mad.

Mediator 1: So you were in a hurry for class. Anthony bumped into you and your books fell. You then became mad at Anthony. Do you have anything to add?

Zina: No.

Mediator 1: Then Anthony, tell us what happened and how you feel.

Anthony (acting very angry): This is all so stupid. I'm innocent. This is all Zina's fault.

Mediator 1: Please, no blaming. Let's concentrate on the problem.

Anthony: I was running to class. My mother forgot to wake me up on time. So I was late. Just like Zina. And I was running to class so I wouldn't get in trouble. I've been late two other times, and the teacher would have been mad at me if I was late again. I accidentally bumped into Zina. I didn't do it on purpose. I'm so frustrated that she thinks that I did it on purpose.

Mediator 2: So you were in a hurry to get to class. You accidentally bumped into Zina. You are frustrated that she thinks that you did it on purpose. Is there anything else you would like to say?

Anthony: Well...Zina gets me so mad. She thinks that I don't like her. I don't know why she thinks that way. Truthfully, she's normally a nice person and I like her. But not now.

Mediator 2: So you sometimes get mad. You think that Zina doesn't think you like her. But you normally do like her. Do you have anything else to add?

Anthony: No. That's all.

ACTIVITY SHEET
MEDIATION ROLE PLAYS

This activity sheet will guide you through the steps of role plays.

1. Choose the roles.
Decide which two students will pretend to be disputants and which two students will mediate.

2. Select a problem to role play.
The mediators should not know what the problem is until the role play begins.

3. Mediators explain the scene.
Mediators decide where they will pretend that the mediation takes place. In a school room? On the playground? Or where else?

Mediators explain how the available props are being used. Is the school chair really a sofa? Is the ceiling really the sky?

4. Do the role play!
The disputants and mediators role play.

5. The rest of the students observe the role play.
During the role play, the other students observe. Things for students to think about include:
   * What are the mediators doing that is very good?
   * What things can the mediators do to improve the mediation?
   * What is each disputant's argument?
   * What is each disputant's underlying interest?
   * In what ways can the argument be resolved?

6. Discuss the role play after it has ended.

Ask each disputant:
- * In what ways did the role play go well?
- * What was difficult about this role play?
- * How did the mediators help you resolve the conflict?
- * What else could the mediators have done or said to help you resolve the conflict?

Ask each mediator:
- * How did you feel about this role play?
- * What was most difficult about the role play?
- * What was easiest?
- * What was the argument about?
- * What do you think each disputant's underlying interests were?

Ask the students who observed:
- * Discuss answers to the questions in step 5.

Ask the teacher:
- * What made this role play successful?
- * In what ways can the mediators mediate even more effectively?

OBSERVATION SHEET
ANSWER THE QUESTIONS ABOUT EACH MEDIATOR

	Mediator 1	Mediator 2
1. Describe how the mediator showed he/she was listening.		
2. Describe what gestures and facial expressions the mediator used.		
3. Describe how the mediator looked at the person.		
4. What parts of the mediation process did the mediator follow correctly?		

STUDENT MEDIATION - SESSION FIVE

OBJECTIVES

Upon completing this session, students will be able to:

1. Recognize "feeling words" and determine the related emotions.
2. Use open and closed questions.
3. Explain the uses of open and closed questions during conflict situations.
4. Explain the reasons for avoiding questions that begin with why.

MATERIALS

List of Common Student Conflicts
"Mediation Role Plays" activity sheet (page 232)
Observation Sheet (page 234)
Student Mediation Guide

SESSION

I. WELCOME/ ICEBREAKER

Have the group sit in one big circle. Facilitate an icebreaker from Appendix II. Following the icebreaker, ask the students to return to the circle.

II. REVIEW PAST SESSION

Review the past sessions (you can use the Magic Ball of Wisdom to liven the review session):

Ask students to explain:

    a. The five essential characteristics of a good mediator.
    b. The difference between cooperation and competition.
    c. Why cooperation is more effective during mediation sessions.
    c. The ground rules for mediation.
    e. What reflective listening is. When do mediators use reflective statements? What is an example of a reflective statement?

III. ACTIVITY

Step 1: Important Communication Skills for Mediation

Facilitate the lesson "The Feeling List," located on page 101. Tell the students that when mediators listen to disputants, they pay attention to all the "feeling words" mentioned. So when mediators summarize each disputant's side of the conflict, they make sure to mention the "feeling words."

Have the students divide into groups of six for role plays. Two people in the group are mediators, two are disputants, and two watch the role play as observers. The mediators can use the Student Mediation Guide for help if they want it. The group role plays according to the steps on the "Mediation Role Plays" activity sheet. The observers can give constructive, positive feedback to the mediators using the Observation Sheet. After each role play, have students switch roles until everyone in the group has had a chance to be a mediator.

Step 2: Open vs. Closed Questions

Facilitate "The Guessing Game," located on page 94. Ask students:

a. When are open questions useful during mediation? (Answer: Open questions are useful in helping students open up and verbalize their feelings and problems. When students find it difficult to talk, open questions can be useful.)

b. When are closed questions useful during mediation? (Answer: Closed questions are useful in stopping students from speaking too much and dominating the discussion during the mediation session.)

c. If disputants do not stop talking, should the mediator ask them open or closed questions? Why?

Step 3: Avoid "Why" Questions

Facilitate "Why Ask Why?" located on page 96. Ask students: If you ask disputants questions that begin with why, how do you think they will feel when they respond?

Step 4: Role Play

Tell the class that it is going to role play again, using the same process explained in step 1 of this session. Before role plays, ask the students what things they should remember when they role play.

They should remember things such as:

* use good body language.
* don't ask questions beginning with why.
* ask open questions when appropriate.
* use reflective statements after each disputant tells his/her side of the story.
* reflect "feeling words."

As a reminder, you may want to write this list on the chalkboard.

IV. REVIEW

V. CLOSING

Compliment the students on something positive they accomplished during the session. Tell them you will see them at the next session.

List of Common Student Conflicts

Role play ideas:

- A student neglects or doesn't complete homework assignments.
- A student does not complete chores.
- A student is scared to tell his/her family about poor school grades.
- A student tries hard in school and still does poorly.
- One student forgets to do something for another student.
- A student has conflicts with parents, who drink, quarrel, or are involved in a divorce.
- A student is resentful about others that have more money or prettier things.
- A student has a fear of teachers.
- Students lie or gossip about one another.
- Students have no money and encounter conflicts.
- Students fight with sisters, brothers, friends, mothers, fathers, or grandparents.
- A child/parent fight continues even though the parents sometimes "finish" the conflict, refusing to deal with it anymore.
- A student finds it hard to study at home because of distractions.
- A student cheats and gets caught.
- Two friends are attracted to the same boy or girl.
- A student continually teases another student.
- A student's father says that another student is not good enough to be his child's friend.
- A teacher says a student cheated; the student claims he/she did not.
- A friend borrows something and returns it broken or dirty.

The best role play ideas are those you think of on your own!

2004 © Open Society Institute

The Publisher grants permission for the reproduction of this worksheet for non-profit educational purposes only.
Activity sheets may be downloaded from www.idebate.org/conflictandcommunication.htm

STUDENT MEDIATION - SESSION SIX

OBJECTIVES

Upon completing this session, students will be able to:

1. Identify shared interests of disputants.
2. Recognize similarities between disputants.

MATERIALS

"Alcohol" and "Mediation Role Plays" (page 232) activity sheets
List of Common Student Conflicts (page 237)
Magic Ball of Wisdom

SESSION

I. WELCOME/ ICEBREAKER

After all students have arrived, welcome everyone back to the student mediation training session. Facilitate an icebreaker from Appendix II. After the icebreaker, ask students to form a large circle.

II. REVIEW PAST SESSION

Get out the Magic Ball of Wisdom and throw it to students as you review the past sessions.
(*NOTE: Make sure that you are familiar with answers to these questions.*)

   a. Suppose two students are fighting. They walk up to a mediator and ask the mediator for advice on how to solve their problem. Should the mediator give them advice? Why not?

   b. Have two volunteers demonstrate reflective listening. One student pretends to talk about a conflict. The other student acts as the mediator and reflects what the student talks about. Make sure the mediator reflects feeling words.

   c. What are some of the ground rules of mediation?

   d. Why are rules so important in mediation?

   e. How can you show disputants that you understand how they are feeling?

   f. What are some examples of open questions?

III. ACTIVITY

Step 1: Discovering Shared Interests

Tell the students that today they will be learning step 5 of the mediation process: discovering shared interests.

Facilitate the lesson "The Milk Bottle," located on page 151.

Step 2: The Newspaper Problem

Divide the class into pairs. The pairs will have 5 minutes to solve the following problem: How can both students in a group stand on an open newspaper in such a way that even if they try, they cannot touch each other? After 5 minutes, ask if any group has figured out the solution.

Explain that in most conflicts, it might seem that there is no solution that satisfies both people. For example, in the story about the milk bottle, it seemed that there was no solution as to who should get the milk bottle. But if you think creatively, most conflicts can be solved. The solution to the newspaper problem is a creative one: Place the newspaper at the bottom of a door and close the door; have one student stand on the newspaper in the room, the other standing on the newspaper on the other side of the door.

Divide students into groups of three and have them think of a conflict that initially appears unsolvable, but that has a creative solution.

Everyone then gathers in a large circle, and each group shares its creative conflict solutions.

Step 3: There Are Similarities (Shared Interests) in Any Conflict!

This game is called "Objects." First, ask the students to think of any object and picture it in their minds. They shouldn't tell anyone what their object is. Second, have a volunteer say what his/her object is. Third, each person in the circle then has to say how their object is similar to the object named. Tell students that they may have to be creative! For example, suppose you are thinking of a horse and the object named is a boat. You could say that your object is like the named object because both can be used for transportation. Finally, have other students name their objects. Students are usually surprised that their different objects had similarities. Repeat the activity.

Explain to the group that sometimes people in arguments think their views are so different that the argument can never be solved. Ask the group:

    a. What do the last activities show us about that?
    b. Why is it important for disputants to find similarities between them?

Step 4: Questions to Encourage Discovery of Shared Interests

Have the class form a circle. Tell students that in almost every argument people have some shared interests. If they can discover these shared interests, it is more likely that the conflict will be resolved. There are some specific questions that can help people discover their shared interests. Ask for a volunteer to read the questions in step 5 on the Student Mediation Guide.

Step 5: Role Play

Have the students take out the "Mediation Role Plays" activity sheet.

Have four volunteers come to the center of the circle. Give each of the four volunteers a copy of the "Alcohol" activity sheet. Tell two of the students that they are mediators; the other two are disputants. The mediators prepare the area in the center of the circle for a mediation session. The four volunteers role play Alcohol. (You may want to give the volunteers time to privately practice the role play before presenting it to the class.) The volunteers should use the "Mediation Role Plays" activity sheet to guide them through the process of role playing. Inform the class that this role play is an example of steps 1-5 of student mediation. Remind the mediators that they should use good body language.

After the role play, ask the group:

    a. What was Harry and Maria's argument about?
    b. What was Harry's position?
    c. What was Maria's position?
    d. What were Harry and Maria's shared interests?
    e. How did the mediators discover Maria and Harry's shared interests?

Divide students into groups of six and have them create their own role plays. Two people in each group are mediators, two are disputants, and two watch the role play as observers. The mediators may use the Student Mediation Guide for help. The groups role play according to the steps on the "Mediation Role Plays" activity sheet. After each role play, have everyone switch roles until everyone in the group has had a chance to be a mediator.

Students should practice the first five steps listed on the Student Mediation Guide.

Students can think of their own conflicts to role play; you could suggest a conflict to them, or you or they could refer to the List of Common Student Conflicts (page 237).

IV. REVIEW

V. CLOSING

Compliment the students on something positive they accomplished during the session. Tell them you will see them at the next session.

ACTIVITY SHEET
ALCOHOL

The disputants walk to the center of the circle.

Mediator 1: Hello and welcome to this mediation session. Please sit down.

Harry: Okay.

Maria: Thanks.

Mediator 2: Welcome to mediation. My name is Theodore. What are your names?

Maria: I'm Maria.

Harry: I'm Harry.

Mediator 1: I'm Thomas. Now, before we begin, I would like to explain a few things. Mediation will give both of you the opportunity to work together and understand more about each other. Through this process, you can try to find a solution that improves your situation. Mediation can make it possible for both of you to win.

Mediator 2: Before we start, we want to tell you about a few rules that will be followed during the mediation. Two rules that we, as mediators, will follow are:

   * We don't take sides or judge either of you.
   * Everything said here is confidential.

Now there are ground rules we would like you to agree to:

   * No name-calling, insults, or blaming
   * No interrupting
   * Be honest
   * Work hard to solve the problem
   * Everything said here is confidential

Maria, do you agree to follow the rules?

Maria: Yes.

Mediator 2: Do you agree to follow the rules, Harry?

Harry: But Maria's being a jerk.

Mediator 1: Harry, to be involved in this mediation, you have to agree to follow the rules. Now do you agree?

Harry: Fine, I agree.

Mediator 1: Good. Then let's begin. Maria, can you tell us what happened and how you feel?

Maria: Are you sure that no one will find out about what I say?

Mediator 1: Everything in the mediation session is confidential.

Maria: Okay. I don't really know where to start. This is hard to say. Not many people know about it, but my mother is an alcoholic. Ever since I was young, my mother has been an alcoholic. She just can't stop drinking. And it hurts me to see her in such a bad condition.

Mediator 1: You feel hurt seeing your mother drinking all the time.

Maria: Yes. And I have all of these different feelings. I'm so sad sometimes. My mother drinks and then yells at me all the time. It's so hard to live in my house. I find it helpful talking to someone about my mother. So I talked a lot with Harry. He is my best friend. Well... he was my best friend until now. Yesterday I found out that he told his mother about my mother. I can't believe he would do that! I told him never to tell anyone about my mother's alcoholism. I don't want the whole school to know about her problem. Everyone will think I'm strange then. I'm so mad at Harry!

Mediator 1: You feel sad when your mother yells at you. So you used to talk about your problems with Harry. You told Harry never to tell anyone about your mother's problem. But you are mad at Harry because he told his mother. Is there anything you would like to add?

Maria: I am just so upset that my best friend would do that to me. I don't think I should ever talk to Harry again!

Mediator 1: You are upset that Harry told his mother about your mother's problem. Anything else?

Maria: No. That's it.

Mediator 2: Then, Harry, please tell us what happened and how you feel.

Harry: Like Maria says, she tells me everything about her mother. Her mother really has a bad drinking habit. Recently, Maria's mother started yelling at her more and more. I told my mother about Maria's mother. Yes I did. Because I feel so sad for Maria. I feel so helpless, as though there is nothing I can do except listen to Maria's pain. I had to do something! So I told my mother.

Maria: I can't believe you did that!

Mediator 1: We agreed not to interrupt each other.

Maria: Sorry.

Mediator 2: Harry, Maria tells you everything about her mother's alcoholism. You felt sad and helpless, and you felt the need to tell your mother about Maria's mother. Do you have anything else to add?

Harry: No. That's it. Except that I hoped my mother would have some idea about how I could help Maria.

Mediator 1: In this part of mediation, we want you to talk with each other. Harry, can you please describe to Maria what she said?

Harry: Sure. She is mad at me. She talked about how I told my mother about her mother. She doesn't want all the people at school to find out about her mother's problem. That's it.

Mediator 1: Maria, is that an accurate description of what you said?

Maria: Yes.

Mediator 2: So Maria, can you please describe to Harry what he said?

Maria: Harry talked about how he wants to help my mother. So he told his mother about my mother's problem.

Mediator 2: Harry, is that an accurate description of what you said?

Harry: Not exactly. I do care about Maria's mother. But the real reason I told my mother is because I care about Maria. I feel sad for her. I want to be a good friend. I want to help her. That's it.

Mediator 1: Maria, what are some things you and Harry agree on?

Maria: Nothing. I can't trust him anymore.

Mediator 2: Harry, what are some things you and Maria agree on?

Harry: Difficult question. I think that we both care about Maria's mother. I want Maria not to feel so sad, and I think Maria doesn't want to feel sad, either.

Mediator 1: It seems as though you and Maria agree about a couple of things. You both care about Maria's mother and you don't want Maria to be sad.

Maria: And we both want to be friends with each other.

Mediator 2: So it seems as though you both also agree that you want to be friends. Is that right?

Harry: Yes.

Maria: Yes.

STUDENT MEDIATION - SESSION SEVEN

OBJECTIVES

Upon completing this session, students will be able to:

1. Describe the guidelines of brainstorming.
2. Describe how to help disputants evaluate possible solutions and choose the most satisfying one.
3. Describe how to help disputants think of solutions to conflicts.

MATERIALS

Ideas Sheet
"The Prison Cell" and "Mediation Role Plays" (page 232) activity sheets
Student Mediation Guide (page 222)
watch that displays minutes and seconds
Magic Ball of Wisdom

SESSION

I. WELCOME/ ICEBREAKER

After students have arrived, welcome everyone back to the student mediation training session. Facilitate an icebreaker from Appendix II. Following the icebreaker, ask the students to form a large circle.

II. REVIEW PAST SESSION

Get out the Magic Ball of Wisdom and throw it to students as you review the past sessions:

a. Why is it important for mediators to be nonjudgmental?
b. What are some of the ground rules of mediation?
c. When are closed questions helpful?
d. What are some questions you can ask disputants to discover shared interests?
e. Have two volunteers demonstrate reflective listening. One student pretends to talk about a conflict. The other student acts as a mediator and reflects what the student talks about (especially the "feeling words").
f. Review the first five steps of mediation in the Student Mediation Guide. Tell the students that they will be exploring steps 6 and 7: how to help disputants think of and evaluate solutions to their problems.

III. ACTIVITY

Step 1:

Explain that after helping disputants discover shared interests, the mediators ask them to think of possible solutions to their problem. The more solutions disputants think of the better. The students may recognize this process as brainstorming. There are four guidelines that help the disputants generate as many different solutions as possible (tell students that the four guidelines are listed in the Student Mediation Guide). Briefly explain them to the students:

   a. *The disputants should say every idea they can imagine.* Some ideas may sound impossible or silly, but that's okay. Sometimes the most outrageous ideas cause others to think of workable solutions to problems.
   b. *The disputants should think of as many ideas as possible.* The more ideas disputants can think of, the greater the chance a good solution will be found.
   c. *During the brainstorming process, don't judge any idea as good or bad.* Evaluating the different possible solutions comes later in the mediation session.
   d. *Don't talk about the ideas yet. Just say them.* The mediators should be careful that the disputants do not talk about the ideas while brainstorming. Have disputants just say as many different possible solutions that they can think of. Tell the students that in a real mediation, one of the mediators should write down all the ideas on the Ideas Sheet.

Step 2: The Prison Cell

Hand out the Ideas Sheet and The Prison Cell activities sheet. Students divide into groups of four to six. Students individually read The Prison Cell. For 10 minutes, each group thinks of as many creative solutions as possible, writing the solutions on the Ideas Sheet. The groups should follow the brainstorming guidelines discussed earlier and, for the time being, ignore the positive and negative consequences.

Evaluate the positive and negative consequences: Explain to students that after the disputants think of as many solutions as possible, mediators ask the disputants to think about the positive and negative consequences of each idea.

Have each group evaluate the solutions it thought of by analyzing each one's positive and negative consequences. To clarify, offer the following example: A possible solution is that John could yell loudly all day and all night. The king wouldn't be able to sleep, so a positive consequence might be that John is freed. With John gone from the castle, the king could sleep. But this solution has negative consequences. John might develop a sore throat. Or the king might become angry with John and order him moved to a dirtier prison cell.

After the groups list their solutions and consequences, they decide which solution would be most helpful. Once each group has completed the activity, it shares its possible solutions, consequences, and the solution chosen for John.

Step 3: Role Plays

Ask the students to return to the circle and get out their "Mediation Role Plays" activity sheets. Four volunteers come to the center of the circle. Tell two of the students that they are mediators; the other two are disputants. The mediators prepare the area in the center of the circle for a mediation session. (They can use the Student Mediation Guide if needed.) Meanwhile, tell the two disputants that they are best friends. One of them borrowed the other's radio. When the radio was returned, it was broken. Now they are in a fight and have decided to go to student mediation to help them resolve their conflict.

Before beginning the role play, tell the students that today's role play, called Tag Role Play, is slightly different than normal role plays. Two mediators and two disputants role play in the center of the circle, with the entire group surrounding them to observe. At any time, students observing the role play can tap either a mediator or disputant on the shoulder, taking over that student's role. For example, if a student observer has a good question to ask the disputants, he/she stands up and taps a mediator on the shoulder. The mediator moves to the outer circle and becomes an observer. The new mediator or disputant continues the role play as if there had been no interruption. Make it clear that by the end of the role play everyone should have been involved at some point.

The students should use the "Mediation Role Plays" activity sheet to guide them through the process of role plays. Inform the class that this role play is an example of steps 1–7 of student mediation. Remind the role playing mediators that they should use positive body language and be aware of the body language of the disputants.

Step 4: Icebreaker

Role plays are often very tiring, but they are a very important and effective way for students to practice the mediation skills. The following is an icebreaker to rejuvenate the students:

> Have the entire group stand in a large circle and hold hands. Designate one person in the circle as president. The president squeezes the hand of the person to his/her right. That person squeezes the hand of the person to his/her right, and so on, until the squeeze has gone around the circle, reaching the president's left hand. Tell the group that you are now going to time how quickly everyone can get the squeeze around the circle. When you say, "Go," the president starts the squeeze around the circle. When the president feels the squeeze arrive at his/her left hand, he/she screams, "Stop!" Inform the group how long it took for the squeeze to go around the circle. Repeat the activity, but first announce that you think they can beat that time by at least 4 seconds!

After the icebreaker, ask the class whether the activity was competitive or cooperative. Why?

Step 5: More role plays

Have the students divide up into groups of six for role plays. Two people in the group are mediators, two are disputants, and two watch the role play as observers. The mediators can use the Student Mediation Guide for help if they need it. The groups role play according to the steps on the "Mediation Role Plays" activity sheet. After each role play, have everyone switch roles until everyone in the group has had a chance to be a mediator.

Students can think of their own conflicts to role play, you could suggest a conflict to them, or you or they could refer to the List of Common Student Conflicts (page 237).

IV. REVIEW

V. CLOSING

Compliment the students about something positive they accomplished during the session. Tell them you will see them at the next session.

ACTIVITY SHEET
THE PRISON CELL

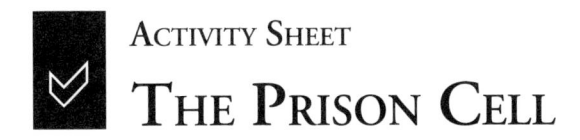

John is in a small prison cell. The walls surrounding him are very tall. There is no ceiling, so he can see the blue sky above him. The room beside his cell is the king's bedroom. John wants to escape somehow, but the only things he has in the cell are two bottles, tape, and twenty pencils. How can he escape?

When thinking of solutions, remember to think of as many as possible. Don't criticize anybody's suggestions. Just say them. Write all ideas on the Ideas Sheet.

IDEAS SHEET

Possible Solutions	Beneficial Consequences	Harmful Consequences

2004 © Open Society Institute

The Publisher grants permission for the reproduction of this worksheet for non-profit educational purposes only.
Activity sheets may be downloaded from www.idebate.org/conflictandcommunication.htm

STUDENT MEDIATION - SESSION EIGHT

OBJECTIVES

Upon completing this session, students will be able to:

1. Summarize agreements of disputants involved in mediation sessions.
2. Answer questions on How Did The Mediation Go?
3. Describe their support systems (e.g., the responsibilities of their adviser).

MATERIALS

Mediation Resolution Form
What Disputants Learned Mediation Form
Mediator Evaluation Form
Student Mediation Guide (page 222)
How Did The Mediation Go? (page 255) and Mediation Role Plays (page 232) activities sheets
List of Common Student Conflicts (page 237)
spherical object (orange, ball, apple)
Magic Ball of Wisdom

SESSION

I. WELCOME/ ICEBREAKER

Ask everyone to sit in a large circle. Welcome everyone back to the mediation training sessions. Tell them that this session will begin with a fun activity! First, everyone must stand up. Take a spherical object and tell everybody that the aim of this game is to pass the object around the circle. Hand the object to the student beside you, and have the object passed around until it is handed back to you. Congratulate everyone. Now tell them that the object is going to be passed around again, but this time they may not use their hands. Put the object on your neck, holding it there by pressure from your chin. Pass it from neck to neck until the object gets back to you.

II. REVIEW PAST SESSION

Get out the Magic Ball of Wisdom and throw it to students as you review the past sessions:

   a. What are the guidelines for thinking of possible solutions to problems? (The guidelines are listed on the Student Mediation Guide.) Why are these guidelines important in the mediation process?
   b. What is empathy? How can mediators show empathy?
   c. Have two volunteers demonstrate reflective listening. One student pretends to talk about a conflict. The other student acts as a mediator and reflects what the student talks about.

    d. What are some of the ground rules of mediation? (These rules are listed on the Student Mediation Guide.)
    e. Suppose a student is mad at his sister. The brother and the sister come for mediation. What are some open questions you could ask to help them talk about their conflict?
    f. What are some questions you can ask the brother and sister to discover shared interests?

III. ACTIVITY

Step 1: Mediation Resolution Form

Explain that in many mediation sessions students not only learn about the conflict and each other, they also find a solution to their conflict. So, during a mediation session, if students agree on a solution, the mediators and disputants together fill out a Mediation Resolution Form. This form is confidential, and the only person who sees it (besides the mediators and disputants) is the mediation adviser.

Hand out the Mediation Resolution Form and read it with your students.

Step 2: Role Plays

Divide students into groups of six and have them role play. (Students can choose a role play from the List of Common Student Conflicts.) Two people in the group are mediators, two are disputants, and two watch the role play as observers. The mediators can use the Student Mediation Guide for help. After each role play, have students switch roles until everyone in the group has had a chance to be a mediator. The groups role play according to the steps on the "Mediation Role Plays" activity sheet. Stress that during each role play, the students should go through the eight steps of mediation learned. This means that students should even fill out a Mediation Resolution Form with the disputants.

Step 3: Icebreakers

Here are fun icebreakers to facilitate after the groups finish their role plays. (If all the groups finish role playing at the same time, facilitate these activities with the whole group. Otherwise, explain the activities to individual groups once they complete their role plays.)

    * A group member pretends to yawn until he/she causes someone else to truly yawn.
    * While keeping their eyes closed, the group members try to line up by order of height. The shortest person should be at the front of the line; the tallest should stand in the back.

Step 4: What Disputants Learned

Distribute the What Disputants Learned Mediation Form to each student. Read over the form with the students. Explain that it must be filled out at the end of every mediation session before the disputants leave. It tells who the disputants are and what they learned from the mediation session. The form is confidential, and the only person who sees it (besides the mediators and disputants) is the mediation adviser.

Ask students for possible answers to each of the questions on the form.

Step 5: Becoming Acquainted With the Mediation Forms

The following activity acquaints students with the mediation forms. Divide students into pairs. Each pair agrees on a common student conflict. They imagine and discuss how two disputants might resolve the conflict. Then they decide how they would fill out the Mediation Resolution Form and What Disputants Learned Mediation Form. Finally, the large group reassembles. Have groups briefly share their conflicts and how they would fill out the forms.

Step 6: Mediator Evaluation

At the conclusion of the mediation session, mediators can give disputants the Mediator Evaluation Form. If desired, disputants can fill out the form and return it to the mediation adviser (or to a designated location).

Step 7: Mediation Evaluation

Hand out How Did the Mediation Go? and read it with the students. Explain that at the end of each mediation session, after the disputants leave, mediators should fill out one of these forms and give it to the group adviser.

Step 8: Role Plays

Have the students role play again, as done in step 3 of this session. Tell them that after everyone has been mediator, they should each fill out the How Did the Mediation Go? form and hand it to you. Also, stress the importance of talking with the adviser after completing every mediation session. Mediators should openly discuss any problems they encountered, any things they are proud of, and so on.

IV. REVIEW

V. CLOSING

Compliment the students about something positive they accomplished during the session. Tell them you will see them at the next session.

MEDIATION RESOLUTION FORM

This form is to be filled out when disputants reach an agreement.

Mediators' names:_____ Date:_____

What is the conflict about?

_____
_____
_____
_____

The Agreement

The disputants have resolved their conflict. They each agree to the following:

_____ agrees to _____
(Disputant's full name)

_____
_____

_____ agrees to _____
(Disputant's full name)

_____
_____

Both students feel that their conflict has been resolved. They sign their names below, showing that they each agree to fulfill the conditions of their agreement.

Student's signature:_____ Date:_____

Student's signature:_____ Date:_____

Witnessed by:

Student Mediator's signature:_____ Date:_____

Student Mediator's signature:_____ Date:_____

2004 © Open Society Institute

The Publisher grants permission for the reproduction of this worksheet for non-profit educational purposes only.
Activity sheets may be downloaded from www.idebate.org/conflictandcommunication.htm

WHAT DISPUTANTS LEARNED MEDIATION FORM

This form is to be filled out at the end of every mediation session.

Mediators' names:_____ Date:_____

What is the conflict about?
_____
_____
_____

List what _____ learned about:
           (Disputant's full name)

1. The conflict:_____

2. The other student:_____

3. How he/she now understands the conflict differently than before the mediation session began:
_____

List what _____ learned about:
           (Disputant's full name)

1. The conflict:_____

2. The other student:_____

3. How he/she now understands the conflict differently than before the mediation session began:
_____

Both students feel that they have learned about the conflict and about each other today. They sign their names below, showing their increased understanding.

Student's signature:_____ Date:_____

Student's signature:_____ Date:_____

Witnessed by:

Student Mediator's signature:_____ Date:_____

Student Mediator's signature:_____ Date:_____

2004 © Open Society Institute

The Publisher grants permission for the reproduction of this worksheet for non-profit educational purposes only.
Activity sheets may be downloaded from www.idebate.org/conflictandcommunication.htm

Mediator Evaluation Form

This form can be filled out by students after a mediation session.

1. Describe how you feel the mediation session went.

2. Who were the mediators during your session?

3. What were some strengths of the mediators during the session?

4. What are some things that the mediators need to improve during mediation sessions?

5. You can use the space below to describe more specifically your thoughts and feelings about one or both of the mediators.

How did the Mediation Go?

This form is to be filled out after the disputants have left. Each mediator fills out a separate form.

1. In what ways did the mediation go well?

2. Some things that I can do to improve the mediation are:

3. What was difficult about this mediation?

4. Here are some questions that I had while mediating:
    A.
    B.
    C.

5. Give yourself a hug. You did a great job in the mediation!

2004 © Open Society Institute

The Publisher grants permission for the reproduction of this worksheet for non-profit educational purposes only.
Activity sheets may be downloaded from www.idebate.org/conflictandcommunication.htm

STUDENT MEDIATION - SESSION NINE

OBJECTIVES

Upon completing this session, students will be able to:

1. Identify and explain the ten steps of student mediation.
2. Explain the leadership skills of a mediator.
3. Describe methods for relieving stress.

MATERIALS

"Mediation Role Plays" activity sheet (page 232)
List of Common Student Conflicts (page 237)
Student Mediation Guide (page 222)
Magic Ball of Wisdom

SESSION

I. WELCOME/ ICEBREAKER

After all students have arrived, have everyone sit in a large circle. Welcome everyone back to the mediation training.

Tell the students that they all have the potential to become great leaders. Have everyone line up in a straight line. Designate the first person in line as the leader. Whatever he/she does, everyone else must do. Thus, the leader can walk around the room and everyone—still in line—will follow him/her. If the leader crawls under a desk, everyone crawls under the desk one by one. After a short time, the leader goes to the back of the line, and the next person in line becomes the leader. This process continues until every student has had a chance to be the leader.

Have the group sit in a large circle. Ask the students:

    a. What is a leader?
    b. How are student mediators leaders?
    c. Do you think you all can be leaders?

II. REVIEW PAST SESSION

Get out the Magic Ball of Wisdom and throw it to students as you quickly review the past sessions:

    a. When should you fill out the Mediation Resolution Form?
    b. To whom should you give the completed How Did the Mediation Go?
    c. How do students in mediation find a resolution to their problem?

d. Have two volunteers demonstrate reflective listening. One student pretends to talk about a conflict. The other student acts as the mediator and reflects what the student talks about.
e. What are some of the ground rules of mediation?
f. What are some questions you can ask disputants to discover shared interests?

III. ACTIVITY

Step 1:

Students get out the "Mediation Role Plays" activity sheet. Four volunteers come to the center of the circle. Tell two of the students that they are mediators; the other two are disputants. The mediators prepare the area in the center of the circle for a mediation session. (They can use the Student Mediation Guide to aid them in remembering all of the steps and what to say.) Meanwhile, tell the two disputants that they are brother and sister. The brother tried studying for an important math test. He had difficulty concentrating because his sister was practicing the piano for a recital. The brother and sister are now in conflict. He did poorly on his test, and she was not properly prepared for her recital. The brother and sister decided to go to mediation to work out their conflict.

Before beginning the role play, tell the students that today's role play is called Tag Role Play. (The students were introduced to this type of role play in Session Seven). A student observing the role play can tap the mediators or disputants on the shoulder. The observer then takes over that student's role. For example, if a student observer has a good question to ask the disputants, he/she stands up and taps the mediator on the shoulder. The mediator moves to the big circle and becomes an observer. The new mediator or disputant continues the role play as if there had been no interruption. By the end of the role play everyone in the group should have been involved.

NOTE: If students are shy or intimidated, you could designate specific students to substitute in the role play.

The actors should use the "Mediation Role Plays" activity sheet to guide them through the process of role playing. Inform the class that this role play is an example of steps 1–9 of student mediation. Remind mediators that while role playing they should use positive body language.

Step 2:

Inform the group that the last step of student mediation is giving yourself a hug. Have the students wrap their arms around themselves and give themselves a big hug. After mediating, they should feel very proud of themselves for helping others.

Tell the class that to show that we are all supportive of one another, we are going to have a group hug: everyone is going to hug everyone else.

One student, the leader, walks around the circle and hugs everyone. After the leader hugs the person beside him/her, that person follows the leader around the circle and hugs everyone. One by one, a train of huggers is formed: after students have been hugged by all the people hugging, they join the line of huggers.

Step 3:

Tell the students that one of the five essential characteristics of a mediator is that he/she cares. They have decided to become mediators because they care and want to help other people. But sometimes helping someone else can be stressful and difficult. Ask the students what they do when they feel stressed.

Emphasize that stress is a normal reaction during and after a mediation session. Tell students that if they feel stressed after a mediation session they can do some simple activities to reduce their stress level. Teach students some of the activities in Appendix I.

Step 4: Role Plays

Divide the students into groups of six and role play. Two people in the group are mediators, two are disputants, and two watch the role play as observers. The mediators can use the Student Mediation Guide for help if they need it. After each role play, have everyone switch roles until everyone in the group has had a chance to be a mediator. The groups role play according to the steps on the "Mediation Role Play" activity sheet. Stress that the students should go through all of the mediation steps during each role play. This means that students should help the disputants fill out a What the Disputants Learned Mediation Form, a Mediation Resolution Form, and a Mediation Evaluation Form. This also means that after each mediation role play, the mediators should do a stress-relieving activity.

Students can think of their own conflicts to role play, you can suggest a conflict to them, or they can refer to the List of Common Student Conflicts.

IV. REVIEW

V. CLOSING

Compliment the students on something positive they accomplished during the session. Tell them you will see them at the next session.

STUDENT MEDIATION - SESSION TEN

OBJECTIVES

Upon completing this session, students will be able to:

1. Identify and explain the ten steps of student mediation.
2. Create advertisements for mediation services.
3. State the time and date of weekly meetings for practicing skills and keeping in touch.

MATERIALS

List of Common Student Conflicts (page 237)
"Mediation Role Plays" activity sheet (page 232)
Student Mediation Guide (page 222)
Magic Ball of Wisdom
posters, paper, pencils
materials to create advertisements
Student Mediation Certificate filled out for each student who successfully completed the student mediation training program
Student Mediation Guide Card

SESSION

I. WELCOME/ ICEBREAKER

Welcome students to the mediation training session. Facilitate an icebreaker from Appendix II; then have students sit in a circle.

II. REVIEW PAST SESSION

Get out the Magic Ball of Wisdom. Have students toss the ball to each other. Whenever a student catches the ball, he/she says one thing learned from the mediation training.

III. ACTIVITY

Step I: Role Plays

Divide the students into groups of six and have them role play. Students can think of their own conflicts to role play, you can suggest a conflict to them, or you or they can refer to the List of Common Student Conflicts. Two people in the group are mediators, two are disputants, and two watch the role play as observers. (The mediators can use the Student Mediation Guide for help if they need it.) After each role play, have the participants switch roles until everyone in the group has had a chance to be a mediator. The groups role play according to the steps on the "Mediation Role Plays" activity sheet. Stress that the students should go through all of the mediation steps during each role play. This means that students should even have the disputants fill out a Mediation Resolution Form. This also means that the mediators should do a stress-relieving activity after each mediation session.

Step 2: Advertising

Divide students into groups of four. Ask the groups to brainstorm creative ways to advertise the student mediation service. After 20 minutes, everyone returns to the large circle and shares ideas. Next, ask students to use their ideas to create mediation advertisements.

Step 3: Graduation

Tell the students that they are very special people. Congratulate them because they are all now officially student mediators! Distribute the certificates. Also hand the students a small Student Mediation Guide Card. Tell them that anytime they need to mediate, they can pull the card out of their pockets and use it to guide them in the mediation process. Ask everyone how it feels to be a student mediator.

NOTE: If possible, have a school assembly or other event to formally introduce the mediators and start the program. This will give more credibility to the mediation process. The principal could speak and sign the certificates. At the school assembly, the mediators could present the short play "The Three Lovely Little Pigs," which demonstrates the usefulness of mediation in an entertaining manner. (The play is located in Appendix III.)

Step 4: Weekly Meeting Date and Time

Inform the group of the date and time of the weekly mediators meeting.

IV. REVIEW

V. CLOSING

Congratulate the students for becoming official student mediators. Tell them that you will see them at the weekly meeting.

STUDENT MEDIATION CERTIFICATE

This certificate has been granted to

_____

for successful completion of the
Student Mediation Training.

_____   _____
Adviser's signature   Date

_____   _____
Adviser's signature   Date

2004 © Open Society Institute

The Publisher grants permission for the reproduction of this worksheet for non-profit educational purposes only.
Activity sheets may be downloaded from www.idebate.org/conflictandcommunication.htm

STUDENT MEDIATION GUIDE CARD

1. Prepare the area
2. Welcome
3. Explain the rules
4. Listen to the conflict
5. Recognize shared interests
6. Think of solutions
7. Find a resolution (or list information learned)
8. Put it all on paper
9. Do the office work
10. Give yourself a hug

2004 © Open Society Institute

The Publisher grants permission for the reproduction of this worksheet for non-profit educational purposes only. Activity sheets may be downloaded from www.idebate.org/conflictandcommunication.htm

How to Set Up a Student Mediation Program

Implementing a mediation program in your school can benefit your entire community. There are six steps involved in establishing a program:

I. Obtain administrative support.

A. Investigate school resources.

1. What needs can the mediation program fulfill for your school?

2. Which situations are and are not appropriate for student mediation?

[You should check your school's policy on discipline. At most schools, any conflict involving violence and injury does not go to mediation.]

B. Choose an adviser or advisers.

An advisory team is usually best, because one person may not have the flexibility or enough free time to oversee the entire mediation program. It is important that an adult adviser be available to the mediators during mediation sessions.

1. Who would be willing and able to be a good adviser?

2. Does that person understand the program's goals?

3. What are that person's expectations about the program?

4. Can that person help you obtain administrative support?

C. Write a proposal.

A written proposal describing the program is useful in obtaining both financial and verbal support. A basic proposal includes the following:

1. Abstract: A brief statement describing the school's problems and the reasons for the mediation program.

2. Rationale: A brief description of the strengths of the program. See Student Mediation: Purpose (page 203) for information on mediation's strengths.

3. Program Goals: How will the program benefit the students, administration, faculty, and community? Be specific. How will the program resolve the problems mentioned in the abstract?

4. Plan of Action: How are students selected and trained? How is the program evaluated? Include a timeline listing when different events will be completed.

5. Budget: Possible finances are room rental, office supplies (such as photocopying materials, badges or t-shirts identifying the mediators), and so on.

D. Meet with appropriate administrators.

Meet with appropriate administrators and explain the program's goals and training procedures. Emphasize how a student mediation program can benefit the students, faculty, and administration. (Show the administrators this manual's systematic training program, if necessary.)

In most schools, the support of administrators is helpful in implementing and maintaining a mediation program. To gain their support, you could invite them to become members of the mediation advisory committee. The committee's purpose is to act as a council of advisers, helping to build the program's success.

Sometimes administrators might worry about how well prepared students are in handling the responsibilities mediation entails. Explain that mediation training is an intensive ten-week program that thoroughly trains students. You can also assure the administration that students will not mediate conflicts dealing with drugs, weapons, and so on.

If school administrators will not support the program, you can implement it in less traditional settings, such as in a youth group, library, private home, cafe, etc.

II. Obtain student interest.

Advertise the student mediation program through as many sources as possible. You can advertise such things as:

- What a student mediator does.
- How worthwhile student mediation is to the school community.
- How useful student mediation can be in teaching conflict management and leadership skills.
- How student mediation is an exciting way to meet new friends.

Possible advertising techniques to gain student and faculty interest:

1. Present the play "The Three Lovely Little Pigs" (in Appendix III).

2. Word of mouth
   - Talk with students about the mediation program.
   - Ask other faculty to talk with their students about the program.
   - Ask students to talk with other students about the program.

3. Write an article in the school or local newspaper.

4. Design flyers or brochures to distribute to students.

5. Organize an assembly to explain the program.

6. Have a student or teacher explain the program before classes begin in the morning or at some other time.

7. Explain the program over the school's public address program.

8. Design posters.

The advertisements should include the date, time, and place of information sessions on student mediation. Two or more information sessions may be necessary because of students' varied schedules.

At the information session for students, explain what student mediation is and how it is useful to them and to the school. Tell them that mediation skills are taught mostly through games, so the training is a lot of fun. Possibly facilitate a fun activity to get them interested. Give students the date, time, and place of the first training session.

III. Select students.

Typically, no more than thirty student mediators are trained at the same time. In order for the entire school to accept and utilize mediation, the mediators should be representative of the diversity of the student body. For example, if only the academically successful students are mediators, the less academically successful students might feel too intimidated to volunteer to be mediators or, after the program is functioning, too uncomfortable using the mediation service.

Areas of diversity include:
- Grade level
- Troublemakers/Good Students
- Gender
- Religious affiliation
- Race/Ethnicity
- Strong/Weak leadership abilities
- Intellectually talented/Intellectually less talented
- Think of other areas that apply specifically to your school

There are at least four approaches to selecting students. Choose the approach that will help mediation be most effective in your school's environment.

APPROACH 1: Every student in the school completes the student mediation program. Teachers could teach the program to all of the students in their classes. Therefore, if conflicts occur, any classmate could serve as a mediator.

APPROACH 2: All interested students become involved in the mediation program.

APPROACH 3: Advisers and/or trained student mediators interview all interested students. This panel selects twenty to thirty students to be trained in student mediation.

Typical interview questions are:
1. Why do you want to be a mediator?
2. What are some qualities of a good friend?
3. What do you think your role as a student mediator will be?
4. What type of conflicts do you think you will encounter as a student mediator?

Be sure to select a sample of students who are representative of the school's diversity.

APPROACH 4: Students may nominate two classmates who they feel would be good mediators (students may nominate themselves). Tell students that nominations will be kept confidential. Each nomination can be written on a small piece of paper, folded, and handed to the teacher. Teachers then select a sample of the nominated students who represent the diversity of the school. Inform the students selected. If they are interested, have them meet with the mediation program's adviser. If less than thirty students attend the meeting, they can all become trainees. Otherwise, conduct interviews of the interested student leaders using the interviewing process from Approach 3.

IV. Train students.

Organize an hourly, daily, or weekly meeting time and place for the students and adviser(s). Use the ten-step mediation training program in this curriculum. Although you can adapt the sessions' activities and time lengths, try to hold at least one session every week. Once you have trained the initial student mediators, they can assist in training other students.

V. Organize the program.

After students have been trained in mediation, how can other students in conflict locate and utilize the mediators? There are several possible strategies. Use the strategy or strategies that best match the needs, resources, and rules of your school. For example, in some schools, student mediators can miss classes to mediate. In other schools, different strategies are more practical and effective, such as scheduling mediation sessions for a particular period that coincides with free time in the schedule of the mediator and adviser. In any case, it is advisable that all mediation requests first be reviewed by the mediation program's adviser, who usually schedules the mediation session and makes sure that the conflicts to be mediated do not contradict school or regional laws. Most mediation programs do not handle physical conflicts involving weapons, drugs, and so on. These conflicts are usually referred to a school psychologist, faculty member, or administrator.

Here are some strategies you can use so that students in conflict locate and utilize the mediation services:

A. Designate a room as the student mediation center. If this is not feasible or desirable, mediators can conduct sessions in any private area, such as an empty classroom or a private part of the playground.

B. Students in conflict can fill out a Student Mediation Request Form (page 268). If both students agree to try mediation, the adviser selects the student mediators and schedules a session.

C. Depending on your school policy, if mediators see a conflict, they can approach the disputants, explain that they are mediators, and ask the disputants if they would like to try mediation. If either disputant says no, the mediators should not attempt to mediate. Many schools do not use this approach because mediators could wind up in the middle of a violent conflict in an uncontrolled environment.

D. Students can fill out a Student Mediation Request Form and drop it in a box located in an easily accessible school area. At the end of every day, the mediation program's adviser collects the request forms and organizes sessions. Assign mediators with caution. For example, sometimes disputants feel more comfortable with mediators of the same gender. Usually a team of mediators composed of one male and one female is effective.

E. Designated areas could be set aside for mediation at certain hours of the day. Mediators should take turns mediating by rotating on a fixed schedule. Usually, the adviser sets up the schedule.

F. Teachers can use the Mediation Referral Form (page 269) to refer disputing students to student mediation services.

Disputants can arrange to meet with mediators after a mediation session to see if the agreement worked. The mediators can meet each disputant individually, or arrange a new session at the discretion of the adviser. Student mediators are not typically involved in the decision to reschedule a mediation. If the agreement has been broken, the disputants can request another mediation session. All subsequent mediation meetings and sessions must be initiated by one or both disputants, who are responsible for their own actions.

VI. Maintain the program.

Weekly meetings and consultations among the mediation program adviser(s) and students keep the group in touch with the program's progress and problems. Many things can be accomplished at these meetings. First, problems dealt with during the mediations can be discussed so the students can learn from each other's experiences. Remind students that everything discussed is confidential. Second, conflict management activities (from Part I of this curriculum) can be facilitated. Third, students can practice mediation by role playing, as explained within the student mediation training program. Fourth, the group can create or organize advertisements to attract student attention to the mediation service.

Ways to advertise student mediation to students in conflict:

    A. Write articles for school or local newspapers.

    B. Create flyers.

    C. Plan a sports event, dance, or have a speaker who deals with creating peace. Advertise the event as sponsored by the student mediators.

    D. Create brochures.

    E. Make a traveling display.

    F. Create a video presentation of mediation.

    G. Have television/news programs report the program. (They love these kinds of stories.)

    H. Create an assembly. Possibly explain the concepts behind mediation through role play or by presenting "The Three Lovely Little Pigs."

    I. Introduce students to mediation by going into classrooms and role playing a conflict and mediation session.

    J. Wear buttons or stickers with a student mediation logo.

    K. Make announcements on the school's public address system.

    L. Prepare a display or bulletin board advertisement in the hall or school lobby.

Faculty and student feedback on the program is very important. Often faculty and students can provide invaluable suggestions on how to improve the program's effectiveness.

STUDENT MEDIATION REQUEST FORM

My name is:_____ and I'm involved in a conflict with _____

Here is what the conflict is about:

_____
_____
_____
_____
_____
_____
_____
_____
_____

The best times for me to participate in a mediation session are:

_____
_____

Here is how Students Mediators can contact me: _____
_____

I would like to learn more about the conflict and try to solve it by meeting with mediators and the other person involved.

_____   _____
Student's signature   Date

2004 © Open Society Institute

The Publisher grants permission for the reproduction of this worksheet for non-profit educational purposes only.
Activity sheets may be downloaded from www.idebate.org/conflictandcommunication.htm

Student Mediation Referral Form

Student names: _____

_____

_____

_____

Referred by: _____

Conflict description: _____

_____

_____

_____

_____

_____

_____

Where conflict ocurred: (check one)

___Classroom   __Hall   __Lunch   __Schoolyard   __Other

_____   _____
Teacher / Administrator signature   Date

2004 © Open Society Institute

The Publisher grants permission for the reproduction of this worksheet for non-profit educational purposes only.
Activity sheets may be downloaded from www.idebate.org/conflictandcommunication.htm

Student Mediation Acceptance Notification

Dear Parent(s) or Guardian(s):

Congratulations! Your child has been chosen to be a Student Mediator. He / she will be taking part in ___ hours of training. The program will be supervised by _____

_____

Student mediators are students trained in facilitating discussion between two disputing students or groups as they search for a solution. We would appreciate if you would sign the permission slip at the bottom of this page and have your child return it to school.

Again, congratulations!

_____ _____
Mediation Advisor's signature   Date

Student mediators should return this permission slip to the mediation adviser.

I give _____ permission to become trained
            (Student's Name)
in student mediation.

_____ _____
Signature of Parent/ Guardian   Date

2004 © Open Society Institute

The Publisher grants permission for the reproduction of this worksheet for non-profit educational purposes only.
Activity sheets may be downloaded from www.idebate.org/conflictandcommunication.htm

APPENDIXES

Appendix I: Stress-Relieving Activities

Appendix II: Icebreakers

Appendix III: The Three Lovely Little Pigs (A Short Play About Mediation)

Appendix IV: Interdisciplinary Approaches to Conflict Management

Appendix V: Dividing Students into Groups

Appendix I: Stress-Relieving Activities

Conflict can be healthy, promoting growth and change, but it can also bring about stress. Whether dealing with a personal or interpersonal conflict, stress is a natural response to these situations.

The way we handle situations determines how stress affects us. How do we behave when we are stressed? Some people can turn the most tense situations into humorous, stress-free situations. Others cry and shake if they encounter even slightly stressful circumstances. The following activities can help you and your students manage stress. The activities are simple and require very little time.

1. EXERCISE.

A. Taking a fast 5–10 minute walk can reduce tension and increase energy levels. Many people eat snack foods or drink coffee to give them energy, but a short walk increases energy and reduces tension for longer periods of time.

B. Climb up and down stairs for 5–10 minutes.

C. Do any other kind of exercise that increases your heart rate. Even simple exercises—jumping up and down or running in place for a few minutes—can be helpful. Two reasons exercise is so useful in dealing with stress are that it 1) lessens the amount of stress hormones (such as adrenaline) and 2) promotes the production of endorphins, which are natural chemicals in the body that make you feel good.

D. Sit comfortably at your desk with your back straight. Keep your arms and hands relaxed by your sides. Lift one shoulder and move it slowly backward. Then slowly release the tension so the shoulder relaxes. Do this ten times with each shoulder.

E. Have your arms loose by your sides. Shake your hands from your wrists. Your arms should stay relaxed while doing this. Repeat the exercise five times.

F. Clench your hands into fists. Squeeze your hands as tightly as you can. Imagine all the stress and tension of your day draining to your hands. Keep squeezing for 5–10 seconds and then quickly release your squeeze by stretching out all your fingers. Keep your fingers outstretched for 5–10 seconds. Repeat this exercise three times.

G. Stretch your neck. Stand straight. Relax your head so that it is down toward your chest. Slowly and gently roll your head in circles, from shoulder to shoulder.

2. TELL JOKES.

Humor can relieve stress. By telling jokes or by thinking or talking about funny incidents, people laugh. Laughter reduces stress levels.

3. THINK POSITIVE!

A. Look at the positive. For instance, suppose a student is not behaving and is causing you a great deal of stress. Instead of letting him make you feel stressed, focus on how well-behaved the rest of the class is. Or focus on how beautiful the weather is. When stressed, people often forget to acknowledge the positive aspects of their lives. Students, too, can focus on the positives. For example, instead of feeling stressed over bad school grades, students could focus on how much fun it is to play outside.

B. When you find yourself focusing on the negative aspects of your life, write down all the things in your life that make you feel happy and proud.

C. If you can't get the negative aspects of your life off your mind, write a list of all the things that annoy and bother you. Circle all the items that you can change. Pick at least one of the circled items and try to change it. Then you have at least one less annoying thing in your life to cause you stress.

4. WRITE DOWN THE THINGS THAT CAUSE YOU STRESS.

A. Keep a daily journal of all of the things that make you happy and all of the things that make you feel stressed. Writing can also help you to put in order the obsessions that come with stress.

B. Write a letter to a person or organization that is causing you stress. Express all your feelings in the letter. Then tear it up and throw it away.

5. TALK WITH A FRIEND OR RELATIVE.

By talking with someone, we can define and work through the problems that stress us.

6. CHANGE YOUR ENVIRONMENT.

Sometimes environments compound feelings of stress. For instance, you and the students work and feel stress all day in the classroom. Simply taking the class outside for a few minutes breaks the stress of the classroom environment.

7. SCREAM!

A loud scream can be a stress-reliever. Although you cannot perform this activity in crowded places, it is very effective. You could take the class to an empty field, count to three, and then have everyone scream at once. It makes you feel exhilarated.

8. SIT IN SILENCE!

Sitting in silence for 5–15 minutes can reduce tensions.

9. LISTEN TO MUSIC.

A. Close your eyes and listen to calming music. Feel the music and allow it to block out any thoughts that might enter your mind.

B. If you don't have a radio or CD player, close your eyes and imagine music being played in your head.

C. Sing songs.

D. Dance or move to music.

10. GIVE YOURSELF A MASSAGE.

Here are the steps for a simple self-massage:

A. Drop your head forward so that your chin almost touches your chest. The neck should be stretched out, but it should not be strained. Let the muscles in your neck relax. Massage the back of your neck by rubbing the area from your skull to your shoulders.

B. Massage your ears and temples, lightly rubbing them in a circular motion. Move your fingers back up and down your neck.

C. Very lightly brace your scalp with the palms of your hands, one hand above each ear. Rotate your hands lightly in a circular motion.

D. Again massage the back of your neck and then rub your shoulders.

11. READ A BOOK OR WATCH TELEVISION.

12. DO PROGRESSIVE MUSCLE RELAXATION.

Follow these steps:

A. Sit in a comfortable position.

B. Breathe deeply.

C. Feel the tension in your feet. Be conscious of what the tension feels like. Then let the tension disappear. How? Just let it go. Continue this process with the ankles, the calves, the knees, the upper legs, the buttocks, the lower back, the upper back, the shoulders, the arms, the neck, and the head.

D. This activity usually takes at least 15 minutes, and it feels great by the end!

13. IMAGINE SOMETHING RELAXING.

A. Take a few deep breaths. Think of a time when you were totally relaxed. Imagine that place in your mind and pretend that you are there. Try to remember everything you can about the place.

B. Imagine that the word relax is in big letters in front of you. Concentrate on the word, what it looks like and how it feels to be relaxed. If any other thoughts enter your mind, just ignore them (or imagine them flying away) and resume thinking about the word relax.

C. Think of your favorite color. Picture yourself outside on a beautiful day, looking at the clouds. Magically, the clouds turn into your favorite color. Breathe in the clouds, letting their color fill your lungs and your body. Then exhale. Each time you exhale, stress flows out of you. Continue this exercise for 10 minutes.

14. BREATHE DEEPLY.

Here are some breathing exercises:

A. Take slow, deep breaths. Breathe in through your nose, holding the air in your lungs for 3 seconds before slowly releasing it. Inhale and exhale for the same amount of time. Repeat this style of breathing for 5 minutes. Once it is easy to hold your breath for 3 seconds, try holding it for longer periods (up to 10 seconds). Try breathing in through your nose and out through your mouth.

B. Try diaphragmatic breathing. Your diaphragm is located below your lungs. Put your hand right above your belly button when you breathe deeply. If your hand rises, you are breathing through your diaphragm. Do this deep breathing for 5–10 minutes.

15. SAY A CREATIVE VISUALIZATION.

Develop your own creative visualization. Here is a sample one. Read it aloud very soothingly and slowly:

Close your eyes, take a deep breath, and relax. Imagine yourself standing in front of a beautiful mountain. The sky is blue and a few small clouds drift by. The sun shines on the trees. You hear birds chirping. In the distance you hear the sound of a running river.

(Tell everyone to take a deep breath and exhale.)

Your bones feel light and your muscles are relaxed. Suddenly, your body, like a balloon, begins to float. You feel yourself slowly rising up toward the sky. The higher you get, the more relaxed you feel.

(Tell everyone to take a deep breath and exhale.)

You float. Higher and higher you rise. Trees and leaves pass by you. At last, you see the top of the mountain. The sun's light shines on you. It feels so good. You keep rising, higher and higher. You feel more and more relaxed.

(Tell everyone to take another deep breath and exhale.)

You float into the blue sky. The sky feels soft. Very soft and warm. As you float higher, the mountain fades into the distance. Now all you can see below is the green color of the mountains and the grass. You are relaxed. The white clouds surround you. You float through them and breathe deeply.

(Tell everyone to take a deep breath and exhale.)

The air is so soft and comfortable. You float higher and higher. Now you are above the clouds. You see the earth below you. You are in space. Your body feels light. Your arms are light. Your legs are light. Your shoulders are light. You feel light and float higher and higher. You are relaxed.

(Tell everyone to take a deep breath and exhale.)

Then, you slowly float back down. You float back through the clouds. You are relaxed. You descend down. You can see the mountain now. You keep floating downward. Your body and your mind are relaxed. There are the trees. There is the grass. You slowly land back on the ground. You hear the river running. You hear the birds chirping. You are relaxed.

(Tell everyone to take a deep breath and exhale.)

NOTE: Music can accompany the visualization, if you wish.

Appendix II: Icebreakers

The following are very short icebreakers. Icebreakers are fun activities that allow students to feel comfortable revealing information about themselves and participating. The activities also promote group cohesion.

THE OBJECTS

Put approximately fifteen small objects (such as a fork, spoon, sock, hat, etc.) on a desk. Have the students stand in a line and pass by the desk, quickly trying to memorize the objects. They go to their seats while you place the objects out of their sight. They write down all the objects they can recall. Then tell them what the objects were. Which objects were easiest/hardest to remember? How many objects did students remember?

10 SECONDS

The class decides on a specific color or shape. The students sit in a circle. Clockwise, each person in the circle has to name two objects in the room that are that color or shape. They have 10 seconds to name two things. A person in the class (or you) yells "Next" after each person's 10 seconds have ended. Once everyone has had an opportunity to name two things, the class decides on a new color or shape. Each person must now name two objects within 7 seconds. Students could then try to name two objects within 5 seconds. This is not easy!

PASS THE COIN

The class is divided into two groups, which stand in two straight lines facing each other. The first person in each line has a coin in his/her hand. The first person in each group passes his/her coin down the line. The next students either pass or pretend to pass the coin to the end of the line. Each group must guess who has the other group's coin.

THE GUESSER

Students sit in a circle. One person, the guesser, leaves the room. The circle chooses a leaser. Whenever the leader makes a motion, everyone imitates him/her. The guesser returns to the room. The leader makes many motions, and everyone follows them. The guesser tries to figure out who is initiating the motions. When he/she guesses correctly, the guesser names the person who gave away the leader. That person becomes the new guesser.

LAUGH

Divide students into pairs. One person in each pair tries to make the other laugh. After a minute, the two people switch roles.

THE SOCK

Out of sight of the students, fill a box, bag, or sock with a fork, ball, or any other small objects. During class, pass the sock to the students. Each student has 10 seconds to feel the sock. Afterward, the students write down what they think is in the sock. Students share their guesses, and then the sock's contents are revealed.

THE PENCILS

Three students, the finders, leave the room and the class hides a pencil. The finders return to the room and try to find the pencil. The closer any of the finders get to the pencil, the louder the class claps. The further away the finders are, the softer the students clap. Students keep clapping, loudly or softly, until the pencil is found.

THE SIGNATURE

Students must shake each of their classmate's hands and get his/her signature.

I SEE IT!

One student is chosen to be the Eye. The Eye looks around the room, locates a specific object, and notes its color. Everyone in the room must be able to see the object. The Eye says, "I see the color…". and names the color. The rest of the class tries to guess what object the Eye sees. Whoever guesses correctly becomes the new Eye.

THE INCLINE

Tell students to close their eyes, and while remaining silent, create one straight line in the order of their heights: The shortest person is first, the tallest is last.

BIRTHDAY LINE

Students must quickly stand in a straight line in the order of their birthdays, the youngest student first, the oldest last. Students are not allowed to speak.

TAP TAP

Six students, the Heads, walk to the front of the room. The rest of the class sits at their desks with their heads on their desks and their eyes closed. Each of the six Heads lightly taps one student on the head. That person raises his/her arm so that no one else taps him/her. The Heads return to the front of the room. Then all of the students raise their heads and open their eyes. Each student with a raised arm tries to guess who tapped him/her. The students who guess correctly become Heads, and the old Heads sit down.

ONE FOOT

Students stand and balance on one leg. The other leg is in the air. See who can balance the longest.

TIME

One person, the guesser, stands in the center of the room and closes his/her eyes. Twelve people stand around the guesser. Each one represents one hour on the clock. The guesser says, "The alarm goes off at .... o'clock." Whoever represents that number makes a funny sound. The guesser tries to guess the name of the person who made the sound. The guesser stays in the middle until he/she guesses correctly. The person guessed becomes the new guesser.

SHAPING THE SCULPTURE

Students stand in a circle. One person makes a funny movement and sound. The next person in line repeats the movement and sound, changing them slightly. The movement and sound are changed and passed from person to person around the circle.

Appendix III: The Three Lovely Little Pigs (A Short Play About Mediation)

The following is a short play illustrating the usefulness of student mediation. Trained student mediators can present this play to students in classrooms, at a school assembly introducing students to student mediation, and so on. This play is a great way to advertise student mediation to students. Because the play is entertaining, the audience becomes familiar with the usefulness of mediation in a fun, non-intimidating fashion. The play is also a useful tool for students training to become student mediators.

The Three Lovely Little Pigs: The Mediation

Characters:

The Third Lovely Little Pig

The Mean Hungry Wolf

Mediator 1 (who is also the story-reader)

Mediator 2

The Setting:

There should be four chairs set up at the front of the room. The middle two chairs should be facing the audience, and the two side chairs should be turned slightly inward. Two pieces of paper and a pencil are near the middle chair.

(Mediator 1 reads the following excerpt of the story of "The Three Lovely Little Pigs." The mediator could hold up pictures that correspond with the story. Mediator 2 sits quietly beside Mediator 1. The Third Lovely Little Pig and The Mean Hungry Wolf sit with the audience and listen to the story.)

Mediator 1: Once on a time, there lived three lovely little pigs. The pigs were all moving to a new town called Pigsville, and they needed places to live.

The First Lovely Little Pig liked to play in haystacks as a child. So he built a house made of hay. One day, The Mean Hungry Wolf walked up to the pig's house, knocked on the door, and growled, "I need to come in!"

The First Lovely Little Pig said, "No. No way!" And he locked his door. The wolf became angry and yelled, "If you don't open the door, I'll blow, I won't go, I'll blow and I'll blow. I'll blow until your house falls to the ground!" The First Lovely Little Pig squealed, "No way! I may be little, but I'm not stupid. I'm not opening this door." So the wolf blew and he blew, and down the house fell.

The Second Lovely Little Pig liked to climb trees as a child. So she built a house made of logs and branches. Late one day, The Mean Hungry Wolf walked up to her house, knocked on the door, and grumbled, "I need to come in!" The Second Lovely Little Pig said, "I never open my door for strangers. Sorry." The wolf became annoyed and said, "I'm not a stranger. I'm The Mean Hungry Wolf. Everyone knows me! Now, if you don't open the door, I'll blow, I won't go, I'll blow and I'll blow. I'll blow until your house falls to the ground!" The Second Lovely Little Pig squealed, "I really don't know you. I'm not going to open this door. Sorry, stranger." So the wolf blew and he blew and down the house fell.

The Third Lovely Little Pig liked to strengthen his muscles by lifting bricks as a child. So he built a house made of brick. Early one morning, The Mean Hungry Wolf walked up to his house, knocked on the door, and growled, "I need to come in!" The Third Lovely Little Pig said, "No way! My house is too messy for anyone to see." The wolf got angry and yelled, "I don't mind messes. So, if you don't open the door, I'll blow, I won't go, I'll blow and I'll blow. I'll blow until your house falls to the ground. AND THEN I'LL EAT YOU!"

Wolf: *(jumping up out of the audience angrily and screaming)*: THAT'S NOT TRUE! None of it is true. It's all lies. I can't believe what that story says. None of it's true…

Pig: *(jumping up out of the audience angrily and screaming)*: It's all true. I can't believe you would even think that the story has any lies. It's all true. Every word.

(Wolf and Pig walk toward each other, calling each other liars. Mediator 1 and Mediator 2 walk toward them.)

Mediator 1: Hold on a minute! Stop yelling at each other!

Mediator 2: Wait! Be quiet.

Wolf: But he called me a liar!

Pig: He is a liar!

Mediator 2: Calm down.

Pig: *(Turning toward the mediators):* Who are you both?

Mediator 1: My name is_____.

Mediator 2: And my name is _____. We're student mediators.

Wolf: What's a student mediator?

Mediator 2: Student mediators are students. Just like you. But we're trained to help people in conflicts to clarify their feelings and thoughts.

Mediator 1: And we help people in conflicts to communicate with one another and try to find solutions to their problems. So would you like to try mediation?

Wolf: Sure.

Mediator 1: *(Looking at Pig)* Would you like to try mediation?

Pig: But what if that mean hungry wolf growls the whole time?

Mediator 2: In mediation, each person gets an opportunity to talk with no interruptions. So you would get a chance to talk. Want to try mediation?

Pig: I guess so. Yes.

Mediator 2: Great! Then both of you follow us to the mediation room.

Wolf: Okay.

Pig: Okay.

(Wolf, Pig, and the mediators walk toward the seats set up in the front of the room.)

Mediator 1: The two of you can sit down.

(All four characters sit down. The mediators sit in the middle seats.)

Mediator 2: Welcome to the mediation session. Once again, my name is_____.

Mediator 1: And my name is_____. What are your names?

Wolf: Everybody calls me The Mean Hungry Wolf. But my real name is just Wolf.

Pig: You don't know who I am??? I'm The Third Lovely Little Pig. Friends just call me Pig.

Mediator 1: Okay. We welcome both of you to the mediation room. Mediation will give both of you the opportunity to work together and understand more about each other. Through this process, you can try to find a solution that improves your situation. Mediation can make it possible for both of you to win.

Pig: So what are the rules?

Mediator 2: Two rules that we, as mediators, will follow are:

* We don't take sides or judge either of you.

* Everything said here is confidential.

Now there are ground rules we would like you to agree to:

* No name-calling, insults, or blaming

* No interrupting

* Be honest

* Work hard to solve the problem

* Everything said here is confidential

Pig, do you agree to the rules?

Pig: Yes.

Mediator 2: Wolf, how about you?

Wolf: Well....Okay.

Mediator 2: Great! Now, Pig, please explain what happened and how you feel.

Pig: Let me first tell you about pigs. Everybody thinks we are dirty and like to roll in the mud. The truth is, we have style, we are educated, and we like to live in classy areas, not in pig pens. My brother, sister, and I all decided to move to Pigsville. It's a beautiful area.

We each had childhood dreams about what kind of house to build. My brother wanted a house of hay and my sister wanted one of trees. I wanted mine built of bricks. We spent weeks building, and we finally had three splendid houses. We were three happy pigs!

But then, one cloudy day, our happy lives became very sad. I discovered that this evil wolf frightened my brother and sister. What's worse, their houses were blown down!

Wolf: That's ridiculous!

Mediator 1: Wolf. Please no interrupting. And Pig, no name calling.

Wolf: Sorry.

Mediator 2: Pig, please continue.

Pig: You can imagine how terrified I was the next day when I heard a knock at my door and saw Wolf standing there. "I need to come in," he growled. He breathed loudly. It was all so scary. I told him that my house was too messy to let him in. But he stood still and kept breathing loudly...HE WAS TRYING TO BLOW DOWN MY HOUSE! Fortunately, he did not succeed.

I hid in my closet all night, ran to the market this morning for vegetables, and ended up here. I'm now scared that Wolf is going to try to blow down my house again. I'm really scared. He even said he wanted to eat me!

Mediator 2: So you think Wolf blew down your brother and sister's houses. And when he appeared at your door, you felt terrified that he was going to blow down your house and eat you. Anything to add?

Pig: No, that's the whole story.

Mediator 1: Wolf, will you please tell us what happened and how you feel.

Wolf *(sneezes loudly):* HACHOO! Excuse me, but I can't stop sneezing. I've had this cold for months. I just can't get rid of it. So two days ago, I decided to visit a doctor. I traveled to a town called Pigsville. They have excellent doctors there. I located a doctor named Doctor First Lovely Little Pig. The moment I knocked on his door, I started sneezing...and I couldn't stop. HACHOO! I started breathing louder and louder, trying to catch my breath.

The Doctor asked, "Who's there?" The only word I could say was, "Wolf...Wolf...WOLF!"

And before I could catch my breath, I sneezed as hard as a tornado and blew down the house. The doctor must have needed extra help to cure me: Without saying a word, he rushed to his neighbor's house. His neighbor, the world famous expert on sneezing, is named Doctor Second Lovely Little Pig.

I walked to the second doctor's house, and again I started sneezing and sneezing. The moment I knocked on the door, I felt a big, big sneeze crawling from my stomach toward my nose. So I told the doctor to open the door and cure me or else I would blow down her house. Doctor Second Lovely Little Pig said she didn't open the door for strangers.

Before I could control myself, I again sneezed as hard as a tornado and blew down the house. Both doctors ran into the forest.

I was desperate for a doctor to cure me, so I ran to Pig's brick house. Pig is a well-known doctor, and I begged him to let me in. But he wouldn't. I felt so frustrated and angry that I told him I would eat him if he didn't help me. But that's ridiculous! I would never eat a pig. I'm a vegetarian.

Mediator 1: So you have a very bad cold, bad enough that you blew down houses. You searched for a doctor to cure you, and you felt frustrated and angry because no one would help you. Do you have anything to add?

Wolf: I certainly do. In the forest, animals tease me and call me The Mean Hungry Wolf. But I'm hungry all the time because I don't have much money. Instead of eating food this week, I was going to pay Pig to cure my cold. I'm afraid that I might not even have enough money to pay for a doctor, though!

Mediator 1: So you feel afraid that you might not have enough money to pay for a doctor. Is that correct?

Wolf: Yes it is.

Mediator 2: Now in this next part of mediation, we want you to talk with each other. Wolf, please describe what Pig said.

Wolf: Okay. Pig said I frightened his brother and sister and blew down their houses. He even thinks I was going to blow down his house and eat him. It's all so ridiculous!

Mediator 2: Pig, is that description accurate?

Pig: Yes, except that it's not ridiculous. It's all true!

Mediator 2: Both of you, please remember that during mediation you have to work together, okay?

Pig: Okay.

Wolf: Yes.

Mediator 1: Now Pig, please describe what Wolf said.

Wolf *(sneezing)*: Yes.

Pig: Wolf said he has a bad cold. So he searched for a doctor. My brother and sister wouldn't help him. He said he sneezed and blew down their houses. He came to me for help. I wouldn't help him either.

Mediator 1: Wolf, is that description accurate?

Mediator 2: Pig, what do you want to get out of this conflict?

Pig: I want to feel safe in Pigsville. I don't want Wolf to eat me or anyone else. And I don't want my house blown down.

Mediator 2: So you want to feel safe everywhere in Pigsville. Wolf, what do you want to get out of this conflict?

Wolf: I just want to get rid of my cold.

Mediator 1: Okay. We have discovered what each of you wants out of this conflict. Now let's think of possible solutions that allow both of you to get what you want at the same time.

Mediator 2: Here are the guidelines: Say every idea that you can think of. Think of as many ideas as possible. Don't judge any idea as good or bad. And don't talk about the ideas yet. Just say them. So what are some ideas?

(Mediator 2 takes out a pencil and paper. When ideas are called out, he/she pretends to write them down.)

Pig: Well...Wolf could go to jail.

Mediator 1: What are some other ideas?

Wolf: I can't think of any. Oh, wait! I just thought of an idea. Now that Pig knows who I am, he can be my doctor.

Mediator 1: Great! Two good ideas. Can you think of any others?

Wolf: No.

Pig: No, I can't either.

Mediator 2: So now let's look at the positives and negatives of each suggested solution. What are the positives of Wolf going to jail?

Pig: Well, Wolf couldn't eat me or blow down houses. And if Wolf remains in jail, his cold may go away since he will be inside all the time.

Mediator 1: Okay. What are the negative aspects of Wolf going to jail?

Wolf: I like my freedom. I like to walk around the forest. I don't want to leave my family. And those prison uniforms are so ugly.

Pig: And maybe Wolf's cold will get worse in jail.

Mediator 1: How about if Pig becomes Wolfs doctor? What are the positive aspects?

Pig: Wolf's cold would go away. He would feel much healthier.

Wolf: And if my cold disappears, I wouldn't sneeze and blow down houses.

I would never harm Pig because he would be my doctor.

Mediator 2: What are the negative aspects of this solution?

Wolf: I can't think of any.

Pig: I can't think of any, either.

Mediator 2: Then let me summarize. Pig can be your doctor. And Wolf, you can become Pig's friend, never harming him or his house. Do you each agree to this solution?

Wolf: Yes.

Pig: Yes.

(Mediator 2 gets out a pencil and piece of paper and pretends to be writing.)

Mediator 2: I'm going to write the agreement on this form here. Now each of you should sign it.

(Wolf and Pig each pretend to sign the paper.)

Mediator 1: Now let's think of how mediation has helped us clarify the conflict. Pig, what did you learn today?

Pig: I learned that wolves have very powerful sneezes! And I learned that Wolf is not mean. He just has a bad, bad cold.

Mediator 1: Wolf, what did you learn?

Wolf: I didn't know that the Three Lovely Little Pigs thought I was intentionally trying to blow down their houses. I hope we can all become friends.

Mediator 2: Great. And congratulations! You have now officially resolved your conflict. And you have learned a lot about each other in the process. Thanks for coming to mediation.

Appendix IV: Interdisciplinary Approaches to Conflict Management

For the conflict management program to be most effective, conflict management studies must be integrated into all aspects of a student's life, including at school, with family, and with peer groups.

I. THE ROLE OF THE SCHOOL

Schools are not only where students gain information, but they are also the major forum for youth socialization. It is at school where friendships are formed and broken; where individuals learn how to communicate effectively; where students excel in team partnership with others; and where students are most likely to experience conflicts that can affect their personal growth. The school setting is a natural location for teaching students about conflict management. The following are several areas of study and sample activities to teach conflict management during regular school hours. The activities listed function as both a pedagogical resource and as a reminder: Conflict management studies can be creatively incorporated into many areas of students' lives.

LANGUAGE ARTS/WRITING

- Students write daily in a journal about conflicts they faced the day before and how they solved them (or are trying to solve them).
- Students write essays on what peace means to them.
- Students write stories about conflict or a fight two people had and how it was peacefully resolved or, if it is unresolved, how they might resolve the issue.
- Students read and discuss books that emphasize concepts such as friendship, compassion, cooperation, responsibility, and nonviolent problem-solving strategies.
- Students write and act out role plays demonstrating the problems causing conflict and their possible solutions.
- Students research and evaluate stories and books containing stereotypes and negative images of groups.

MATHEMATICS

Mathematics deals largely with logic and problem-solving skills that are important in the process of conflict resolution. Therefore, almost any mathematics studies are useful for handling conflicts effectively.

- Students compute mathematics problems that relate to conflict resolution. For example, have students count the number of conflicts they faced yesterday. Have them multiply that number by 365. The result is the approximate number of conflicts they face in a year. A school or district survey could be compiled.
- Students graph how many conflicts they face each week and also how many they solved peacefully.
- Students graph the number of conflicts their friends experience by using a survey or questionnaire.

SCIENCE

Students discuss the dangers of violence. Possible questions include:

- What happens to the body when you get angry?
- What happens to the body when someone hurts or punches you? What are important alternatives to violence?
- How is the world community trying to control nuclear weapons? What if someone uses nuclear weapons to resolve conflict?
- What are our basic human needs? What happens if they are not satisfied?

HISTORY/SOCIAL STUDIES

- Students discuss events in history in which nonviolent tactics were used to bring about change. Nonviolence has and continues to be a force for change in areas such as governmental revolutions, labor strikes, goods boycotts, and alternative institutions like the United Nations.
- Students analyze whether violent actions help to create a peaceful world. Find events in history in which violence was used. Ask the class to think up different solutions to the problem: How could the problem have been solved without the use of violence? What role could conflict resolution have played?
- Students read a newspaper/magazine article about a problem or crisis. Discuss possible solutions to the problem.
- Students discuss individuals, historic and current, who could be called peacemakers (local, national, international).

PHYSICAL EDUCATION

- Students play games that encourage cooperation, not competition—games in which no one loses and that emphasize friendship are cooperative games.
- You and your students design team sports so that everyone plays others of comparable ability.

ART

- Students draw anything related to conflict, communication, violence, nonviolence, etc.
- Students draw a picture of conflict and one depicting a resolution method.
- Students create posters for the school showing peaceful activities, e.g. pupils sharing, talking, engaged in a group activity, helping a younger or older person.

MUSIC

- The class sings songs about peace and cooperation.
- Students write songs about a conflict and how it is resolved. They teach these songs to the rest of the class.

STUDENT CONDUCT

- The students and the teacher write a constitution. The constitution should address what happens when students do not follow the rules. Everyone should sign the document. Both the teacher and the students enforce the rules
- Students become peer mediators, helping other students solve disputes nonviolently.

These are just a few ideas about how conflict management activities can be incorporated into different areas of the students' classroom studies. Many of the activities in this book can be utilized in different subject areas. Create your own activities, use some of the ones in this curriculum, and do whatever you can to guide your students through the labyrinth of conflict management.

II. THE ROLE OF THE FAMILY

Families are the major source of personal and social development. They are key to the success of a conflict resolution curriculum, for it is at home and in the community that students can practice conflict management skills. Parents can become partners with students in monitoring TV and other media, noting stereotyping and violence. Since siblings learn from each other, the student learning conflict management skills can become a role model and teacher to younger siblings. Many of the activities in this curriculum can be adapted for family or parent education.

III. THE ROLE OF PEERS

Peers are another major source of personal and social development. Students struggle with issues of identity and acceptance, and they often model their behavior on the actions of others. Part II of this book uses peer relationships as a pathway for students to positively influence one another.

Appendix V: Dividing Students into Groups

Many activities in this curriculum require the class to be divided into small groups. While students feel more comfortable participating in small groups, they often feel anxious or worried when they must choose a partner for an activity. They think thoughts such as: What if I don't get picked? What if I'm the last one picked? What if the group I'm in ignores me?

The following are some suggestions about ways students can be divided into groups in a nonthreatening manner:

1. Instruct students to raise either their right or left arm in the air and find someone else with the same arm raised.
2. Have students count off numbers, and all people with the same number are in the same group. (For example, if you need to divide the group into four smaller groups you would have the students count off one through four until all students have a number.)
3. Have students find someone else with a piece of clothing the same color as theirs.
4. Tell students to hop around the room on their right or left foot and find someone else who is hopping on the same foot.
5. Tell students to write down the number one or two on a piece of paper. They find someone else with the other number.
6. Instruct students to find someone with a letter in his/her name that is the same as theirs.
7. You can randomly divide the students into groups.

GLOSSARY

This glossary contains definitions of the key concepts.

Analytical thinking: A way of thinking in which one breaks down complex ideas into their essential components.

Appreciating diversity: Understanding the unique qualities of people of different ethnic, racial, and other backgrounds.

Attitudes: People's usual positive or negative opinions toward a person, place, situation, etc.

Behavior: How one conducts oneself.

Brainstorming: A simple, effective method for generating ideas.

Communication: The act of sharing and exchanging information such as thoughts and feelings.

Community conflict: Conflicts that occur in or affect the community.

Confidentiality: The maintenance of a secret or something private.

Conflict analysis: Investigating the basic components of conflict.

Conflict resolution: The process of finding solutions to conflicts that satisfy disputants' interests.

Cooperation: Working together to complete a task.

Decision-making: The process of arriving at a choice between at least two possible options.

Discrimination: The act of treating someone differently on the basis of age, religion, ethnicity, nationality, handicap, gender, class, race, and so on. It is prejudice acted out. Discrimination is similar to scapegoating, which is when a person or group is blamed for mistakes or events caused by others.

Empathy: Stepping into another person's shoes and trying to understand how he/she feels.

Enemy image: Viewing all members of an opposing warring nation as evil, unworthy, cold-hearted people who are unable to be trusted.

Environmental conflicts: Conflicts that occur in or affect the environment. Often environmental conflicts relate to human and animals' dependency on the environment in order to survive.

Ethnocentrism: Notion that one's country and the citizens within it are superior to those in other countries. It is excessive nationalism.

Family conflict: Conflict that occurs in or affects the family or its members.

Feelings: Emotions.

Friendship: The state of respecting and holding affection for another.

Group bonding: The process of building connections of friendship and appreciation between people.

Human rights: Inherent, justly due rights of all humans.

Internal conflicts: Conflicts that occur within one's head; self-conflicts.

Leadership Skills: Skills useful in guiding or directing others.

Media: Forms of public communication, such as television, radio, etc.

Nationalism: Pride in one's own country.

Needs: Those things necessary for survival, such as food or water.

Nonverbal communication: The act of sharing and exchanging information through body movements and other nonverbal pathways.

Peer conflicts: Conflicts between friends or people of one's own level of maturity.

Perceptions: Ways of viewing information, ideas, situations, etc.

Personal responsibility: Accepting ownership of one's actions.

Positional arguments: Arguments in which the disputants stick to their positions, irrespective of their true interests.

Power/authority: Power is the ability to have others listen and comply with one's requests. Authority gives one the power to expect submission of requests.

Prejudice: An opinion, often unfavorable, about a subject or group that is formed before exploring all of its facets. Often, prejudice is formed due to a lack of effort to understand perceived differences.

Pride: A feeling of self-worth and self-respect.

Problem-solving: The process of finding a satisfying solution to a problem.

Propaganda: A systematic effort to spread opinions and beliefs; the spread of information to further a group's goals.

Recognizing conflict: Becoming aware of the mental and physical symptoms that indicate that one is in a conflict situation.

School conflicts: Conflicts that occur in or affect the people at school.

Self-concept: The overall view that people have of themselves. It consists of all of the person's attitudes, perceptions, and ideas about themselves.

Self-efficacy: The feeling of confidence that one can successfully complete a task.

Self-empowerment: The authority every individual can access and possess within himself/herself.

Self-esteem: How one views oneself. The higher one's self-esteem, the more positive one's view is.

Self-understanding: Understanding the essential components of oneself.

Self-worth: How much one values oneself.

Sibling conflicts: Conflicts between siblings.

Social norms: Standards, values, and typical patterns of behavior of a society.

Sources of conflict: The fundamental causes of conflicts.

Stereotype: The belief that a group of people possesses certain similar qualities and does not have individual differences.

Trust: A confident reliance on another individual.

Underlying interests: The objects one desires in a conflict situation.

Values: Things of importance, worth, or utility.

Verbal communication: Communication through speech and oral sounds.

Violence: Exertion of force that injures or abuses.

Wants: Something desired or wished for, but which is not necessary for survival.

INDEX OF LESSONS

The Bargots and the Rooters! - 59
Bigger and Bigger - 37
Body Talk - 91
Bottle Caps - 162
Can You Keep a Secret? - 87
Climbing the Ladder - 168
Coloring in the Outlines of People - 147
The Conflict Dictionary - 118
Conflict in the News - 123
Confusing Decisions - 159
Creating a Conflict Management
  Activity - 196
Don't Push Me - 193
Drawing Me - 13
The Evening News - 55
An Eye for an Eye - 125
Faces of Violence - 128
Fact and Fiction - 68
The Factory - 174
The Feel-Good Chair - 34
The Feeling List - 101
Friend or Foe - 73
The Guessing Game - 94
How Many People Am I? - 25
In Trust We Trust - 31
Me and the Mirror - 29
The Milk Bottle - 151
Mind and Heart - 143
The Mirror - 98
Mountains and Valleys - 19
Movie Auditions - 21
My Emotional Property - 103
My Picture of Conflict - 112
My Pounding Heart - 138
My Protective Shield - 178
Positive Self-Talk - 27
Prejudice's Many Shapes and Sizes - 63
Propaganda Fight - 80
The Propaganda Party - 77
The Right Choice - 165
The Roots of Conflict - 114
The Same Differences - 47
Same Script, Different Play - 190
The Same Side of the Road - 53

Self-Esteem Boosters - 40
Snowflakes - 44
The Soap Opera - 172
The Spaceship - 156
Special People of the Week - 23
Stepping Across the Line - 185
Susan Says - 106
Tangled - 89
Telephone Game - 75
Thoughts on Conflict Management - 10
The Tower of Babel - 70
The Two Sides of Me - 38
Watch Your Step - 84
What Do I Need? - 154
What's the Stereotype? - 50
Where is Violence? - 131
Who Am I? - 16
Whose Shoes? - 149
Why Ask Why? - 96
The Yellows and the Blues - 66

INDEX OF KEY CONCEPTS

Analytical Thinking Page
The Evening News 55
Fact and Fiction 68
How Many People Am I? 25
Telephone Game 75
Thoughts on Conflict Management 10

Appreciating Diversity
The Feeling List 101
Prejudice's Many Shapes and Sizes 63
The Same Differences 47
The Same Side of the Road 53
Snowflakes

Attitudes
Confusing Decisions 159
Drawing Me 13
An Eye for an Eye 125
The Feel-Good Chair 34
How Many People Am I? 25
Mind and Heart 143
Mountains and Valleys 19
Movie Auditions 21
Stepping Across the Line 185
The Tower of Babel 70

Behavior
Coloring the Outlines of People 147
Confusing Decisions 159
Drawing Me 13
An Eye for an Eye 125
The Feel-Good Chair 34
Mind and Heart 143
Mountains and Valleys 19
Movie Auditions 21
My Emotional Property 103
Stepping Across the Line 185
The Tower of Babel 70

Brainstorming
Bottle Caps 162
Me and the Mirror 29
The Right Choice 165

Communication
Creating a Conflict Management Activity 196

Community Conflict
The Roots of Conflict 114

Confidentiality
Can You Keep a Secret? 87

Conflict Analysis
Bottle Caps 162
Coloring in the Outlines of People 147
The Conflict Dictionary 118
Conflict in the News 123
Confusing Decisions 159
Creating a Conflict Management Activity 196
An Eye for an Eye 125
Faces of Violence 128
The Feel-Good Chair 34
The Guessing Game 94
The Milk Bottle 151
Mind and Heart 143
My Emotional Property 103
My Picture of Conflict 112
My Protective Shield 178
Propaganda Fight 80
The Right Choice 165
Tangled 89
Thoughts on Conflict Management 10
The Two Sides of Me 38
Watch Your Step 84
What Do I Need? 154
Where is Violence? 131
Why Ask Why? 96

Conflict Resolution
Climbing the Ladder 168
The Conflict Dictionary 118
Creating a Conflict Management Activity 196
The Factory 174
The Right Choice 165
Same Script, Different Play 190
The Soap Opera 172

292| Conflict and Communication

Cooperation
Tangled 89

Decision-Making
Confusing Decisions 159
The Factory 174
The Spaceship 156
Susan Says 106

Discrimination
The Bargots and the Rooters! 59
The Evening News 55
Fact and Fiction 68
Friend or Foe 73
Prejudice's Many Shapes and Sizes 63
The Same Differences 47
The Same Side of the Road 53
The Tower of Babel 70
The Yellows and the Blues 66

Empathy
My Picture of Conflict 112
Whose Shoes? 149

Enemy Image
Friend or Foe 73

Environmental Conflict
The Factory 174

Family Conflict
Climbing the Ladder 168
The Roots of Conflict 114
The Soap Opera 172

Feelings
Coloring in the Outlines of People 147
Drawing Me 13
An Eye for an Eye 125
The Feel-Good Chair 34
The Feeling List 101
Mind and Heart 143
Mountains and Valleys 19
Movie Auditions 21
My Emotional Property 103
Stepping Across the Line 185
The Tower of Babel 70
Whose Shoes? 149

Friendship
Watch Your Step 84

Group Bonding
Can You Keep a Secret? 87
The Guessing Game 94
Mountains and Valleys 19
Self-Esteem Boosters 40
Tangled 89
Watch Your Step 84
Why Ask Why? 96

Human Rights
Don't Push Me 193
My Protective Shield 178
Same Script, Different Play 190
Stepping Across the Line 185

Internal Conflicts
The Two Sides of Me 38

Leadership Skills
Creating a Conflict Management Activity 196

Media
Conflict in the News 123
The Propaganda Party 77
Telephone Game 75

Nationalism/Ethnocentrism
The Bargots and the Rooters! 59
Friend or Foe 73
The Same Side of the Road 53

Needs/Wants
The Spaceship 156
What Do I Need? 154

Non-Verbal Communication
Body Talk 91
The Feeling List 101
The Mirror 98
Tangled 89

Peer Conflicts
The Mirror 98
Propaganda Fight 80
The Roots of Conflict 114

Perceptions
Tangled 89

Personal Responsibility
Susan Says 106

Index of Key Concepts |293

Positional Arguments
The Milk Bottle   151

Power/Authority
Susan Says   106

Prejudice
The Bargots and the Rooters!   59
The Evening News   55
Fact and Fiction   68
Friend or Foe   73
Prejudice's Many Shapes and Sizes   63
The Same Side of the Road   53
The Tower of Babel   70
The Yellows and the Blues   66

Pride
Drawing Me   13
Movie Auditions   21

Problem-Solving
Tangled   89

Propaganda
Propaganda Fight   80
The Propaganda Party   77
Telephone Game   75

Recognizing Conflict
My Pounding Heart   138

School Conflicts
Don't Push Me   193
Propaganda Fight   80
The Roots of Conflict   114

Self-Concept
How Many People Am I?   25
Positive Self-Talk   27
Me and the Mirror   29

Self-Efficacy
Bigger and Bigger   37

Self-Empowerment
Susan Says   106

Self-Esteem
Bigger and Bigger   37
Drawing Me   13
The Feel-Good Chair   34
The Feeling List   101

How Many People Am I?   25
In Trust We Trust   31
Me and the Mirror   29
Mountains and Valleys   19
Movie Auditions   21
Positive Self-Talk   27
Self-Esteem Boosters   40
Special People of the Week   23
Who Am I?   16

Self-Understanding
Confusing Decisions   159
The Same Differences   47
The Same Side of the Road   53
The Spaceship   156
The Two Sides of Me   38

Sibling Conflicts
The Milk Bottle   151
The Soap Opera   172

Social Norms
Same Script, Different Play   190

Sources of Conflict
The Roots of Conflict   114

Stereotypes
The Evening New   55
The Same Side of the Road   53
The Tower of Babel   70
What's the Stereotype?   50

Trust
Can You Keep a Secret?   87
In Trust We Trust   31
Mountains and Valleys   19
Self-Esteem Boosters   40
Watch Your Step   84

Underlying Interests
The Milk Bottle   151

Values
Confusing Decisions   159
An Eye for an Eye   125
Mountains and Valleys   19
Movie Auditions   21
The Spaceship   156
Special People of the Week   23
What Do I Need?   154

Verbal Communication
Body Talk   91
The Feeling List   101
The Guessing Game   94
The Mirror   98
My Emotional Property   103
Tangled   89
Why Ask Why?   96

Violence
Faces of Violence   128
Where is Violence?   131